The Official

Diary of the Season

2003-2004

Torquay United

Reporter: David Thomas

Herald Express

First published in 2004 by:
First Edition Limited, 32 Stamford Street,
Altrincham, Cheshire, WA14 1EY
in conjunction with Herald Express Publications Ltd,
Westcountry Publications Ltd, Harmsworth House, Barton
Hill Road, Torquay, TQ2 8JN.

Statistics provided by: The Press Association.

Text provided by: Herald Express.

Photographs provided by: Paul Levie.

ISBN: 1-84547-086-9

Contents

Celebrations at the end of the game. Southend v Torquay
HPL01591_TNA_010

Chairman's Foreword

Dear Reader,

I give this publication my fullest support for two reasons. Firstly it is a must-read for all avid Gulls fans and secondly it may well provide a get-out for me having to answer so many questions via email!

History is an important part of football and there is no more precise a form of history as when it is laid out in diary form.

I trust that this book will be a success and that it is the first of a series ongoing for many years.

Enjoy the read.

Mike Bateson
Chairman,
Torquay United AFC

Northampton [0] 0 TORQUAY [0] 1 — 9th August

Torquay United brilliantly took the heat out of Northampton Town on their way to one of the best first-day victories in their history at sweltering Sixfields.

Nothing summed up their performance better than the winning goal by midfielder Jason Fowler in the 61st minute, for five men linked up in a slide-rule passing move to set Fowler up for an easy finish.

Northampton had slightly the better of the first-half chances. The highlight of the opening 45 minutes was a miraculous goalline clearance by Lee Canoville, who threw himself across the six-yard box to keep out Low's shot after he had gone past Arjan Van Heusden on a Smith through-ball in the 36th minute.

But at the other end, Jo Kuffour also should have hit the target with a close-range near-post volley and defender Steve Woods headed wide at the far-post, both on right-wing crosses by Russell.

Northampton had a little go after the restart. Van Heusden, whose handling was spot-on throughout, saved a Marc Richards header on the line and Russell came up with a great block to deny a Richards volley.

The teams worked hard, but it was when Graham replaced Kuffour on the hour that United moved up a gear. Within a minute the Scot helped in the left-wing move which finished with Kevin Hill slipping the ball inside for Fowler.

Shaping to curl a 20-yard shot inside the far-post, Fowler fooled 'keeper Glyn Thompson and cut it past his right-hand and inside the near-post - a quality move and a class finish. Three minutes later United produced something even better, and it should have brought the house down.

Seven players joined in as Hill shot from outside the area, Woozley deliberately deflected the ball, which hit the far-post, rebounded on to Thompson's head and looped agonisingly over the bar when it seemed certain that it must drop into the net.

Result.......Result.......Result.

NORTHAMPTON (0) **0** **TORQUAY** ......(0) **1**
Fowler 62

Att 5,675
Referee: Lee Probert

Stats......Stats.......Stats......Stats

NORTHAMPTON				TORQUAY		
1st	2nd	Total		Total	2nd	1st
1	3	4	**Corners**	4	2	2
9	5	14	**Fouls**	15	8	7
0	1	1	**Yellow cards**	1	1	0
0	0	0	**Red cards**	0	0	0
1	2	3	**Caught Offside**	5	3	2
4	2	6	**Shots on target**	3	2	1
0	2	2	**Shots off target**	9	5	4
0	0	0	**Hit woodwork**	1	1	0
49	51	50%	**Possession**	50%	49	51

"I can't take anything away from Torquay, they were well organised and didn't give the ball away. We created enough chances and didn't put the ball away.

Martin Wilkinson"

"**IT** was very hot so it was vitally important that we kept possession and I think we knocked the stuffing out of Northampton.

Leroy Rosenior"

Other Div 3 Results

Carlisle 1 York 2, Huddersfield 2 Cambridge Utd 2, Hull 4 Darlington 1, Kidderminster 2 Mansfield 1, Leyton Orient 1 Doncaster 3, Macclesfield 0 Boston Utd 0, Rochdale 1 Yeovil 3, Scunthorpe 1 Bristol Rovers 2, Southend 2 Cheltenham 0, Swansea 4 Bury 2

Northampton [0] 0 TORQUAY [0] 1

Goalkeeper Stats: Arjan Van Heusden Saves: Catch 8, Crosses: Catch 8

No.	Torquay Player Stats		Shots on target L/R/H/Oth	Shots off target L/R/H/Oth	Caught offside	Fouls conceded	Free-kicks won	Corners taken	Clearances	Defensive blocks
17	Sean Hankin	1st	-/-/-/-	-/-/-/-	-	1	-	-	-	-
		2nd	-/-/-/-	1/-/-/-	-	-	-	-	-	-
5	Craig Taylor	1st	-/-/-/-	-/-/-/-	-	1	3	-	-	-
		2nd	-/-/-/-	-/-/-/-	-	1	-	-	1	-
3	David Woozley	1st	-/-/-/-	-/-/1/-	2	2	1	-	-	-
		2nd	-/-/-/-	1/-/-/-	1	1	1	-	1	-
4	Lee Canoville	1st	-/-/-/-	-/-/-/-	-	-	1	-	1	-
		2nd	-/-/-/-	-/-/-/-	-	-	-	-	-	-
18	Steve Woods	1st	-/1/-/-	-/-/-/-	-	1	-	-	-	-
		2nd	-/-/-/-	-/-/-/-	-	-	-	-	-	-
6	Alex Russell	1st	-/-/-/-	-/2/-/-	-	-	-	2	-	-
	▪ 57	2nd	-/-/-/-	-/-/-/-	-	1	1	2	-	-
11	Kevin Hill	1st	-/-/-/-	-/-/-/-	-	1	2	-	-	-
	▼ 89	2nd	-/-/-/-	1/-/-/-	-	1	1	-	-	-
10	David Graham	1st	-/-/-/-	-/-/-/-	-	-	-	-	-	-
	▲ 61	2nd	-/-/-/-	1/-/-/-	1	2	-	-	-	-
15	Kevin Wills	1st	-/-/-/-	-/-/-/-	-	-	-	-	-	-
	▲ 89	2nd	-/-/-/-	-/-/-/-	-	1	-	-	-	-
14	Matthew Hockley	1st	-/-/-/-	-/-/-/-	-	-	-	-	-	-
		2nd	-/1/-/-	-/1/-/-	-	-	1	-	-	-
8	Jason Fowler	1st	-/-/-/-	-/-/-/-	-	-	2	-	-	-
		2nd	-/1/-/-	-/-/-/-	1	1	1	-	-	-
12	Jo Kuffour	1st	-/-/-/-	-/1/-/-	-	1	-	-	-	-
	▼ 61	2nd	-/-/-/-	-/-/-/-	-	-	-	-	-	-

Subs not used: Benefield, Dearden, Burgess. - **Formation: 4-5-1**

Goalkeeper Stats: Glyn Thompson Saves: Catch 4, Crosses: Catch 2

No.	Player Stats	Shots on target	Shots off target	Caught offside	Fouls conceded	Free-kicks won	Corners taken	Clearances	Defensive blocks
19	Martin Smith	1/1/-/-	-/1/-/-	-	-	1	-	-	-
9	Marc Richards	-/-/1/-	-/-/-/-	1	3	3	-	-	-
11	Paul Trollope ▪ 90	-/-/-/-	-/-/-/-	-	4	-	2	-	-
7	Martin Reeves	-/-/-/-	-/-/-/-	-	1	-	2	-	-
5	Chris Willmott	-/1/-/-	-/-/-/-	-	1	1	-	-	-
25	Derek Asamoah ▲ 82	-/-/-/-	-/-/-/-	-	-	-	-	-	-
16	Lawrie Dudfield ▼ 69	-/-/-/-	-/-/-/-	1	2	-	-	-	-
6	Paul Reid	-/-/-/-	-/-/-/-	-	1	1	-	-	-
2	Luke Chambers ▼ 82	-/-/-/-	-/-/-/-	-	-	3	-	1	1
30	Oliver Burgess ▲ 69	-/-/-/-	-/1/-/-	-	-	-	-	-	-
10	Joshua Low	-/2/-/-	-/-/-/-	1	1	3	-	1	-
3	Peter Clark	-/-/-/-	-/-/-/-	-	1	3	-	-	-

Subs not used: Sampson, Hargreaves, Harper. - **Formation: 4-3-3**

Torquay Played: 1 **Won** 1 **Drawn** 0 **Lost** 0 **For** 1 **Against** 0 **Pos** 10

Torquay [0] 1 CRYSTAL PALACE [1] 1 — 12th August

The Penalty shoot-out may have been a step too far in the end, but Torquay United's fans cheered them to the rafters at Plainmoor against Palace, and rightly so.

The First Division Eagles, semi-finalists in 2001 and quarter-finalists in 2002, had to pull out all the stops to reach the second round this time.

United, with Fowler in terrific form, lived up to Rosenior's attacking pre-match plan with a start which could easily have produced two goals in the first quarter of an hour.

Unfortunately, Fowler hobbled off after half an hour and just when United were getting to grips with his absence Palace caught them with a sucker punch.

In the 29th minute Neil Shipperley flicked on French 'keeper Cedric Berthelin's long ball and Dougie Freedman took one touch before slamming a 25-yard volley over Van Heusden and into the net.

The pace of Kuffour always worried the Palace defence and United kept their passing game going into the second half with constant applause from the stands.

The equaliser came in the 61st minute. Graham cut in from the left past Danny Butterfield and, just when it seemed as if he had been closed down, he shot from 18 yards and the bounce gave Berthelin no chance.

There was hardly a dull moment and the match got even better in the second half. Van Heusden, outstanding in goal, dived to keep out shots by Freedman and Black. Johnson was perpetual motion in the Palace attack.

Palace had to hang on grimly in the closing stages of normal time as Russell Kuffour and Hockley all went close.

Into extra-time, the pace and the quality never slackened and the atmosphere inside Plainmoor was electric.

Chances were missed by both teams and the game went into extra-time then penalties. Palace were bound to be favourites when the tie went to penalties, and so it proved.

No disgrace, and there weren't too many glum faces either as United trudged off to a standing ovation.

Result.......Result.......Result.

TORQUAY ....(0) **1** **CRYSTAL PAL**(1) **1**
Graham 61 — Freedman 29

Att 3,366
Referee: Steve Tomlinson

Stats......Stats.......Stats......Stats

TORQUAY				CRYSTAL PALACE		
1st	**2nd**	**Total**		**Total**	**2nd**	**1st**
4	3	7	**Corners**	6	3	3
6	5	11	**Fouls**	12	3	9
0	1	1	**Yellow cards**	1	0	1
0	0	0	**Red cards**	1	1	0
1	1	2	**Caught Offside**	4	3	1
3	5	8	**Shots on target**	7	3	4
1	5	6	**Shots off target**	2	1	1
0	0	0	**Hit woodwork**	1	1	0
44	46	45%	**Possession**	55%	54	56

> **IT** was a great game of football. Several of my players were exhausted at the finish, but they still had the courage to volunteer to take the penalties.
>
> **Leroy Rosenior**

> **TORQUAY** played really well and I am certainly relieved that we are through.
>
> **Steve Kember**

Other League Cup Results

Barnsley 1 Blackpool 2, Bradford 0 Darlington 0, Bristol R 0 Brighton 1, Cambridge Utd 1 Gillingham 2, Cardiff 4 Leyton Orient 1, Cheltenham 1 QPR 2, Chesterfield 0 Burnley 0, Colchester 2 Plymouth 1, Crewe 2 Wrexham 0, Doncaster 3 Grimsby 2, Luton 4 Yeovil 1, Macclesfield 1 Sheff Utd 2, Millwall 0 Oxford Utd 1, Northampton 1 Norwich 0, Port Vale 0 Nottm For 0, Preston 0 Notts Co 0, Rotherham 2 York 1, Scunthorpe 2 Oldham 1, Southend 2 Swindon 3, Tranmere 1 Bury 0, Walsall 2 Carlisle 1, Watford 0 Bournemouth 0, West Brom 4 Brentford 0, Wigan 2 Hull 0, Wycombe 2 Wimbledon 0

12th August

TORQUAY [0] 1 Crystal Palace [1] 1

Goalkeeper Stats: Arjan Van Heusden Saves: Catch 3, Parry 6, Crosses: Catch 15

#	Torquay Player Stats		Shots on target L/R/H/Oth	Shots off target L/R/H/Oth	Caught offside	Fouls conceded	Free-kicks won	Corners taken	Clearances	Defensive blocks
17	Sean Hankin	1st	-/-/-/-	-/-/-/-	-	-	1	-	1	1
		2nd	-/-/-/-	-/-/-/-	-	-	-	-	2	-
3	David Woozley	1st	-/-/-/-	-/-/-/-	-	-	1	-	1	-
		2nd	-/-/1/-	-/-/-/-	-	-	3	-	1	-
5	Craig Taylor	1st	1/-/-/-	-/-/-/-	-	-	-	-	1	-
		2nd	-/-/-/-	-/-/1/-	-	2	-	-	-	-
18	Steve Woods	1st	-/-/-/-	-/-/-/-	-	-	-	-	-	-
		2nd	-/-/-/-	-/-/-/-	-	-	-	-	4	-
4	Lee Canoville	1st	-/-/-/-	-/-/-/-	-	-	1	-	-	-
		2nd	-/-/-/-	-/1/-/-	1	1	1	-	-	-
6	Alex Russell	1st	-/-/-/-	1/-/-/-	-	-	-	4	-	-
		2nd	-/3/-/-	-/1/-/-	-	1	-	3	-	-
16	Jimmy Benefield	1st	-/-/-/-	-/-/-/-	-	-	-	-	-	-
	▲ 95	2nd	-/-/-/-	-/-/-/-	-	-	-	-	-	-
11	Kevin Hill	1st	-/-/-/-	-/-/-/-	-	2	1	-	1	-
	▼ 110 ■ 90	2nd	-/-/-/-	-/-/-/-	-	3	1	-	1	-
10	David Graham	1st	-/-/-/-	-/-/-/-	-	-	2	-	-	-
	▲ 20	2nd	-/1/-/-	-/1/-/-	1	2	-	-	-	1
15	Kevin Wills	1st	-/-/-/-	-/-/-/-	-	-	-	-	-	-
	▲ 110	2nd	-/-/-/-	-/-/-/-	-	-	-	-	-	-
14	Matthew Hockley	1st	-/-/-/-	-/-/-/-	-	4	1	-	-	-
		2nd	-/1/-/-	-/1/-/-	-	-	-	-	-	-
8	Jason Fowler	1st	-/2/-/-	-/-/-/-	-	-	1	-	-	-
	▼ 20	2nd	-/-/-/-	-/-/-/-	-	-	-	-	-	-
12	Jo Kuffour	1st	-/-/-/-	-/-/-/-	1	-	1	-	-	-
	▼ 95	2nd	-/-/-/-	-/-/1/-	-	-	1	-	-	-

Subs not used: Dearden, Burgess. - **Formation: 4-4-2**

Goalkeeper Stats: Cedric Berthelin Saves: Catch 15, Parry 3, Crosses: Catch 9, Punch 3

#	Player Stats	Shots on target	Shots off target	Caught offside	Fouls conceded	Free-kicks won	Corners taken	Clearances	Defensive blocks
8	Andrew Johnson	-/-/-/-	-/-/-/-	-	1	2	-	-	-
5	Kit Symons ▼ 67	-/-/3/-	-/-/-/-	-	-	-	-	1	2
14	Ben Watson ▲ 55	-/-/-/-	-/2/-/-	-	-	-	4	-	-
16	Tommy Black ▲ 67	1/-/-/-	-/1/-/-	1	1	-	-	-	-
4	Danny Butterfield	-/-/-/-	-/-/-/-	-	1	-	-	-	-
10	Shaun Derry	-/-/-/-	-/1/-/-	-	1	3	-	2	-
6	Tony Popovic ■ 3 ■ 74	-/-/-/-	-/-/-/-	-	4	-	-	1	1
12	Jamie Smith ▲ 55 ■ 98	-/-/-/-	-/-/-/-	-	1	-	-	-	-
15	Aki Riihilahti ▼ 55	-/-/1/-	-/-/-/-	-	1	1	-	-	-
11	Neil Shipperley	-/-/-/-	-/-/1/-	1	-	1	-	3	-
32	Darren Powell	-/-/-/-	-/-/-/-	-	1	1	-	5	-
9	Dougie Freedman	-/2/-/-	1/2/-/-	2	1	5	-	-	-
22	Wayne Routledge ▼ 55	-/-/-/-	-/-/-/-	-	3	2	3	-	-

Subs not used: Clarke, Williams. - **Formation: 3-4-3**

Torquay [0] 1 LINCOLN CITY [0] 0

16th August

Torquay's spirit and determination was summed up perfectly in this match by Hockley, whose 89th minute winner secured a precious victory for the Gulls.

The goal came courtesy of a quality counter-attack. The end-to-end move went through seven United players - Arjan Van Heusden, Alex Russell, Martin Gritton, Russell again, Hockley, Lee Canoville and finally Hockley again for the brave, close-range finish.

Statistics can often lie, but Van Heusden had to make only one save in the whole match, and that was in stoppage-time.

Simon Yeo was a pacy threat for Lincoln in the first half, even though no one finished off several of his inviting crosses.

Ben Futcher, City's tall central defender, headed one free-kick against the foot of a post early on, and Yeo cut in from the right in the 22nd minute and fired just wide.

But United, who started with Kevin Hill at left-back in place of the injured Sean Hankin, still dominated possession, even if they were often disappointing near goal.

Leroy Rosenior tactics opened up the midfield, where United went to town.

Kuffour and Graham both went close before Kuffour was clearly hauled down by Paul Mayo but failed to win a penalty.

And the second was even more of a mismatch with Lincoln's defence looking increasingly desperate as United mounted almost non-stop pressure. The Gulls amassed 14 shots or headers, five on target and nine off.

It seemed only a matter of time before United forced the winner. And Hockley's late goal was greeted rapturously by the crowd.

It had been the sort of game which United often drew, or maybe even lost, at home in the past. And in stoppage-time they nearly dropped their guard, Futcher laying the ball off for Yeo, clear on the left of the box.

Thankfully, Yeo snatched at his volley and the ball thumped into Van Heusden's stomach. An equaliser then would have been a travesty of justice.

Result.......Result.......Result.

TORQUAY ....(0) **1** **LINCOLN CITY** (0) **0**
Hockley 89

Att 2,920
Referee: M Cooper

Stats......Stats.......Stats......Stats

TORQUAY				LINCOLN CITY		
1st	**2nd**	**Total**		**Total**	**2nd**	**1st**
1	4	5	**Corners**	2	0	2
7	4	11	**Fouls**	16	11	5
1	0	1	**Yellow cards**	5	5	0
0	0	0	**Red cards**	0	0	0
3	4	7	**Caught Offside**	9	3	6
3	6	9	**Shots on target**	1	1	0
2	8	10	**Shots off target**	3	1	2
0	0	0	**Hit woodwork**	1	0	1
52	62	57%	**Possession**	43%	38	48

MATT Hockley's goal encapsulated the spirits in the side at the moment. They just never give up. It was no more than we deserved.

Leroy Rosenior

AT 0-0 with 10 minutes to go, we should have held on. We were caught on the break and it has cost us dearly.

Keith Alexander

Other Div 3 Results

Boston Utd 2 Huddersfield 2, Bristol Rovers 0 Rochdale 0, Bury 2 Scunthorpe 3, Cambridge Utd 3 Macclesfield 1, Cheltenham 3 Swansea 4, Darlington 0 Kidderminster 2, Doncaster 2 Southend 0, Mansfield 1 Leyton Orient 1, Oxford Utd 2 Hull 1, Yeovil 3 Carlisle 0, York 1 Northampton 0

TORQUAY [0] 1 Lincoln City [0] 0

Goalkeeper Stats: Arjan Van Heusden Saves: Catch 1, Crosses: Catch 1

No.	Torquay Player Stats	Half	Shots on target L/R/H/Oth	Shots off target L/R/H/Oth	Caught offside	Fouls conceded	Free-kicks won	Corners taken	Clearances	Defensive blocks
5	Craig Taylor	1st	-/-/-/-	-/-/-/-	-	2	1	-	3	1
		2nd	-/1/-/-	-/-/-/-	-	-	1	-	-	-
3	David Woozley	1st	1/-/-/-	-/-/-/-	-	2	1	-	-	-
	▼ 59	2nd	-/-/-/-	-/-/-/-	-	-	2	-	-	-
9	Martin Gritton	1st	-/-/-/-	-/-/-/-	-	-	-	-	-	-
	▲ 59	2nd	-/-/-/-	-/-/-/-	1	-	-	-	-	-
18	Steve Woods	1st	-/-/-/-	-/-/-/-	-	1	1	-	1	-
		2nd	-/-/-/-	-/-/-/-	1	3	-	-	-	-
4	Lee Canoville	1st	-/-/-/-	-/-/-/-	-	1	-	-	-	-
	■ 45	2nd	-/-/-/-	2/-/-/-	-	-	-	-	-	-
6	Alex Russell	1st	-/1/-/-	-/-/-/-	-	-	-	1	-	-
		2nd	-/1/-/-	-/-/-/-	1	-	2	3	-	-
16	Jimmy Benefield	1st	-/-/-/-	-/-/-/-	-	-	-	-	-	-
	▲ 72	2nd	-/-/-/-	-/1/-/-	-	-	1	-	-	-
11	Kevin Hill	1st	-/-/-/-	-/-/-/-	-	-	-	-	-	-
		2nd	-/-/-/-	1/-/-/-	-	-	1	-	-	-
15	Kevin Wills	1st	-/-/-/-	-/-/-/-	-	-	-	-	-	-
	▲ 88	2nd	-/-/-/-	-/-/-/-	-	-	-	-	-	-
10	David Graham	1st	-/1/-/-	-/-/-/-	3	-	1	-	-	-
		2nd	-/1/-/-	-/1/-/-	1	1	1	-	-	-
14	Matthew Hockley	1st	-/-/-/-	-/1/-/-	-	1	-	-	-	-
		2nd	-/2/-/-	-/1/-/-	-	-	-	-	-	-
8	Jason Fowler	1st	-/-/-/-	-/-/-/-	-	-	1	-	-	-
	▼ 88	2nd	-/1/-/-	-/1/-/-	-	-	-	1	-	-
12	Jo Kuffour	1st	-/-/-/-	-/1/-/-	-	-	-	-	-	-
	▼ 72	2nd	-/-/-/-	-/1/-/-	-	-	3	-	-	-

Subs not used: Dearden, Burgess. - **Formation: 4-4-2**

Goalkeeper Stats: Alan Marriott Saves: Catch 2, Feet 1, Crosses: Catch 3, Punch 1

No.	Player Stats	Shots on target	Shots off target	Caught offside	Fouls conceded	Free-kicks won	Corners taken	Clearances	Defensive blocks
15	Simon Weaver	-/-/-/-	-/-/-/-	-	2	1	-	4	1
27	Gary Fletcher	-/-/-/-	-/-/-/-	4	1	1	-	-	-
25	Niall McNamara ▲ 90	-/-/-/-	-/-/-/-	-	-	-	-	-	-
6	Ben Sedgemore ▼ 90 ■ 48	-/-/-/-	-/-/-/-	-	1	-	2	-	-
9	Simon Yeo	1/-/-/-	1/1/-/-	4	2	3	-	-	-
16	Rory May ▲ 68	-/-/-/-	-/-/-/-	-	1	1	-	-	-
5	Paul Morgan ■ 71	-/-/-/-	-/-/-/-	-	1	2	-	3	-
4	Ben Futcher ■ 50	-/-/-/-	-/-/1/-	-	2	-	-	5	1
3	Paul Mayo ■ 80	-/-/-/-	-/-/-/-	-	3	1	-	1	-
8	Richard Butcher	-/-/-/-	-/-/-/-	-	1	-	-	-	-
26	Richard Liburd ▼ 68 ■ 68	-/-/-/-	-/-/-/-	1	2	1	-	-	-

Subs not used: Willis, Wattley, Bailey. - **Formation: 3-5-2**

Torquay Played: 2 **Won** 2 **Drawn** 0 **Lost** 0 **For** 2 **Against** 0 **Pos** 7

Macclesfield [1] 1 TORQUAY [0] 1

23rd August

An afternoon which started with a dreadful tackle by Macclesfield Town captain David Flitcroft on Torquay United midfielder Alex Russell finished with the Gulls stretching their unbeaten league run to three games.

After only eight seconds, Flitcroft lunged at Russell with a reckless challenge that should have seen him sent off. Russell needed prolonged treatment before he could continue, but like the rest of his team-mates, he gritted his teeth and helped to earn a vital point.

After goalkeeper Arjan Van Heusden had kept the Silkmen at bay with a brilliant display just after half-time, an inspired double-substitution by Leroy Rosenior turned the match.

After 52 minutes, Rosenior took off both his wide players, Jo Kuffour and Jason Fowler, and sent on Jimmy Benefield and Kevin Wills.

The pair had been on the pitch only two minutes when Wills dashed round the back of Macclesfield right-back George Abbey to score United's equaliser with his first touch.

United must have feared the worst at the start of the game after Van Heusden saved Danny Whitaker's well taken 25-yard volley.

Gritton went clear on a Graham pass in the 20th minute before pulling his shot inches wide with Myhill to beat, and four minutes later Woods powered a header just wide from Russell's first-time cross from the left.

Torquay were not at their fluent best and injuries continued to affect the team.

Macclesfield went for the kill early in the second half, and it was then that Van Heusden kept United in the match.

But just when the opposition seemed to be well on top United scored. In the 55th minute Benefield won a header in midfield, Gritton carried on the move, spotted Wills on the move and delivered a terrific through ball inside Town right-back Abbey.

The pass was perfect and Wills dashed clear to score with a cool left-foot shot across Myhill and in off the right-hand post.

At the start of stoppage-time Taylor blocked a goalbound shot by Miles to make sure of United's point.

Result.......Result.......Result.

MACCLESFIELD..(1) **1** **TORQUAY** ......(0) **1**
Miles 8 Wills 55

Att 1,970
Referee: A Penn

Stats......Stats.......Stats......Stats

MACCLESFIELD				TORQUAY		
1st	2nd	Total		Total	2nd	1st
1	0	1	**Corners**	1	0	1
4	0	4	**Fouls**	6	0	6
1	0	1	**Yellow cards**	0	0	0
0	0	0	**Red cards**	0	0	0
0	0	0	**Caught Offside**	0	0	0
5	0	5	**Shots on target**	4	0	4
0	0	0	**Shots off target**	0	0	0
0	0	0	**Hit woodwork**	0	0	0
48	49	48%	**Possession**	52%	51	52

"**WE** got off to a magnificent start, but then we gifted them an equaliser with some poor defending. The rest was history.

David Moss"

"**IT** was warm and difficult, we were under the cosh a lot in the second half, but we deserved a point for the way we stuck at it.

Leroy Rosenior"

Other Div 3 Results

Carlisle 0 Bristol Rovers 2, Huddersfield 0 York 1, Hull 3 Cheltenham 3, Kidderminster 0 Bury 2, Leyton Orient 2 Yeovil 0, Rochdale 2 Cambridge Utd 2, Scunthorpe 1 Oxford Utd 1, Southend 0 Mansfield 3

23rd August

Macclesfield [1] 1 TORQUAY [0] 1

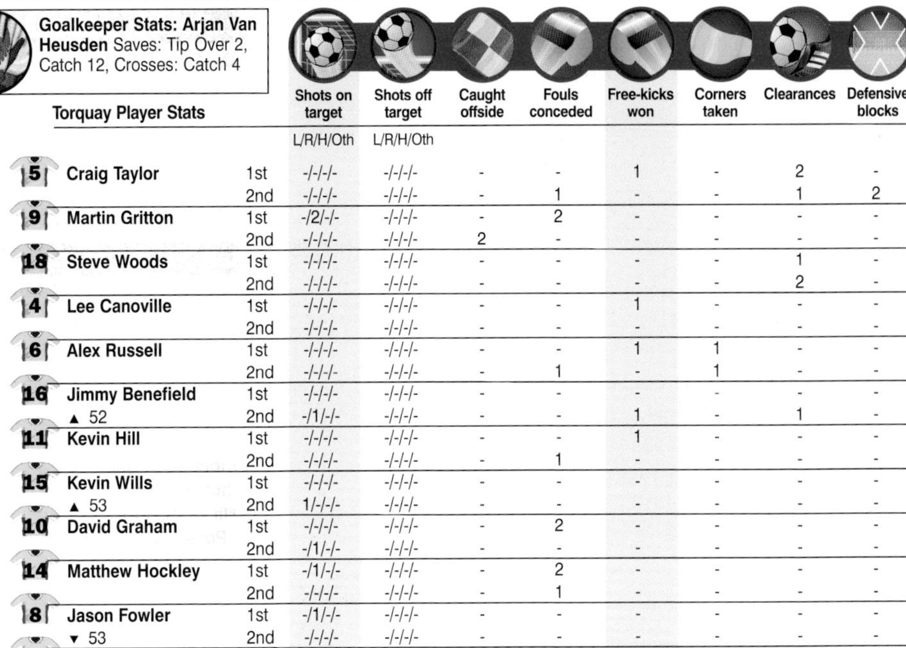

Goalkeeper Stats: Arjan Van Heusden Saves: Tip Over 2, Catch 12, Crosses: Catch 4

No.	Torquay Player Stats	Half	Shots on target L/R/H/Oth	Shots off target L/R/H/Oth	Caught offside	Fouls conceded	Free-kicks won	Corners taken	Clearances	Defensive blocks
5	Craig Taylor	1st	-/-/-/-	-/-/-/-	-	-	1	-	2	-
		2nd	-/-/-/-	-/-/-/-	-	1	-	-	1	2
9	Martin Gritton	1st	-/2/-/-	-/-/-/-	-	2	-	-	-	-
		2nd	-/-/-/-	-/-/-/-	2	-	-	-	-	-
18	Steve Woods	1st	-/-/-/-	-/-/-/-	-	-	-	-	1	-
		2nd	-/-/-/-	-/-/-/-	-	-	-	-	2	-
4	Lee Canoville	1st	-/-/-/-	-/-/-/-	-	-	1	-	-	-
		2nd	-/-/-/-	-/-/-/-	-	-	-	-	-	-
6	Alex Russell	1st	-/-/-/-	-/-/-/-	-	-	1	1	-	-
		2nd	-/-/-/-	-/-/-/-	-	1	-	1	-	-
16	Jimmy Benefield	1st	-/-/-/-	-/-/-/-	-	-	-	-	-	-
	▲ 52	2nd	-/1/-/-	-/-/-/-	-	-	1	-	1	-
11	Kevin Hill	1st	-/-/-/-	-/-/-/-	-	-	1	-	-	-
		2nd	-/-/-/-	-/-/-/-	-	1	-	-	-	-
15	Kevin Wills	1st	-/-/-/-	-/-/-/-	-	-	-	-	-	-
	▲ 53	2nd	1/-/-/-	-/-/-/-	-	-	-	-	-	-
10	David Graham	1st	-/-/-/-	-/-/-/-	-	2	-	-	-	-
		2nd	-/1/-/-	-/-/-/-	-	-	-	-	-	-
14	Matthew Hockley	1st	-/1/-/-	-/-/-/-	-	2	-	-	-	-
		2nd	-/-/-/-	-/-/-/-	-	1	-	-	-	-
8	Jason Fowler	1st	-/1/-/-	-/-/-/-	-	-	-	-	-	-
	▼ 53	2nd	-/-/-/-	-/-/-/-	-	-	-	-	-	-
12	Jo Kuffour	1st	-/-/-/-	-/-/-/-	-	-	-	-	-	-
	▼ 52	2nd	-/-/-/-	-/-/-/-	-	-	-	-	1	-

Subs not used: Dearden, Burgess, Killoughery. - **Formation: 4-4-2**

Goalkeeper Stats: Boaz Myhill Saves: Catch 6

No.	Player Stats	Shots on target	Shots off target	Caught offside	Fouls conceded	Free-kicks won	Corners taken	Clearances	Defensive blocks
3	Danny Adams	-/-/-/-	-/-/-/-	-	1	-	-	-	1
5	Karl Munroe	-/-/-/-	-/-/-/-	-	-	2	-	2	-
6	Steve Macauley	-/-/-/-	-/-/-/-	-	-	-	1	1	-
9	Matthew Tipton ▲ 64	-/1/-/-	-/-/-/-	-	-	-	-	1	-
12	Danny Whitaker	1/1/2/-	-/-/-/-	-	-	2	3	-	-
10	John Miles	-/3/-/-	-/-/-/-	3	1	2	-	-	-
18	Colin Little ▼ 64	1/-/-/-	-/-/-/-	-	-	-	-	-	-
16	George Abbey	-/1/-/-	-/-/-/-	-	-	1	-	-	-
4	David Smith	-/-/-/-	-/-/-/-	-	-	1	-	-	-
7	David Flitcroft ■ 1	1/1/-/-	-/-/-/-	-	2	1	-	-	-
14	Martin Carruthers	-/4/-/-	-/-/-/-	2	1	1	-	1	-

Subs not used: Wilson, Widdrington, Welch, Ross. - **Formation: 4-4-2**

Torquay Played: 3 **Won** 2 **Drawn** 1 **Lost** 0 **For** 3 **Against** 1 **Pos** 6

Torquay [0] 1 ROCHDALE [0] 3

25th August

Just when they should have been setting themselves up for a knock-out blow of their own, Torquay United walked on to a series of sucker-punches against Rochdale.

United failed to capitalise on an impressive start in which they forced three corners in the first four minutes and, although a David Graham goal briefly gave them some hope of salvaging a point, the Gull's reshuffled defence was split open far too often.

In the 57th minute United fell behind. Rochdale seized on a Kevin Wills header inside their own area, broke quickly and, after beating Benefield just outside United's box, he went down under Arjan Van Heusden's challenge.

The referee pointed to the spot and Lee McEvilly drove home the penalty.

United immediately sent on Jo Kuffour for Benefield, but within another minute they were two down.

This time Rochdale's Paul Connor hit United on the counter, sweeping past Hockley's hesitant challenge before shooting against the advancing Van Heusden. The ball rebounded and hit midfielder Robert Betts before bouncing into the empty net.

Hockley must have known that one more mistimed tackle would end his afternoon, and it came in the 73rd minute. His foul on McClare looked fairly innocuous, but referee Mr.Kettle's showed him the red card.

A match-winning hero against Lincoln just days before, sent off in his next home game - the fate of a committed footballer.

Just when it looked all over for Torquay, they pulled a goal back. Craig Taylor's long, diagonal ball put Kuffour in on the right and his short cross was buried by Graham from ten yards.

After Hockley's departure, Fowler was withdrawn to play as sweeper in a three-man defence, but in the 78th minute yet another counter-attack by the visitors saw Connor put McClare away on the left and his square ball left Betts with an easy chance for the third.

Result.......Result.......Result.

TORQUAY ....(0) **1** **ROCHDALE**....(0) **3**
Graham 75 — McEvilly 59(p), Betts 63, 78

Att 3,003
Referee: T Kettle

Stats......Stats.......Stats......Stats

TORQUAY				ROCHDALE		
1st	**2nd**	**Total**		**Total**	**2nd**	**1st**
5	3	8	**Corners**	6	1	5
8	8	16	**Fouls**	12	5	7
0	4	4	**Yellow cards**	4	3	1
0	1	1	**Red cards**	1	0	1
1	0	1	**Caught Offside**	7	3	4
2	3	5	**Shots on target**	5	4	1
3	9	12	**Shots off target**	7	0	7
0	0	0	**Hit woodwork**	0	0	0
44	48	46%	**Possession**	54%	52	56

WE needed to score in the first 20 minutes, but after we lost Lee Canoville (to injury) we fell away and a bad day turned into a horrendous one.

Leroy Rosenior

THE players have been fantastic. On Saturday against Cambridge we came from two goals down to get a point and this result speaks for itself.

Alan Buckley

Other Div 3 Results

Boston Utd 1 Carlisle 0, Bristol Rovers 2 Macclesfield 2, Cambridge Utd 0 Hull 2, Cheltenham 2 Kidderminster 1, Darlington 2 Leyton Orient 1, Doncaster 1 Huddersfield 1, Oxford Utd 3 Swansea 0, Yeovil 0 Northampton 2

TORQUAY [0] 1 Rochdale [0] 3

Goalkeeper Stats: Arjan Van Heusden Saves: Catch 2, Parry 2, Crosses: Catch 4 □ 59

No.	Torquay Player Stats	Half	Shots on target L/R/H/Oth	Shots off target L/R/H/Oth	Caught offside	Fouls conceded	Free-kicks won	Corners taken	Clearances	Defensive blocks
5	Craig Taylor	1st	-/-/-/-	1/-/-/-	-	2	-	-	3	1
		2nd	-/-/-/-	1/1/-/-	-	2	1	-	-	-
9	Martin Gritton	1st	-/-/-/-	-/-/-/-	-	-	-	-	-	-
	□ 87	2nd	-/-/1/-	-/-/-/-	-	1	1	-	-	-
18	Steve Woods	1st	-/-/-/-	-/-/-/-	-	1	1	-	-	-
		2nd	-/-/-/-	1/-/-/-	-	-	2	-	-	-
4	Lee Canoville	1st	-/-/-/-	-/-/-/-	-	-	-	-	-	-
	▼ 12	2nd	-/-/-/-	-/-/-/-	-	-	-	-	-	-
6	Alex Russell	1st	-/-/-/-	-/-/-/-	-	-	-	5	-	-
		2nd	-/-/-/-	1/-/-/-	-	1	-	3	-	-
16	Jimmy Benefield	1st	-/1/-/-	-/1/-/-	-	1	-	-	1	-
	▼ 59	2nd	-/-/-/-	-/-/-/-	-	-	-	-	-	-
11	Kevin Hill	1st	-/-/-/-	-/-/-/-	-	-	-	-	2	-
	▼ 67	2nd	-/-/-/-	-/-/-/-	-	-	-	-	-	-
15	Kevin Wills	1st	-/-/-/-	-/-/-/-	-	2	2	-	-	-
		2nd	-/-/-/-	1/-/-/-	-	-	-	-	-	-
10	David Graham	1st	-/1/-/-	-/1/-/-	1	1	2	-	-	-
		2nd	-/2/-/-	-/1/2/-	-	1	-	-	-	-
14	Matthew Hockley	1st	-/-/-/-	-/-/-/-	-	1	1	-	-	-
	□ 53 ■ 74	2nd	-/-/-/-	-/-/-/-	-	2	-	-	-	-
8	Jason Fowler	1st	-/-/-/-	-/-/-/-	-	-	1	-	1	-
	▲ 12 □ 79	2nd	-/-/-/-	-/-/-/-	-	-	-	-	-	-
12	Jo Kuffour	1st	-/-/-/-	-/-/-/-	-	-	-	-	-	-
	▲ 59	2nd	-/-/-/-	-/1/-/-	-	-	-	-	-	-
19	Graham Killoughery	1st	-/-/-/-	-/-/-/-	-	-	-	-	-	-
	▲ 67	2nd	-/-/-/-	-/-/-/-	-	-	1	-	-	-

Subs not used: Burgess, Dearden. - **Formation: 4-4-2**

Goalkeeper Stats: Matthew Gilks Saves: Catch 8 □ 90

No.	Player Stats	Shots on target	Shots off target	Caught offside	Fouls conceded	Free-kicks won	Corners taken	Clearances	Defensive blocks
15	Robert Betts □ 6	1/1/-/-	-/-/-/-	-	-	-	-	-	-
2	Wayne Evans	-/-/-/-	-/-/-/-	-	1	2	-	2	-
27	Paul Connor	-/1/-/-	-/1/1/-	7	2	4	-	1	-
3	Michael Simpkins □ 4 ■ 45	-/-/-/-	-/-/-/-	-	3	2	-	1	-
26	Simon Grand ▲ 45	-/-/-/-	-/-/-/-	-	-	-	-	1	-
6	Daryl Burgess	-/-/-/-	-/-/-/-	-	1	1	-	4	-
10	Matt Doughty	-/-/-/-	-/-/-/-	-	-	-	-	1	2
9	Chris Shuker ▼ 45	-/-/-/-	-/2/-/-	-	-	-	1	-	-
18	Lee McEvilly □ 90	-/-/-/-	-/-/-/-	-	3	4	-	1	-
4	Sean McClare	-/1/-/-	-/1/-/-	-	1	1	-	1	-
7	Leo Bertos	-/-/-/-	1/1/-/-	-	1	1	5	-	-

Subs not used: Edwards, Townson, McCourt, Beech. - **Formation: 4-4-2**

Torquay Played: 4 **Won** 2 **Drawn** 1 **Lost** 1 **For** 4 **Against** 4 **Pos** 7

Scunthorpe [0] 2 TORQUAY [1] 1

30th August

The importance of Alex Russell to Torquay United will never be more starkly underlined than it was at Glanford Park on, when ten-man Scunthorpe United came from behind to force a controversial victory in the fifth minute of stoppage-time.

United's midfield talisman is recognised as a master at ball retention, as he showed when the Gulls passed Northampton off the Sixfields Stadium pitch on the opening day of the season.

But at Macclesfield the weekend before, he was brutally fouled in the opening ten seconds. In the first couple of minutes on Saturday, Russell went up for a header and was taken out by his marker Ian Kilford. Russell played on for another quarter-of-an-hour before his double-vision got to the point where he could not carry on.

By the time Russell went off, United were a goal up when Gritton, on a through-ball by Fowler, pounced on a defensive mix-up between Scunthorpe goalkeeper Tom Evans and centre-half Jamie McCombe to clip home his first goal of the season.

Without playing with anything like the fluency of their first few performances, United deserved their half-time lead.

With nothing to lose, Scunthorpe threw themselves at a United defence in which Craig Taylor and Steve Woods were outstanding, while Hockley followed the wily Beagrie everywhere.

The Gulls had dealt with everything by the time Beagrie took a right-wing corner in the 86th minute.

Van Heusden went up with Torpey, couldn't hold the ball under the former Bristol City man's challenge and substitute Steve MacLean, on loan from Scottish giants Rangers, forced it home off the underside of the bar from six yards.

As the match moved into stoppage-time Scunthorpe put together a move fit to win any match.

Five men were involved in a move which ended with Calvo-Carcia slamming a right-foot shot into the top right-hand corner from 20 yards.

Result.......Result.......Result.

SCUNTHORPE ....(0) **2** **TORQUAY** ......(1) **1**
McLean 86 Gritton 15
Calvo-Garcia 90

Att 3,080
Referee: P Crossley

Stats......Stats.......Stats......Stats

SCUNTHORPE				TORQUAY		
1st	2nd	Total		Total	2nd	1st
4	4	8	**Corners**	1	0	1
8	2	10	**Fouls**	11	6	5
1	1	2	**Yellow cards**	2	1	1
0	1	1	**Red cards**	0	0	0
1	1	2	**Caught Offside**	7	4	3
4	3	7	**Shots on target**	3	1	2
3	5	8	**Shots off target**	9	5	4
0	0	0	**Hit woodwork**	0	0	0
38	57	47%	**Possession**	53%	43	62

WE had enough chances in the first half to have won but we gave them a Keystone Cops goal and our confidence was shot to pieces.

Brian Laws

IT'S been an interesting day. I was sent off after kicking a water bottle. We were comfortably in control and should have taken the game.

Leroy Rosenior

Other Div 3 Results

Carlisle 0 Cambridge Utd 0, Huddersfield 2 Bristol Rovers 1, Hull 2 Boston Utd 1, Kidderminster 1 Oxford Utd 1, Leyton Orient 1 Cheltenham 4, Macclesfield 4 Yeovil 1, Northampton 1 Doncaster 0, Rochdale 4 Darlington 2, Southend 1 Bury 0, Swansea 4 Mansfield 1

Scunthorpe [0] 2 TORQUAY [1] 1

Goalkeeper Stats: Arjan Van Heusden Saves: Catch 4, Crosses: Catch 4

No.	Torquay Player Stats		Shots on target L/R/H/Oth	Shots off target L/R/H/Oth	Caught offside	Fouls conceded	Free-kicks won	Corners taken	Clearances	Defensive blocks
7	Tony Bedeau	1st	-/-/-/-	-/-/-/-	-	-	-	-	1	-
	▼ 65 □ 22	2nd	-/-/-/-	-/1/-/-	-	-	1	-	-	-
5	Craig Taylor	1st	-/-/-/-	-/-/-/-	-	1	-	-	2	-
		2nd	-/-/-/-	-/-/-/-	-	2	-	-	4	-
9	Martin Gritton	1st	1/1/-/-	1/-/-/-	2	2	1	-	-	-
	□ 90	2nd	1/-/-/-	-/-/-/-	2	1	-	-	-	-
18	Steve Woods	1st	-/-/-/-	-/-/-/-	-	-	-	-	-	-
		2nd	-/-/-/-	-/-/-/-	-	2	1	-	1	-
16	Jimmy Benefield	1st	-/-/-/-	-/-/-/-	-	-	-	-	-	-
	▲ 65	2nd	-/-/-/-	-/-/-/-	-	-	-	-	-	-
6	Alex Russell	1st	-/-/-/-	-/-/-/-	-	-	2	1	-	-
	▼ 21	2nd	-/-/-/-	-/-/-/-	-	-	-	-	-	-
15	Kevin Wills	1st	-/-/-/-	1/-/-/-	-	1	2	-	-	-
		2nd	-/-/-/-	-/-/-/-	-	-	-	-	1	-
10	David Graham	1st	-/-/-/-	-/1/-/-	1	-	1	-	-	-
	▲ 21	2nd	-/-/-/-	1/-/-/-	2	1	-	-	-	-
14	Matthew Hockley	1st	-/-/-/-	-/1/-/-	-	1	1	-	-	-
		2nd	-/-/-/-	-/-/-/-	-	-	-	-	-	-
8	Jason Fowler	1st	-/-/-/-	-/-/-/-	-	-	-	-	-	-
	▼ 90	2nd	-/-/-/-	-/-/-/-	-	-	-	-	-	-
12	Jo Kuffour	1st	-/-/-/-	-/-/-/-	-	-	1	-	-	-
		2nd	-/-/-/-	-/3/-/-	-	-	-	-	-	-
19	Graham Killoughery	1st	-/-/-/-	-/-/-/-	-	-	-	-	-	-
	▲ 90	2nd	-/-/-/-	-/-/-/-	-	-	-	-	1	-

Subs not used: Dearden, Burgess. - **Formation: 4-4-2**

Goalkeeper Stats: Tom Evans Saves: Catch 6, Round Post 2, Crosses: Catch 2

No.	Player Stats	Shots on target	Shots off target	Caught offside	Fouls conceded	Free-kicks won	Corners taken	Clearances	Defensive blocks
11	Alex Calvo-Garcia ▲ 45	-/1/-/-	-/-/-/-	-	-	-	-	-	-
15	Ian Kilford ▼ 45	-/-/-/-	-/-/-/-	-	1	-	-	-	-
6	Cliff Byrne	-/-/-/-	-/-/-/-	-	2	1	-	1	-
5	Mark Jackson	-/-/-/-	-/-/1/-	-	1	1	-	-	-
19	Richard Kell	-/-/-/-	-/-/-/-	-	1	-	-	-	-
22	Steven MacLean ▲ 81	-/1/-/-	-/-/-/-	-	-	-	-	-	-
10	Steve Torpey	-/-/-/-	1/-/1/-	1	2	2	-	-	-
3	Kevin Sharp	-/-/-/-	-/1/-/-	-	-	2	-	-	-
4	Jamie McCombe	-/-/-/-	-/-/-/-	-	-	2	-	1	-
9	Paul Hayes ▼ 81 □ 11	-/2/-/-	-/2/1/-	-	1	3	-	-	-
8	Wayne Graves □ 5 ■ 57	-/-/-/-	-/1/-/-	-	2	-	-	-	-
14	Peter Beagrie	-/3/-/-	-/-/-/-	1	-	-	8	-	-

Subs not used: Featherstone, Ridley, Russell. - **Formation: 4-4-2**

Torquay Played: 5 **Won** 2 **Drawn** 1 **Lost** 2 **For** 5 **Against** 6 **Pos** 12

...August Team Stats.....Team Stats......Team Stats......Team S

League table at the end of August

	HOME						AWAY						
	P	W	D	L	F	A	W	D	L	F	A	Pts	Df
Swansea	5	3	0	0	11	3	1	0	1	4	6	12	6
York	5	2	0	0	3	0	2	0	1	3	4	12	2
Oxford Utd	5	2	0	0	5	1	1	2	0	3	2	11	5
Hull	5	2	1	0	9	5	1	0	1	3	2	10	5
Northampton	5	2	0	1	2	1	1	0	1	2	1	9	2
Doncaster	5	1	1	0	3	1	1	1	1	3	2	8	3
Rochdale	5	1	1	1	7	7	1	1	0	3	1	8	2
Bristol Rovers	5	0	2	0	2	2	2	0	1	5	3	8	2
Mansfield	5	1	1	0	6	1	1	0	2	5	6	7	4
Cheltenham	5	1	0	1	5	5	1	1	1	7	6	7	1
Kidderminster	5	1	1	1	3	4	1	0	1	3	2	7	0
Torquay	**5**	**1**	**0**	**1**	**2**	**3**	**1**	**1**	**1**	**3**	**3**	**7**	**-1**
Scunthorpe	5	1	1	1	4	4	1	0	1	3	7	7	-4
Macclesfield	5	1	2	0	5	2	0	1	1	3	5	6	1
Cambridge U	5	1	0	1	3	3	0	3	0	4	4	6	0
Huddersfield	5	1	1	1	4	4	0	2	0	3	3	6	0
Bury	5	1	0	1	4	4	1	0	2	4	5	6	-1
Yeovil	5	1	0	1	3	2	1	0	2	4	7	6	-2
Southend	5	2	0	1	3	3	0	0	2	0	4	6	-4
Boston Utd	5	1	1	0	3	2	0	1	2	1	5	5	-3
Lincoln City	5	1	1	1	3	1	0	0	2	1	3	4	0
Leyton Orient	5	1	0	2	4	7	0	1	1	2	3	4	-4
Darlington	5	1	0	1	2	3	0	0	3	3	9	3	-7
Carlisle	5	0	1	2	1	4	0	0	2	0	4	1	-7

August matches table

	P	W	D	L	F	A	Pts
Swansea	5	4	0	1	15	9	12
York	5	4	0	1	6	4	12
Oxford Utd	5	3	2	0	8	3	11
Hull	5	3	1	1	12	7	10
Northampton	5	3	0	2	4	2	9
Rochdale	5	2	2	1	10	8	8
Bristol Rovers	5	2	2	1	7	5	8
Doncaster	5	2	2	1	6	3	8
Cheltenham	5	2	1	2	12	11	7
Mansfield	5	2	1	2	11	7	7
Scunthorpe	5	2	1	2	7	11	7
Kidderminster	5	2	1	2	6	6	7
Torquay	**5**	**2**	**1**	**2**	**5**	**6**	**7**
Macclesfield	5	1	3	1	8	7	6
Bury	5	2	0	3	8	9	6
Cambridge Utd	5	1	3	1	7	7	6
Huddersfield	5	1	3	1	7	7	6
Yeovil	5	2	0	3	7	9	6
Southend	5	2	0	3	3	7	6
Boston Utd	5	1	2	2	4	7	5
Leyton Orient	5	1	1	3	6	10	4
Lincoln City	5	1	1	3	4	4	4
Darlington	5	1	0	4	5	12	3
Carlisle	5	0	1	4	1	8	1

August team stats details

Club Name	Ply	Shots On	Shots Off	Corners	Hit W'work	Caught Offside	Offside Trap	Fouls	Yellow Cards	Red Cards	Pens Awarded	Pens Con
Boston Utd	5	23	30	22	3	27	11	63	9	1	- (-)	-
Bristol Rovers	5	26	29	19	0	22	13	72	3	1	- (-)	1
Bury	5	31	28	25	1	21	21	73	15	0	1 (1)	1
Cambridge U	5	28	22	34	0	22	11	62	7	0	- (-)	1
Carlisle	5	28	26	32	0	9	24	68	11	2	- (-)	-
Cheltenham	5	35	27	29	1	27	21	59	10	0	1 (1)	1
Darlington	5	21	23	23	0	20	20	71	13	0	- (-)	1
Doncaster	5	26	27	35	1	27	11	55	8	0	- (-)	1
Huddersfield	5	27	22	19	1	9	30	62	9	1	- (-)	-
Hull	5	39	39	38	2	17	27	68	5	0	- (-)	-
Kidderminster	5	27	25	27	0	16	15	54	5	1	2 (1)	-
Leyton Orient	5	34	26	33	2	16	38	59	7	1	1 (1)	-
Lincoln City	5	16	14	28	1	20	26	74	12	1	1 (1)	1
Macclesfield	5	33	20	14	0	24	13	50	8	0	- (-)	-
Mansfield	5	37	20	31	2	17	5	42	14	2	- (-)	2
Northampton	5	31	14	32	0	14	20	67	9	0	- (-)	-
Oxford Utd	5	19	28	17	1	21	19	71	5	1	2 (2)	2
Rochdale	5	36	30	28	0	15	21	55	12	2	3 (3)	1
Scunthorpe	5	30	29	38	2	16	21	55	9	1	1 (1)	-
Southend	5	26	30	14	0	15	17	36	7	0	2 (1)	-
Swansea	5	45	38	37	1	2	14	52	6	0	1 (1)	2
Torquay	**5**	**24**	**40**	**19**	**1**	**20**	**14**	**59**	**8**	**1**	**- (-)**	**-**
Yeovil	5	35	32	34	0	20	13	54	8	0	- (-)	-
York	5	21	18	19	0	24	16	64	9	2	- (-)	1

 Monthly Match Details: Games 60 **Home Wins** 29 **Away Wins** 17 **Draws** 14

...August Player Stats..... Player Stats...... Player Stats......Pla

Monthly Top scorers

Lee Trundle (Swansea)	5
Danny Allsopp (Hull)	4
Jonathan Stead (Huddersfield)	4
Kevin Gall (Yeovil)	4
Iyseden Christie (Mansfield)	4
Bradley Maylett (Swansea)	3
D Chillingworth (Cambridge Utd)	3
Leo Fortune-West (Doncaster)	3
Jason Price (Hull)	3
Martin Carruthers (Macclesfield)	3

Penalties scored

3 Lee McEvilly (Rochdale), **2** Andy Crosby (Scunthorpe)

Assists

Mitch Ward (York)	3
Paul Connor (Swansea)	3
Lee Trundle (Swansea)	3
Anthony Carss (Huddersfield)	2
Stuart Bimson (Cambridge Utd)	2
Chris Hughes (Darlington)	2
Jamie Paterson (Doncaster)	2

Quickest goals

1:26 mins - Lee Bullock (Carlisle vs York)

1:51 mins - John Miles (Bristol Rovers vs Macclesfield)

3:02 mins - Paul Raven (Carlisle vs York)

3:33 mins - Kevin Gall (Yeovil vs Carlisle)

3:37 mins - Lee Thorpe (Leyton Orient vs Yeovil)

Top Keeper

	Mins	Gls
G Thompson (Northampton)	477	2
Andy Woodman (Oxford U)	480	3
Andy Warrington (Doncaster)	478	3
Mark Ovendale (York)	483	4
Alan Marriott (Lincoln City)	479	4
Kevin Miller (Bristol Rovers)	481	5
Roger Freestone (Swansea)	95	1
Shane Higgs (Cheltenham)	189	2

Shots on target

Lee Trundle (Swansea)	13
Peter Beagrie (Scunthorpe)	13
Iyseden Christie (Mansfield)	13
Jonathan Stead (Huddersfield)	12
Joshua Low (Northampton)	11
Martin Carruthers (Macclesfield)	11
Danny Allsopp (Hull)	10
Jason Price (Hull)	10
Bradley Maylett (Swansea)	10
John Miles (Macclesfield)	10

Shots off target

Ben Burgess (Hull)	12
Neil Redfearn (Boston Utd)	12
Lee Trundle (Swansea)	11
Jonathan Stead (Huddersfield)	9
Iyseden Christie (Mansfield)	9
David Graham (Torquay)	8
Julian Alsop (Oxford Utd)	8
Paul Hayes (Scunthorpe)	8
Drewe Broughton (Southend)	8
Richie Foran (Carlisle)	8

Caught offside

Stuart Douglas (Boston Utd)	13
John Miles (Macclesfield)	13
Martin Carruthers (Macclesfield)	13
Gregg Blundell (Doncaster)	12
Paul Connor (Swansea)	12
Junior Agogo (Bristol Rovers)	11
Steve Basham (Oxford Utd)	11
Steve Torpey (Scunthorpe)	11
Liam George (York)	11

Free-kicks won

Drewe Broughton (Southend)	18
Paul Connor (Swansea)	18
Dave Kitson (Cambridge Utd)	16
Paul Tait (Bristol Rovers)	15
Kirk Jackson (Yeovil)	13
Bradley Maylett (Swansea)	12
Leon Britton (Swansea)	12
Karl Munroe (Macclesfield)	12
Barry Conlon (Darlington)	11

Steve Woods (v Scunthorpe)

Fouls conceded

Ben Burgess (Hull)	14
Drewe Broughton (Southend)	13
Julian Alsop (Oxford Utd)	13
Martin Carruthers (Macclesfield)	13
Danny Swailes (Bury)	12
Darren Dunning (York)	12
Lee Thorpe (Bristol Rovers)	12
Jonathan Stead (Huddersfield)	12
Craig Taylor (Torquay)	12

Fouls without a card

Ben Burgess (Hull)	14
Craig Taylor (Torquay)	12
Richard Butcher (Lincoln City)	12
Junior Agogo (Bristol Rovers)	10
Kevin Nugent (Swansea)	10
Jon Ashton (Oxford Utd)	9
Kirk Jackson (Yeovil)	8
David Graham (Torquay)	8
Richard Kell (Scunthorpe)	8

Martin Gritton can't help showing his delight for Lee Canoville as he celebrates his first half scorcher.
Torquay v Northampton
HPL01273_TNA_013

Substitute Joe Broad had little time to impress after replacing Jason Fowler, but gets in a telling cross soon after coming on.
HPL01273_TNA_004

Woods and Torpey battle it out.
Torquay v Scunthorpe
HPL01386_TNA_004

Steve Woods gets in a headed clearance in the first half.
Torquay v Scunthorpe
HPL01386_TNA_008

Torquay [0] 2 LEYTON ORIENT [0] 1

6th September

If leading scorer David Graham was trying to make a point, after being left on the subs' bench for the second week running, he could hardly have made it more tellingly than he did against Leyton Orient at Plainmoor.

The former Rangers and Scotland Under-21 starlet had two classily taken goals, making his tally for the season four - and a second-half performance which lit up a disjointed match.

The double-dismissal of Craig Taylor and Orient striker Gary Alexander blighted the first half. Taylor's tackle on Alexander prompted what looked like a stamping reaction from the Orient player. Nearly a dozen players joined the melee which followed. With the help of his linesman, referee Clive Penton first sent off Alexander and then showed a red card to Taylor.

Both teams had to reshuffle their formations and chances were scarce. However, Canoville denied Thorpe a scoring header, flicking Lockwood's cross away for a corner. In between, Martin Gritton twice went close for United, but by half-time neither team had come to terms with their new arrangements.

United restarted slowly, and it was only a matter of time before the manager turned to Graham. After fifty minutes, the Scot was on for makeshift striker Kevin Wills. Just three minutes later he struck. Jason Fowler's lobbed through-ball supplied the ammunition and Graham, so cool when he might easily have snatched at the chance, finished with a cushioned first-time left-foot volley which beat advancing keeper Lee Harrison and defender Justin Miller.

David Hunt's long throws for Orient often had United's defence under pressure and it was time for them to dig in. Right-winger Tony Bedeau, who did most of his best work helping out in defence, denied Thorpe with an important defensive header.

But just when United needed a second goal badly, Graham came up trumps again. Isolating Orient's sweeper Matt Joseph one-for-one on the left, Graham produced a burst of pace to skip past him and finished with a toe-poke shot under Harrison.

After collecting a booking for over-celebration , Graham nearly grabbed a third goal, and he also set up Gritton for a shot well saved. Orient finally pulled a goal back when Tom Newey nipped in at the near-post to tap in Hunt's right-wing free-kick.

Result.......Result.......Result.

TORQUAY ....(0) **2** **LEYTON O**......(0) **1**
Graham 54, 73 Newey 86

Att 2,362
Referee: C Penton

Stats......Stats.......Stats......Stats

TORQUAY				LEYTON ORIENT		
1st	2nd	Total		Total	2nd	1st
0	1	1	**Corners**	8	7	1
2	4	6	**Fouls**	20	13	7
1	1	2	**Yellow cards**	2	1	1
1	0	1	**Red cards**	2	1	1
3	1	4	**Caught Offside**	4	1	3
3	3	6	**Shots on target**	3	2	1
2	2	4	**Shots off target**	4	3	1
0	0	0	**Hit woodwork**	0	0	0
50	49	50%	**Possession**	50%	51	50

I'M delighted and proud of my players. We may not have played as well as we can but the determination in the circumstances was exceptional.

Leroy Rosenior

IN the last half hour we had a lot of pressure, with seven or eight corners, but we didn't make their goalkeeper work hard enough.

Paul Brush

Other Div 3 Results

Boston Utd 1 Scunthorpe 1, Bristol Rovers 1 Kidderminster 0, Bury 2 Huddersfield 1, Darlington 2 Carlisle 0, Mansfield 3 Macclesfield 2, Oxford Utd 2 Southend 0, Yeovil 2 Swansea 0, York 1 Rochdale 2

6th September

TORQUAY [0] 2 Leyton Orient [0] 1

Goalkeeper Stats: Arjan Van Heusden Saves: Catch 2, Crosses: Catch 3

No.	Torquay Player Stats		Shots on target L/R/H/Oth	Shots off target L/R/H/Oth	Caught offside	Fouls conceded	Free-kicks won	Corners taken	Clearances	Defensive blocks
7	Tony Bedeau	1st	-/-/-/-	-/-/-/-	-	-	2	-	-	-
		2nd	-/-/-/-	-/-/-/-	-	-	4	-	1	-
5	Craig Taylor	1st	-/-/-/-	-/-/-/-	-	-	-	-	-	-
	■ 11	2nd	-/-/-/-	-/-/-/-	-	-	-	-	-	-
9	Martin Gritton	1st	-/-/-/-	2/-/-/-	2	-	-	-	-	-
		2nd	1/-/-/-	-/-/-/-	-	-	-	-	1	-
18	Steve Woods	1st	-/-/-/-	-/-/-/-	1	-	1	-	-	-
		2nd	-/-/-/-	-/-/-/-	-	-	2	-	3	-
4	Lee Canoville	1st	-/-/-/-	-/-/-/-	-	-	-	-	1	-
		2nd	-/-/-/-	-/-/-/-	-	-	1	-	-	-
6	Alex Russell	1st	-/2/-/-	-/-/-/-	-	-	-	-	-	-
		2nd	-/-/-/-	-/-/-/-	-	1	-	1	-	-
16	Jimmy Benefield	1st	-/-/-/-	-/-/-/-	-	-	-	-	-	-
	▲ 65	2nd	-/-/-/-	-/1/-/-	-	-	-	-	1	-
11	Kevin Hill	1st	-/-/1/-	-/-/-/-	-	-	-	-	-	-
		2nd	-/-/-/-	-/-/-/-	1	-	3	-	3	-
15	Kevin Wills	1st	-/-/-/-	-/-/-/-	-	1	2	-	-	-
	▼ 50 ■ 14	2nd	-/-/-/-	-/-/-/-	-	-	-	-	-	-
10	David Graham	1st	-/-/-/-	-/-/-/-	-	-	-	-	-	-
	▲ 50 ■ 7	2nd	1/1/-/-	1/-/-/-	-	1	2	-	-	-
14	Matthew Hockley	1st	-/-/-/-	-/-/-/-	-	-	1	-	-	-
		2nd	-/-/-/-	-/-/-/-	-	-	1	-	-	-
8	Jason Fowler	1st	-/-/-/-	-/-/-/-	-	1	1	-	-	-
	▼ 65	2nd	-/-/-/-	-/-/-/-	-	2	-	-	-	-

Subs not used: Dearden, Killoughery, Camara. - **Formation: 4-4-2**

Goalkeeper Stats: Lee Harrison Saves: Catch 3, Crosses: Catch 2

No.	Player Stats	Shots on target	Shots off target	Caught offside	Fouls conceded	Free-kicks won	Corners taken	Clearances	Defensive blocks
10	Lee Thorpe	-/-/1/-	-/-/-/-	1	2	1	-	-	-
23	Tom Newey	1/-/-/-	-/-/-/-	2	2	1	-	-	-
7	Justin Miller ▼ 71	-/1/-/-	-/-/-/-	-	-	-	-	-	-
2	Matthew Joseph	-/-/-/-	-/-/-/-	-	1	-	-	-	-
12	Marcus Ebdon	-/-/-/-	-/-/-/-	-	1	2	-	-	-
17	Jabo Ibehre ▲ 71	-/-/-/-	-/-/1/-	-	1	-	-	-	-
4	Greg Heald ■ 35	-/-/-/-	-/-/1/-	-	8	-	-	-	-
3	Matthew Lockwood ■ 90	-/-/-/-	-/-/-/-	1	2	-	3	2	-
27	Alan McCormack ▼ 76 ■ 53	-/-/-/-	1/-/1/-	-	2	1	5	-	-
16	Wayne Purser ▲ 76	-/-/-/-	-/-/-/-	-	-	-	-	-	-
19	David Hunt	-/-/-/-	-/-/-/-	-	1	1	-	-	-
9	Gary Alexander ■ 10	-/-/-/-	-/-/-/-	-	-	-	-	-	-

Subs not used: Morris, Downer, Jones. - **Formation: 3-5-2**

Torquay Played: 6 **Won** 3 **Drawn** 1 **Lost** 2 **For** 7 **Against** 7 **Pos** 9

Cambridge Utd [1] 1 TORQUAY [1] 1 — 13th September

United's decision to stretch their Abbey Stadium pitch by ten yards this season only increased the already draining conditions for both sides.

Despite a bright start, the Gulls often found themselves stretched in defence, and conceded a goal from former Plainmoor trainee Luke Guttridge in the ninth minute.

Jo Kuffour's well-taken equaliser in the 36th minute did not spare United's players from some pretty straight talking by head coach Leroy Rosenior at half-time.They certainly tightened up in a second half in which Cambridge didn't have a single shot or header on target.

Referee Steve Tanner turned down a penalty appeal; booking Graham for diving early in the half. And in the 47th minute Graham clearly beat Cambridge's pushed-up offside-trap on a through-ball by Kuffour, only for linesman John Hayto to stick his flag up late.

But then Cambridge took the lead. Former Exeter midfielder Justin Walker's pass up the right wing gave Dave Kitson the chance to outpace Craig Taylor and Steve Woods. He was able to look up, spot Guttridge on a break from midfield and his square pass found the fair-haired lad from Newton Abbot completely unmarked.

The corner-count was an extraordinary 9-0 in Torquay's favour when former Cambridge schemer Russell swung over his latest flag-kick from the left, Taylor headed the ball back at the far-post for Kuffour to bury a first-time right-foot volley from six yards.

Still United hardly looked secure, and in the 43rd minute Alex Revell put Daniel Chillingworth clear. He seemed certain to score, but his effort was straight at Van Heusden, also playing against his old club, and the Dutchman smothered the shot.

Chances were scarce, but United will look back and feel that they would have gone on and finished the job on a better day.

Result.......Result.......Result.

CAMBRIDGE U....(1) **1** **TORQUAY** ......(1) **1**
Guttridge 9 Kuffour 36

Att 3,723
Referee: S Tanner

Stats......Stats.......Stats......Stats

CAMBRIDGE UTD				TORQUAY		
1st	2nd	Total		Total	2nd	1st
0	3	3	Corners	12	3	9
5	10	15	Fouls	4	0	4
1	2	3	Yellow cards	2	1	1
0	1	1	Red cards	0	0	0
3	1	4	Caught Offside	5	3	2
3	1	4	Shots on target	7	2	5
2	5	7	Shots off target	3	2	1
0	1	1	Hit woodwork	0	0	0
40	41	41%	Possession	59%	59	60

I never thought we looked in danger of losing, but we have to improve as an attacking team if we are going to make progress.

John Taylor

WE were a little slack in defence in the first half, but when we dropped Jason Fowler a bit deeper we looked a lot more solid.

Leroy Rosenior

Other Div 3 Results

Bristol Rovers 2 Boston Utd 0, Bury 1 Cheltenham 1, Carlisle 3 Rochdale 2, Darlington 2 Doncaster 1, Huddersfield 3 Northampton 0, Hull 3 Southend 2, Macclesfield 1 Kidderminster 1, Oxford Utd 1 Mansfield 1, Scunthorpe 2 Swansea 2, Yeovil 3 York 0

Cambridge Utd [1] 1 TORQUAY [1] 1

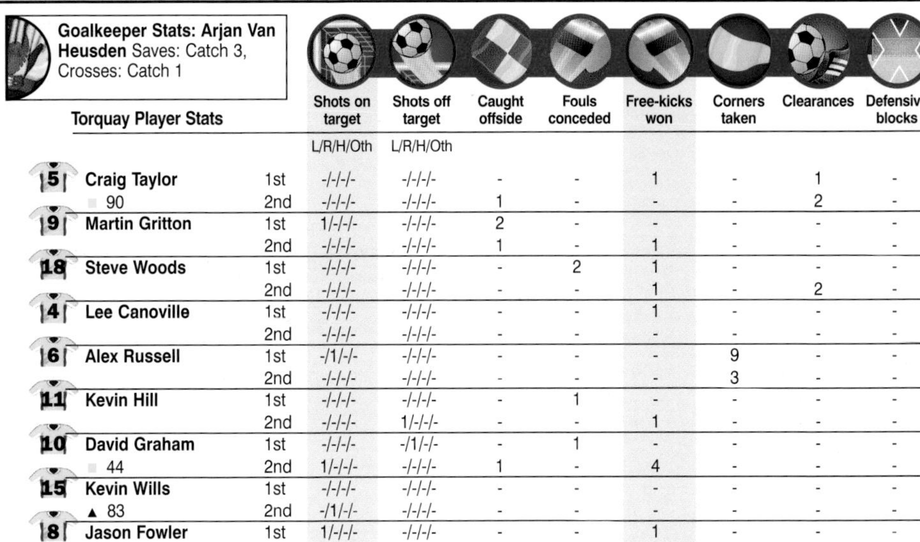

Goalkeeper Stats: Arjan Van Heusden Saves: Catch 3, Crosses: Catch 1

No.	Torquay Player Stats		Shots on target L/R/H/Oth	Shots off target L/R/H/Oth	Caught offside	Fouls conceded	Free-kicks won	Corners taken	Clearances	Defensive blocks
5	Craig Taylor	1st	-/-/-/-	-/-/-/-	-	-	1	-	1	-
	■ 90	2nd	-/-/-/-	-/-/-/-	1	-	-	-	2	-
9	Martin Gritton	1st	1/-/-/-	-/-/-/-	2	-	-	-	-	-
		2nd	-/-/-/-	-/-/-/-	1	-	1	-	-	-
18	Steve Woods	1st	-/-/-/-	-/-/-/-	-	2	1	-	-	-
		2nd	-/-/-/-	-/-/-/-	-	-	1	-	2	-
4	Lee Canoville	1st	-/-/-/-	-/-/-/-	-	-	1	-	-	-
		2nd	-/-/-/-	-/-/-/-	-	-	-	-	-	-
6	Alex Russell	1st	-/1/-/-	-/-/-/-	-	-	-	9	-	-
		2nd	-/-/-/-	-/-/-/-	-	-	-	3	-	-
11	Kevin Hill	1st	-/-/-/-	-/-/-/-	-	1	-	-	-	-
		2nd	-/-/-/-	1/-/-/-	-	-	1	-	-	-
10	David Graham	1st	-/-/-/-	-/1/-/-	-	1	-	-	-	-
	■ 44	2nd	1/-/-/-	-/-/-/-	1	-	4	-	-	-
15	Kevin Wills	1st	-/-/-/-	-/-/-/-	-	-	-	-	-	-
	▲ 83	2nd	-/1/-/-	-/-/-/-	-	-	-	-	-	-
8	Jason Fowler	1st	1/-/-/-	-/-/-/-	-	-	1	-	-	-
		2nd	-/-/-/-	-/-/-/-	-	-	-	-	4	-
12	Jo Kuffour	1st	-/2/-/-	-/-/-/-	-	-	-	-	-	-
	▼ 83	2nd	-/-/-/-	-/-/-/-	-	-	1	-	-	-
17	Brian McGlinchey	1st	-/-/-/-	-/-/-/-	-	-	1	-	-	-
		2nd	-/-/-/-	1/-/-/-	-	-	1	-	1	-

Subs not used: Dearden, Benefield, Killoughery, Burgess. - **Formation: 4-4-2**

Goalkeeper Stats: Shaun Marshall Saves: Catch 4, Parry 1, Crosses: Catch 2

No.	Player Stats	Shots on target	Shots off target	Caught offside	Fouls conceded	Free-kicks won	Corners taken	Clearances	Defensive blocks
14	Luke Guttridge	1/-/-/-	-/-/-/-	2	-	-	-	-	-
3	Fred Murray ▲ 78	-/-/-/-	1/-/-/-	-	-	-	-	-	-
11	Justin Walker	-/-/-/-	-/-/-/-	-	3	-	-	-	-
16	Alex Revell ▼ 74 ■ 21	-/-/-/-	1/2/-/-	-	2	-	-	1	-
4	Andy Duncan	-/-/-/-	-/-/-/-	-	1	1	-	3	-
9	Dave Kitson	-/-/-/-	1/1/-/-	-	3	-	-	4	-
8	Terry Fleming	-/1/-/-	-/-/-/-	-	-	-	-	-	-
22	Stuart Bimson	-/-/-/-	1/-/-/-	-	-	-	3	2	-
12	Daniel Chillingworth ▼ 46	-/1/-/-	-/-/-/-	-	1	1	-	1	-
21	Mark Venus ■ 5	-/-/-/-	-/-/-/-	-	1	-	-	3	1
10	Shane Tudor ▼ 78 ▲ 46	-/1/-/-	-/-/-/-	1	1	-	-	-	-
6	Stevland Angus ■ 52 ■ 90	-/-/-/-	-/-/-/-	1	3	1	-	3	1
15	John Turner ▲ 74	-/-/-/-	-/-/-/-	-	-	-	-	-	-

Subs not used: Brennan, Goodhind. - **Formation: 4-3-3**

Torquay Played: 7 **Won** 3 **Drawn** 2 **Lost** 2 **For** 8 **Against** 8 **Pos** 10

Torquay [2] 2 BRISTOL ROVERS [0] 1 — 16th September

Swaying between sparkling attack and determined defence, Torquay United deservedly beat Bristol Rovers in a riveting West Country derby at Plainmoor.

Inspired by Jason Fowler at his imaginative best in midfield, and with David Graham and skipper Craig Taylor both scoring in the first half, United had the chances to have buried Rovers.

But Rovers substitute Kevin Street's 62nd minute goal, which came against the run of play, threatened to change the course of the match.

Taylor, whose arrival has galvanised United's defence, signed off with a goal before his three-match suspension. And Torquay's passing, especially in the first half, was way above Third Division standard.

After a bright Rovers start, in which the hard running of Junior Agogo sounded a few alarm bells, United hit the bar through Alex Russell's angled shot in the 24th minute.

The breakthrough came in the 31st minute. Jo Kuffour held the ball up for Graham who beat two men in a jinking run and then chipped Rovers keeper Kevin Miller from 20 yards into the top left-hand corner for his fifth goal of the season.

Then on the stroke of half-time United made it 2-0. A Russell corner from the right was only half-cleared to Kevin Hill on the left, he crossed the ball back into the goalmouth where Taylor glanced a 15-yard header into the bottom right-hand corner.

United moved into overdrive in the first 15 minutes of the second half with Graham and Kuffour going close. It seemed only a matter of time before United scored again.

But just when they looked most in charge, Lee Hodges slipped Street through with a clever reverse pass and he stabbed a right-footer past the advancing Arjan Van Heusden.

The closing stages may have been a touch nervy for United fans, but their team held on for a psychologically important victory.

Result.......Result.......Result.

TORQUAY ....(2) **2** **BRISTOL R** ....(0) **1**
Graham 31 — Street 63
Taylor 45

Att 3,691
Referee: P Armstrong

Stats......Stats.......Stats......Stats

TORQUAY — **BRISTOL ROVERS**

1st	2nd	Total		Total	2nd	1st
5	3	8	**Corners**	4	3	1
5	7	12	**Fouls**	21	11	10
0	2	2	**Yellow cards**	2	1	1
0	0	0	**Red cards**	0	0	0
1	1	2	**Caught Offside**	6	1	5
8	5	13	**Shots on target**	6	4	2
0	4	4	**Shots off target**	10	6	4
1	0	1	**Hit woodwork**	1	1	0
47	54	51%	**Possession**	49%	46	53

IT'S an important win for us in terms of our belief in ourselves. We should have been out of sight, by three or four goals, just after half-time.

Leroy Rosenior

WE started well and finished well, but Torquay had a bit too much for us in the middle of the game. They are a very slick side.

Ray Graydon

Other Div 3 Results

Cheltenham 0 Oxford Utd 0, Doncaster 0 Yeovil 1, Kidderminster 0 Scunthorpe 2, Leyton Orient 1 Hull 1, Mansfield 5 Bury 3, Northampton 2 Carlisle 0, Rochdale 1 Huddersfield 1, Swansea 3 Macclesfield 0, York 1 Darlington 1

TORQUAY [2] 2 Bristol Rovers [0] 1

Goalkeeper Stats: Arjan Van Heusden Saves: Tip Over 2, Catch 4, Crosses: Catch 6

Torquay Player Stats		Shots on target L/R/H/Oth	Shots off target L/R/H/Oth	Caught offside	Fouls conceded	Free-kicks won	Corners taken	Clearances	Defensive blocks
5 Craig Taylor	1st	-/-/1/-	-/-/-/-	-	1	2	-	-	-
	2nd	-/-/-/-	-/-/-/-	-	-	2	-	1	-
28 Michael Williamson	1st	-/-/-/-	-/-/-/-	-	-	-	-	-	-
▲ 90	2nd	-/-/-/-	-/-/-/-	-	-	-	-	-	-
18 Steve Woods	1st	-/-/-/-	-/-/-/-	-	-	-	-	1	1
	2nd	-/-/-/-	-/-/-/-	-	-	2	-	1	-
4 Lee Canoville	1st	1/-/-/-	-/-/-/-	-	-	1	-	1	-
	2nd	-/-/-/-	-/-/-/-	-	-	2	-	-	-
6 Alex Russell	1st	-/1/-/-	-/-/-/-	-	-	2	5	-	-
	2nd	-/1/-/-	-/-/-/-	-	-	1	3	-	-
11 Kevin Hill	1st	1/-/-/-	-/-/-/-	-	-	-	-	-	-
	2nd	-/-/-/-	-/1/-/-	1	-	-	-	-	-
10 David Graham	1st	-/2/-/-	-/-/-/-	-	2	3	-	-	-
▼ 90 ■ 77	2nd	-/1/-/-	1/-/-/-	-	3	3	-	-	-
15 Kevin Wills	1st	-/-/-/-	-/-/-/-	-	-	-	-	-	-
▲ 90	2nd	-/-/-/-	-/-/-/-	-	-	-	-	-	-
14 Matthew Hockley	1st	-/1/-/-	-/-/-/-	-	2	-	-	-	-
	2nd	-/-/-/-	-/-/-/-	-	-	-	-	-	-
8 Jason Fowler	1st	-/-/-/-	-/-/-/-	-	-	1	-	-	-
▼ 90 ■ 87	2nd	-/-/-/-	-/-/-/-	-	2	-	-	-	1
12 Jo Kuffour	1st	-/1/-/-	-/-/-/-	-	-	1	-	-	-
	2nd	-/3/-/-	-/2/-/-	-	-	1	-	1	-
17 Brian McGlinchey	1st	-/-/-/-	-/-/-/-	1	-	-	-	-	1
	2nd	-/-/-/-	-/-/-/-	-	2	-	-	-	-

Subs not used: Dearden, Benefield, Camara. - **Formation: 4-4-2**

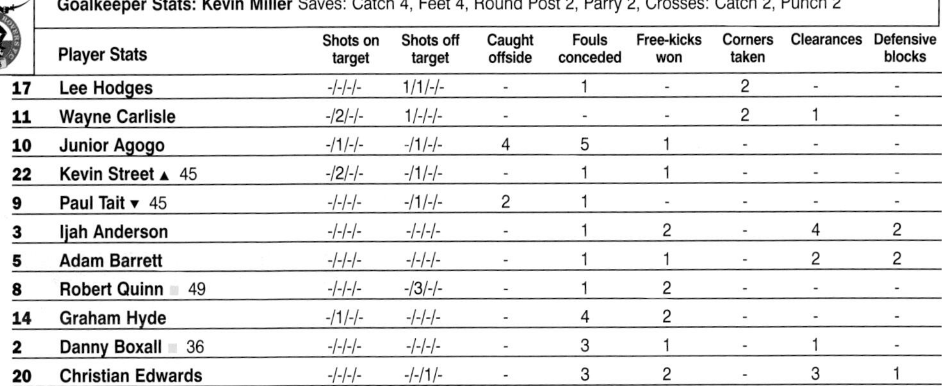

Goalkeeper Stats: Kevin Miller Saves: Catch 4, Feet 4, Round Post 2, Parry 2, Crosses: Catch 2, Punch 2

	Player Stats	Shots on target	Shots off target	Caught offside	Fouls conceded	Free-kicks won	Corners taken	Clearances	Defensive blocks
17	Lee Hodges	-/-/-/-	1/1/-/-	-	1	-	2	-	-
11	Wayne Carlisle	-/2/-/-	1/-/-/-	-	-	-	2	1	-
10	Junior Agogo	-/1/-/-	-/1/-/-	4	5	1	-	-	-
22	Kevin Street ▲ 45	-/2/-/-	-/1/-/-	-	1	1	-	-	-
9	Paul Tait ▼ 45	-/-/-/-	-/1/-/-	2	1	-	-	-	-
3	Ijah Anderson	-/-/-/-	-/-/-/-	-	1	2	-	4	2
5	Adam Barrett	-/-/-/-	-/-/-/-	-	1	1	-	2	2
8	Robert Quinn ■ 49	-/-/-/-	-/3/-/-	-	1	2	-	-	-
14	Graham Hyde	-/1/-/-	-/-/-/-	-	4	2	-	-	-
2	Danny Boxall ■ 36	-/-/-/-	-/-/-/-	-	3	1	-	1	-
20	Christian Edwards	-/-/-/-	-/-/1/-	-	3	2	-	3	1

Subs not used: Austin, Parker, Bryant, Uddin. - **Formation: 4-4-2**

Torquay Played: 8 **Won** 4 **Drawn** 2 **Lost** 2 **For** 10 **Against** 9 **Pos** 7

Torquay [2] 2 DARLINGTON [1] 2

20th September

By his standards, manager Leroy Rosenior was raging after this toothless display in which his team failed to deliver the 3-points.

United looked un-focused from start to finish. They did however take the lead when Woods found the room to rise above the rest and power home Alex Russell's right-wing corner in the eleventh minute.

But less than 60 seconds later Quakers skipper Craig Liddle made a simple run in front of his marker him and nodded the first in from ten yards.

Torquay then took the lead again. Jo Kuffour retrieved the ball on the left of the area, delivered a square ball across, and Graham finished with a rasping first-time left-foot drive into the roof of the net for his sixth of the season.

United seemed poised to win the game comfortably but even during their long spells of possession and superiority, there was an indulgent extra-touch to United's play. Kuffour twice, Hockley, Russell and Woods all went close as Darlington were forced to hang on for the first 20 minutes of the second half.

But the longer it went on without a clinching third goal, the more the visitors believed that they could snatch a point.

In the 71st minute United keeper Arjan Van Heusden had to get down smartly to parry a Conlon shot on the turn, and two minutes later they equalised for the second time.

Ashley Nicholl floated in a long cross and Ian Clark arrived at the far post to score with another free header.

United dominated the last quarter-of-an-hour. But Benefield, Wills and Kuffour all missed chances and in the last minute of stoppage-time Kevin Hill let rip with a goal-bound volley which was blocked by a flailing Darlington defender.

Result.......Result.......Result.

TORQUAY ....(2) **2** **DARLINGTON** (1) **2**

Torquay	Darlington
Woods 11	Liddle 13
Graham 36	Clark 73

Att 2,420
Referee: M Fletcher

Stats......Stats.......Stats......Stats

TORQUAY				DARLINGTON		
1st	2nd	Total		Total	2nd	1st
3	3	6	Corners	4	2	2
5	5	10	Fouls	23	13	10
0	0	0	Yellow cards	3	2	1
0	0	0	Red cards	1	1	0
2	1	3	Caught Offside	4	1	3
4	5	9	Shots on target	6	2	4
3	4	7	Shots off target	5	3	2
0	0	0	Hit woodwork	0	0	0
51	51	51%	Possession	49%	49	49

IF you score twice at home, you should be looking to keep a clean sheet and we haven't done that for seven games now.

Leroy Rosenior

A few strong words were said at half-time and we were much better and much more together in the second half.

Mick Tait

Other Div 3 Results

Boston Utd 1 Bury 0, Cheltenham 0 Cambridge Utd 3, Doncaster 2 Oxford Utd 0, Leyton Orient 1 Scunthorpe 1, Mansfield 0 Yeovil 1, Northampton 0 Macclesfield 0, Rochdale 0 Hull 2, Southend 2 Carlisle 2, Swansea 2 Huddersfield 0, York 2 Bristol Rovers 1

TORQUAY [2] 2 Darlington [1] 2

Goalkeeper Stats: Arjan Van Heusden Saves: Round Post 2, Crosses: Catch 2, Parry 2

Torquay Player Stats		Shots on target L/R/H/Oth	Shots off target L/R/H/Oth	Caught offside	Fouls conceded	Free-kicks won	Corners taken	Clearances	Defensive blocks
28 Michael Williamson	1st	-/-/-/-	-/-/-/-	-	1	1	-	-	1
	2nd	-/-/-/-	-/-/-/-	-	-	-	-	-	-
9 Martin Gritton	1st	-/-/-/-	-/-/-/-	2	1	3	-	-	-
▼ 45	2nd	-/-/-/-	-/-/-/-	-	-	-	-	-	-
4 Lee Canoville	1st	-/-/-/-	-/-/-/-	-	-	-	-	-	-
▼ 87	2nd	-/-/-/-	-/-/-/-	-	1	-	-	-	-
18 Steve Woods	1st	-/-/1/-	-/-/-/-	-	-	-	-	-	1
	2nd	-/-/-/-	-/1/-/-	-	1	-	-	2	-
6 Alex Russell	1st	-/1/-/-	-/1/-/-	-	1	1	3	-	-
	2nd	-/-/-/-	-/2/-/-	-	-	1	3	-	-
16 Jimmy Benefield	1st	-/-/-/-	-/-/-/-	-	-	-	-	-	-
▲ 56	2nd	-/-/-/-	-/-/-/-	-	-	2	-	-	-
11 Kevin Hill	1st	-/-/-/-	-/-/-/-	-	-	1	-	1	-
	2nd	1/-/-/-	-/-/-/-	-	-	3	-	1	-
10 David Graham	1st	1/-/-/-	1/1/-/-	-	-	1	-	-	-
	2nd	-/-/-/-	-/-/1/-	1	1	3	-	-	-
15 Kevin Wills	1st	-/-/-/-	-/-/-/-	-	-	-	-	-	-
▲ 45	2nd	-/-/-/-	-/-/-/-	-	1	2	-	-	-
14 Matthew Hockley	1st	-/-/-/-	-/-/-/-	-	-	-	-	-	-
	2nd	-/1/1/-	-/-/-/-	-	-	-	-	-	-
8 Jason Fowler	1st	-/-/-/-	-/-/-/-	-	1	1	-	-	-
▼ 56	2nd	-/-/-/-	-/-/-/-	-	-	-	-	-	-
12 Jo Kuffour	1st	-/1/-/-	-/-/-/-	-	1	2	-	-	-
	2nd	1/1/-/-	-/-/-/-	-	-	2	-	-	-
19 Graham Killoughery	1st	-/-/-/-	-/-/-/-	-	-	-	-	-	-
▲ 87	2nd	-/-/-/-	-/-/-/-	-	1	-	-	-	-

Subs not used: Dearden, Burgess. - **Formation: 4-4-2**

Goalkeeper Stats: Andy Collett Saves: Catch 2, Round Post 2, Crosses: Catch 16

	Player Stats	Shots on target	Shots off target	Caught offside	Fouls conceded	Free-kicks won	Corners taken	Clearances	Defensive blocks
2	Ryan Valentine ▼ 69	-/-/-/-	-/-/-/-	-	-	-	-	2	1
15	David McGurk	-/-/-/-	-/-/-/-	-	1	-	-	1	-
11	Ashley Nicholls	-/-/-/-	-/2/-/-	1	2	1	3	-	-
4	Craig Liddle ■ 6	-/-/1/-	-/-/-/-	-	5	3	-	2	-
6	Fabien Bossy ▼ 61 ■ 60	-/-/-/-	-/-/-/-	-	4	-	-	-	-
8	Ian Clark ▲ 4	1/2/1/-	1/-/1/-	2	2	-	1	-	-
21	Jonathan Hutchinson ■ 40	-/-/-/-	-/-/-/-	-	5	-	-	-	-
13	Barry Conlon	1/-/-/-	-/-/1/-	1	2	1	-	2	1
5	Matthew Clarke	-/-/-/-	-/-/-/-	-	1	2	-	-	-
14	Neil Wainwright ▼ 4	-/-/-/-	-/-/-/-	-	-	1	-	-	-
17	Chris Hughes ▲ 69	-/-/-/-	-/-/-/-	-	-	1	-	-	-
10	Danny Mellanby ▲ 61 ■ 76	-/-/-/-	-/-/-/-	-	1	-	-	1	-

Subs not used: Price, Robson. - **Formation: 4-4-2**

Torquay Played: 9 **Won** 4 **Drawn** 3 **Lost** 2 **For** 12 **Against** 11 **Pos** 6

Yeovil [0] 0 TORQUAY [1] 2 — 27th September

Yeovil Town were taught a footballing lesson by Leroy Rosenior's cool, calm and so collected United side in a brilliant counter-attacking performance. Soaking up wave after wave of home attacks, United broke out to score two sumptuously-crafted goals.

Yet the afternoon nearly started with a costly mistake by Gulls goalkeeper Arjan Van Heusden. And then Yeovil began to go forward, pinning United in their own half, until they dropped their guard and were hit on the break in the 15th minute.

Showing great strength against Nick Crittenden, Kuffour made the most of a clearance and dashed away down the centre of the pitch. Realising that Graham was making unmarked ground fast to his left, Kuffour rolled the ball into his path and Graham ran on into the area before waiting for goalkeeper Chris Weale to commit himself and then lifting his finishing shot over him from 12 yards.

With United constantly threatening on the counter, Graham, Hill and Russel all went close .At the other end a Williamson clearance hit McGlinchey and rebounded into Van Heusden's arms.

Yeovil poured on the pressure again in the first 20 minutes of the second half and they were always capable of producing a searing break that could seal the game.

It came in the 66th minute. A good build-up, epitomising United's passing philosophy, saw Graham, Jason Fowler, Lee Canoville and Russell all join in before Canoville jinked outside Darren Way, crossed low and Kuffour, running towards the near-post, back-heeled the ball past Yeovil's wrong-footed defence and inside the far-post.

In the closing stages Yeovil had two goals disallowed, one for a push by Gall on McGlinchey and another for offside.

At the final whistle, the normally reserved Rosenior punched the air before directing his players towards their celebrating fans. Everybody in United's camp knew the significance of this result.

Result.......Result.......Result.

YEOVIL ....(0) **0** **TORQUAY** ......(1) **2**
Graham 15
Kuffour 67

Att 7,718
Referee: I Williamson

Stats......Stats.......Stats......Stats

YEOVIL 1st	2nd	Total		TORQUAY Total	2nd	1st
2	5	7	**Corners**	3	1	2
4	8	12	**Fouls**	11	6	5
0	0	0	**Yellow cards**	0	0	0
0	0	0	**Red cards**	0	0	0
0	4	4	**Caught Offside**	5	3	2
3	8	11	**Shots on target**	8	3	5
5	2	7	**Shots off target**	6	3	3
0	0	0	**Hit woodwork**	0	0	0
56	61	59%	**Possession**	41%	39	44

WE sometimes have to hold our hands up and admit we didn't do well. We were second best and Torquay fully deserved to win.

Gary Johnson

WE know Yeovil are a good footballing side and I couldn't have asked for more, especially as we only had six players in for training on Thursday.

Leroy Rosenior

Other Div 3 Results

Bristol Rovers 2 Cheltenham 0, Bury 1 Doncaster 3, Cambridge Utd 1 Mansfield 2, Carlisle 1 Swansea 2, Darlington 3 Boston Utd 0, Huddersfield 3 Leyton Orient 0, Hull 6 Kidderminster 1, Macclesfield 0 York 0, Oxford Utd 3 Northampton 0, Scunthorpe 1 Southend 1

Yeovil [0] 0 TORQUAY [1] 2

Goalkeeper Stats: Arjan Van Heusden Saves: Catch 4, Round Post 2, Parry 6, Crosses: Catch 6

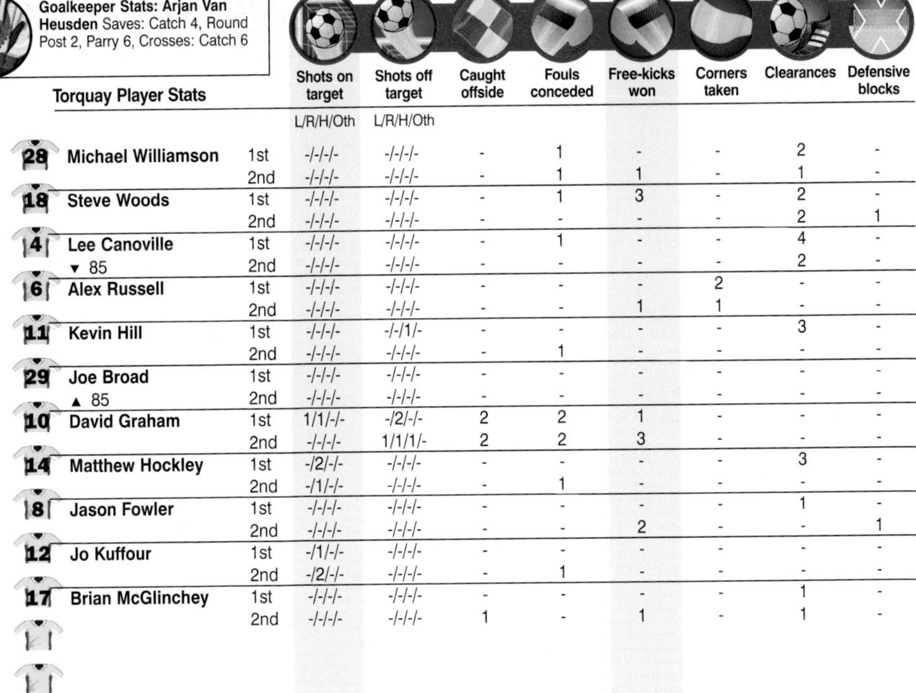

No.	Torquay Player Stats		Shots on target L/R/H/Oth	Shots off target L/R/H/Oth	Caught offside	Fouls conceded	Free-kicks won	Corners taken	Clearances	Defensive blocks
28	Michael Williamson	1st	-/-/-/-	-/-/-/-	-	1	-	-	2	-
		2nd	-/-/-/-	-/-/-/-	-	1	1	-	1	-
18	Steve Woods	1st	-/-/-/-	-/-/-/-	-	1	3	-	2	-
		2nd	-/-/-/-	-/-/-/-	-	-	-	-	2	1
4	Lee Canoville	1st	-/-/-/-	-/-/-/-	-	1	-	-	4	-
	▼ 85	2nd	-/-/-/-	-/-/-/-	-	-	-	-	2	-
6	Alex Russell	1st	-/-/-/-	-/-/-/-	-	-	-	2	-	-
		2nd	-/-/-/-	-/-/-/-	-	-	1	1	-	-
11	Kevin Hill	1st	-/-/-/-	-/-/1/-	-	-	-	-	3	-
		2nd	-/-/-/-	-/-/-/-	-	1	-	-	-	-
29	Joe Broad	1st	-/-/-/-	-/-/-/-	-	-	-	-	-	-
	▲ 85	2nd	-/-/-/-	-/-/-/-	-	-	-	-	-	-
10	David Graham	1st	1/1/-/-	-/2/-/-	2	2	1	-	-	-
		2nd	-/-/-/-	1/1/1/-	2	2	3	-	-	-
14	Matthew Hockley	1st	-/2/-/-	-/-/-/-	-	-	-	-	3	-
		2nd	-/1/-/-	-/-/-/-	-	1	-	-	-	-
8	Jason Fowler	1st	-/-/-/-	-/-/-/-	-	-	-	-	1	-
		2nd	-/-/-/-	-/-/-/-	-	-	2	-	-	1
12	Jo Kuffour	1st	-/1/-/-	-/-/-/-	-	-	-	-	-	-
		2nd	-/2/-/-	-/-/-/-	-	1	-	-	-	-
17	Brian McGlinchey	1st	-/-/-/-	-/-/-/-	-	-	-	-	1	-
		2nd	-/-/-/-	-/-/-/-	1	-	1	-	1	-

Subs not used: Dearden, Benefield, Wills, Killoughery. - **Formation: 4-4-2**

Goalkeeper Stats: Chris Weale Saves: Catch 8, Parry 2, Crosses: Catch 4

No.	Player Stats	Shots on target	Shots off target	Caught offside	Fouls conceded	Free-kicks won	Corners taken	Clearances	Defensive blocks
14	Roy O'Brien	-/1/1/-	-/1/-/-	-	1	2	-	1	-
7	Adam Stansfield ▲ 71	-/-/-/-	-/-/-/-	1	-	-	-	-	-
23	Jamie Gosling ▲ 66	-/-/-/-	-/-/-/-	-	-	-	-	-	-
18	Kirk Jackson ▼ 71	-/1/-/-	-/-/1/-	-	4	1	-	-	-
11	Ronnie Bull ▼ 66	-/-/-/-	-/-/-/-	-	-	1	-	-	-
5	Colin Pluck ▼ 57	-/-/-/-	-/-/-/-	-	1	-	-	1	-
6	Darren Way	-/1/-/-	-/-/-/-	-	-	-	-	-	-
2	Adam Lockwood	-/-/1/-	-/-/-/-	-	1	2	-	1	1
8	Lee Johnson	-/1/-/-	-/1/-/-	-	-	-	6	-	-
9	Kevin Gall	1/-/-/-	-/2/-/-	-	1	1	-	-	-
10	Nick Crittenden	-/1/1/-	-/2/-/-	1	3	3	1	-	-
20	Gavin Williams	-/2/-/-	-/-/-/-	1	-	-	-	-	-
12	Hugo Rodrigues ▲ 57	-/-/-/-	-/-/-/-	1	1	1	-	1	-

Subs not used: Collis, Terry. - **Formation: 4-4-2**

Torquay Played: 10 **Won** 5 **Drawn** 3 **Lost** 2 **For** 14 **Against** 11 **Pos** 4

...September Team Stats.....Team Stats......Team Stats......Team S

League table at the end of September

	HOME						AWAY						
	P	W	D	L	F	A	W	D	L	F	A	Pts	Df
Hull	11	5	1	0	19	8	2	2	1	6	3	24	14
Swansea	11	5	0	0	16	3	2	1	3	8	12	22	9
Yeovil	11	4	0	2	10	4	3	0	2	6	7	21	5
Mansfield	11	3	1	1	14	7	3	1	2	11	9	20	9
Oxford Utd	10	4	1	0	11	2	1	3	1	3	4	19	8
Torquay	**10**	**3**	**1**	**1**	**8**	**7**	**2**	**2**	**1**	**6**	**4**	**18**	**3**
Bristol Rovers	11	3	2	1	8	5	2	0	3	7	7	17	3
Scunthorpe	11	2	3	1	12	9	2	2	1	7	9	17	1
York	11	3	1	1	7	4	2	1	3	3	9	17	-3
Doncaster	11	2	2	1	5	2	2	2	2	10	8	16	5
Huddersfield	11	4	1	1	11	4	0	3	2	5	8	16	4
Cambridge Utd	11	1	3	2	8	9	2	3	0	9	5	15	3
Darlington	11	4	1	1	9	4	0	2	3	6	12	15	-1
Lincoln City	11	1	4	1	4	2	2	1	2	5	4	14	3
Northampton	11	3	1	1	4	1	1	1	4	5	11	14	-3
Rochdale	11	1	2	2	8	10	2	2	2	9	8	13	-1
Bury	11	3	1	2	10	9	1	0	4	7	11	13	-3
Macclesfield	11	2	4	0	8	4	0	2	3	5	11	12	-2
Cheltenham	11	2	1	2	9	11	1	2	3	10	14	12	-6
Leyton Orient	11	1	2	2	6	9	1	2	3	4	8	10	-7
Southend	11	2	1	2	5	7	0	2	4	3	10	9	-9
Boston Utd	11	2	2	1	6	5	0	1	5	1	12	9	-10
Kidderminster	11	1	1	3	4	8	1	1	4	5	11	8	-10
Carlisle	11	1	1	4	5	9	0	1	4	2	10	5	-12

September matches table

	P	W	D	L	F	A	Pts
Yeovil	6	5	0	1	9	2	15
Hull	6	4	2	0	13	4	14
Mansfield	6	4	1	1	14	9	13
Darlington	6	3	3	0	10	4	12
Torquay	**5**	**3**	**2**	**0**	**9**	**5**	**11**
Scunthorpe	6	2	4	0	12	7	10
Huddersfield	6	3	1	2	9	5	10
Swansea	6	3	1	2	9	6	10
Lincoln City	6	2	4	0	5	2	10
Cambridge Utd	6	2	3	1	10	7	9
Bristol Rovers	6	3	0	3	8	7	9
Doncaster	6	2	2	2	9	7	8
Oxford Utd	5	2	2	1	6	3	8
Bury	6	2	1	3	9	11	7
Macclesfield	6	1	3	2	5	8	6
Leyton Orient	6	1	3	2	4	7	6
Rochdale	6	1	2	3	7	10	5
Cheltenham	6	1	2	3	7	14	5
Northampton	6	1	2	3	5	10	5
York	6	1	2	3	4	9	5
Carlisle	6	1	1	4	6	11	4
Boston Utd	6	1	1	4	3	10	4
Southend	6	0	3	3	5	10	3
Kidderminster	6	0	1	5	3	13	1

September team stats details

Club Name	Ply	Shots On	Shots Off	Corners	Hit W'work	Caught Offside	Offside Trap	Fouls	Yellow Cards	Red Cards	Pens Awarded	Pens Con
Boston Utd	6	24	34	35	1	16	20	83	16	0	- (-)	1
Bristol Rovers	6	35	30	33	1	30	10	91	9	1	2 (2)	-
Bury	6	41	30	20	0	29	18	74	10	0	2 (2)	-
Cambridge U	6	40	28	28	4	34	12	88	9	2	1 (-)	-
Carlisle	6	29	27	35	2	27	20	83	12	0	1 (1)	2
Cheltenham	6	40	34	32	0	20	27	74	14	1	3 (3)	4
Darlington	6	33	30	35	1	24	17	83	8	3	- (-)	-
Doncaster	6	43	49	50	0	28	45	66	9	1	2 (1)	3
Huddersfield	6	46	42	38	3	21	22	68	9	3	1 (1)	-
Hull	6	39	39	31	0	21	23	64	8	0	- (-)	-
Kidderminster	6	17	35	33	0	19	22	75	9	0	- (-)	-
Leyton Orient	6	26	30	44	0	19	26	95	9	3	1 (-)	-
Lincoln City	6	27	46	42	3	24	22	77	9	0	- (-)	1
Macclesfield	6	28	30	30	2	26	18	60	10	0	- (-)	1
Mansfield	6	41	31	25	2	19	28	64	9	2	2 (2)	3
Northampton	6	19	16	29	1	22	41	66	7	0	2 (2)	4
Oxford Utd	5	32	28	24	3	24	12	63	5	1	- (-)	-
Rochdale	6	30	20	40	1	27	11	74	14	2	- (-)	-
Scunthorpe	6	38	21	43	2	31	29	86	13	0	4 (3)	2
Southend	6	40	30	33	0	22	29	60	6	1	3 (-)	1
Swansea	6	37	26	31	2	21	32	69	16	2	1 (1)	4
Torquay	**5**	**43**	**24**	**30**	**1**	**19**	**22**	**43**	**6**	**1**	**- (-)**	**-**
Yeovil	6	53	29	31	4	21	26	72	11	0	1 (1)	-
York	6	39	33	38	1	16	28	66	9	1	- (-)	-

Monthly Match Details: Games 71 **Home Wins** 33 **Away Wins** 15 **Draws** 23

...September Player Stats..... Player Stats...... Player Stats......Pla

Monthly Top scorers

David Graham (Torquay)	5
Steven MacLean (Scunthorpe)	4
Dave Kitson (Cambridge Utd)	4
Ben Burgess (Hull)	4
Junior Mendes (Mansfield)	3
Kirk Jackson (Yeovil)	3
Marcus Richardson (Lincoln City)	3
Lee Trundle (Swansea)	3
Jonathan Stead (Huddersfield)	3
Lee Connell (Bury)	3

Penalties scored

2 S MacLean (Scunthorpe), R Forsyth (Cheltenham), A Preece (Bury), L Lawrence (Mansfield)

Assists

Liam Lawrence (Mansfield)	4
Junior Mendes (Mansfield)	3
Mark Wilson (Swansea)	3
John Turner (Cambridge Utd)	3
Jonathan Stead (Huddersfield)	2
Tom Newey (Leyton Orient)	2
Ben Thornley (Bury)	2

Quickest goals

0:21 mins - Paul Connor (Rochdale vs Huddersfield)

0:55 mins - Steve Basham (Oxford Utd vs Northampton)

2:37 mins - Leon Constantine (Hull vs Southend)

5:00 mins - Ben Burgess (Hull vs Kidderminster)

5:52 mins - Steven MacLean (Scunthorpe vs Southend)

Top Keeper

	Mins	Gls
Chris Weale (Yeovil)	573	2
Alan Marriott (Lincoln City)	572	2
Paul Musselwhite (Hull)	285	1
Darryl Flahavan (Southend)	189	1
Andy Woodman (Oxford Utd)	478	3
Ian Gray (Huddersfield)	572	5
Andy Collett (Darlington)	384	4
Sam Russell (Scunthorpe)	384	4

Shots on target

Steven MacLean (Scunthorpe)	13
Steve Basham (Oxford Utd)	12
Jo Kuffour (Torquay)	12
Jonathan Stead (Huddersfield)	12
Andy Booth (Huddersfield)	11
Ben Burgess (Hull)	10
Dave Kitson (Cambridge Utd)	10
Danny Allsopp (Hull)	10
Liam George (York)	9
David Graham (Torquay)	9

Shots off target

Danny Allsopp (Hull)	15
David Graham (Torquay)	11
Jonathan Stead (Huddersfield)	10
Michael McIndoe (Doncaster)	10
Gary Fletcher (Lincoln City)	10
Leo Fortune-West (Doncaster)	9
Anthony Carss (Huddersfield)	9
Paul Green (Doncaster)	9
Liam Lawrence (Mansfield)	8
Andy Booth (Huddersfield)	8

Caught offside

Junior Agogo (Bristol Rovers)	17
Steven MacLean (Scunthorpe)	15
Dave Kitson (Cambridge Utd)	14
Richie Foran (Carlisle)	13
John Turner (Cambridge Utd)	13
Gareth Seddon (Rushden & D)	13
Kevin Townson (Rochdale)	12
Kevin Nugent (Swansea)	12
Martin Carruthers (Macclesfield)	12

Free-kicks won

Liam Lawrence (Mansfield)	22
David Graham (Torquay)	20
Dave Kitson (Cambridge Utd)	16
Bob Taylor (Cheltenham)	15
Lee Trundle (Swansea)	15
Mark Warren (Southend)	15
Steven MacLean (Scunthorpe)	15
Bo Henriksen (Kidderminster)	14
Ijah Anderson (Bristol Rovers)	14

Steve Woods shows his joy

Fouls conceded

Ben Futcher (Lincoln City)	18
Dave Kitson (Cambridge Utd)	18
Richie Foran (Carlisle)	17
Paul O'Shaughnessy (Bury)	16
Paul Tait (Bristol Rovers)	14
Barry Conlon (Darlington)	14
Bob Taylor (Cheltenham)	13
Mark Warren (Southend)	13
Andy Duncan (Cambridge Utd)	13

Fouls without a card

Nick Crittenden (Yeovil)	11
Colin Pluck (Yeovil)	11
Richard Butcher (Lincoln City)	10
Jamie McCombe (Lincoln City)	10
Junior Agogo (Bristol Rovers)	10
Lee Thorpe (Bristol Rovers)	9
Scott McNiven (Oxford Utd)	9
Adam Barrett (Bristol Rovers)	9
Danny Allsopp (Hull)	9

Yeovil keeper Collis beats Martin Gritton to the ball in the first half of the 2-2 draw.
HPL01456_TNA_005

Goal, goal, goal. . . skipper Craig Taylor hits Torquay's first from an indirect free kick.
Torquay v Yeovil.
HPL01456_TNA_013

Steve Woods is mobbed by team mates after equalising.
Torquay v Yeovil.
HPL01456_TNA_035

Liam Rosenior.
Torquay v Yeovil.
HPL01456_TNA_045

Oxford Utd [0] 1 TORQUAY [0] 0 — 1st October

Head coach Leroy Rosenior quashed any suggestion of blame for stand-in Torquay United captain Steve Woods over Oxford United's second-half winner at the Kassam Stadium.

Woods was beaten to a header by lanky Oxford striker Julian Alsop in the 70th minute, a goal that proved to be decisive. It was the first time this season that Torquay have not scored in a match, showing just how well Oxford performed on the night.

After dominating for long periods, Gulls manager Rosenior was very disappointed that his team got nothing out of the game.

David Graham had a good chance but hit it straight at the Oxford keeper early in the first half, and the final ball just wasn't good enough for the Gulls. Time and again, their neat style of play did not get them anywhere and they let their opponents grab hold of the game.

In the second half, Oxford began to severely pressure Torquay's defence and the Gulls normal passing game was stifled time and time again.

Just when it began to look like the pressure was over Oxford scored the vital goal . It was a bad time to concede and the Gulls never recovered. Even though they did react well to Alsop's strike the result was never really in doubt.

The men in the centre of defence performed superbly for the Gulls. But even they seemed unsure as wave after wave of attacks came from the Oxford attack. And eventually this pressure resulted in the goal.

Rosenior was delighted with the way his payers attempted to come back from the goal. Even though they were defeated they never gave up and "lost in the right manner".

Result.......Result.......Result.

OXFORD UTD ......(0) **1** **TORQUAY** ......(0) **0**
Alsop 70

Att 5,479
Referee: L Cable

Stats......Stats.......Stats......Stats

OXFORD UTD				TORQUAY		
1st	**2nd**	**Total**		**Total**	**2nd**	**1st**
0	3	3	**Corners**	4	2	2
10	9	19	**Fouls**	11	4	7
1	2	3	**Yellow cards**	3	1	2
0	0	0	**Red cards**	0	0	0
0	1	1	**Caught Offside**	4	3	1
1	5	6	**Shots on target**	3	1	2
7	4	11	**Shots off target**	3	2	1
0	0	0	**Hit woodwork**	0	0	0
39	54	46%	**Possession**	54%	46	61

"**YOU** could see us getting stronger and stronger in the second half, I was just a little bit worried that we might get done by a counter-punch.

Ian Atkins"

THEY just about deserved it, but I was still disappointed that we didn't get something out of the game. We didn't give up.

Leroy Rosenior

Other Div 3 Results

No other results

Oxford Utd [0] 1 TORQUAY [0] 0

Goalkeeper Stats: Arjan Van Heusden Saves: Catch 2, Parry 1, Crosses: Catch 6

#	Torquay Player Stats		Shots on target L/R/H/Oth	Shots off target L/R/H/Oth	Caught offside	Fouls conceded	Free-kicks won	Corners taken	Clearances	Defensive blocks
28	Michael Williamson	1st	-/-/-/-	-/-/-/-	-	-	3	-	1	-
	■ 78	2nd	-/-/-/-	-/1/-/-	-	2	-	-	2	-
18	Steve Woods	1st	-/-/-/-	-/-/-/-	-	-	1	-	-	-
		2nd	-/-/-/-	-/-/-/-	-	1	1	-	1	-
6	Alex Russell	1st	-/-/-/-	-/-/-/-	-	-	-	-	-	-
		2nd	-/-/-/-	-/-/-/-	-	-	-	2	-	-
16	Jimmy Benefield	1st	-/-/-/-	-/-/-/-	-	-	-	-	-	-
	▲ 73	2nd	-/-/1/-	-/-/-/-	-	-	-	-	-	-
29	Joe Broad	1st	-/-/-/-	-/-/-/-	-	1	1	1	-	1
	▼ 73	2nd	-/-/-/-	-/-/-/-	-	-	-	-	-	-
11	Kevin Hill	1st	-/-/-/-	-/-/-/-	-	3	-	1	-	-
	■ 16	2nd	-/-/-/-	-/-/-/-	-	-	1	-	-	-
15	Kevin Wills	1st	-/-/-/-	-/-/-/-	-	-	-	-	-	-
	▲ 63	2nd	-/-/-/-	-/-/-/-	1	-	-	-	-	-
10	David Graham	1st	1/-/-/-	-/-/-/-	-	1	3	-	-	-
		2nd	-/-/-/-	1/-/-/-	1	1	4	-	-	-
14	Matthew Hockley	1st	-/-/-/-	-/-/-/-	-	1	-	-	-	1
	■ 20	2nd	-/-/-/-	-/-/-/-	-	-	2	-	-	-
8	Jason Fowler	1st	-/-/-/-	-/1/-/-	-	-	2	-	-	-
		2nd	-/-/-/-	-/-/-/-	-	-	-	-	-	-
12	Jo Kuffour	1st	-/1/-/-	-/-/-/-	1	1	-	-	-	-
	▼ 63	2nd	-/-/-/-	-/-/-/-	1	-	-	-	-	-
17	Brian McGlinchey	1st	-/-/-/-	-/-/-/-	-	-	-	-	-	-
		2nd	-/-/-/-	-/-/-/-	-	-	1	-	-	-

Subs not used: Dearden, Camara, Orchard. - **Formation: 4-4-2**

OXFORD UNITED F.C.

Goalkeeper Stats: Andy Woodman Saves: Catch 2, Crosses: Catch 1

#	Player Stats	Shots on target	Shots off target	Caught offside	Fouls conceded	Free-kicks won	Corners taken	Clearances	Defensive blocks
18	Matthew Bound ■ 84	-/-/-/-	-/-/-/-	-	2	-	-	2	-
15	Julian Alsop ▼ 76	-/-/1/-	-/3/1/-	-	6	1	-	-	-
12	Dean Whitehead	1/-/-/-	1/1/-/-	1	-	1	3	-	-
23	Steve Basham	1/-/2/-	-/1/-/-	-	2	1	-	-	-
29	Jon Ashton	-/-/-/-	-/-/-/-	-	4	-	-	3	-
3	Matthew Robinson ■ 17	-/-/-/-	-/2/-/-	-	1	-	-	1	-
21	Paul McCarthy	-/-/-/-	-/-/-/-	-	2	3	-	2	-
2	Scott McNiven ■ 69	-/-/-/-	-/-/-/-	-	1	2	-	1	-
17	Jefferson Louis ▲ 76	-/1/-/-	-/1/-/-	-	-	-	-	-	-
27	Paul Wanless	-/-/-/-	-/-/-/-	-	1	1	-	-	-
8	James Hunt	-/-/-/-	1/-/-/-	-	-	2	-	-	-

Subs not used: Hackett, Scott, Rawle, Brown. - **Formation: 3-5-2**

Torquay Played: 11 **Won** 5 **Drawn** 3 **Lost** 3 **For** 14 **Against** 12 **Pos** 6

Torquay [1] 3 BURY [1] 1

4th October

Head coach Leroy Rosenior never considered it a risk, but his decision to ask young centre-half Mike Williamson to play at right-back, and allow Matt Hockley to do what he does best in midfield, paid off spectacularly on both scores at Plainmoor.

Rosenior's Gulls had to wait until six minutes from time before Alex Russell's first goal of the season finally clinched an emphatic victory.

But, even on a pitch which had started to show signs of bobble and wear, the Shakers were effectively outplayed for most of the match. Kevin Hill and Steve Woods, who had yet another outstanding match in defence, both went close before the breakthrough came in the 26th minute.

Brian McGlinchey's diagonal cross from the left was deflected out to Jo Kuffour on the right, he made ground, crossed to the near-post where Graham glanced the ball home into the opposite corner for his eighth of the season.

Twice Garner dived to deny Kuffour, who was giving the Bury defence a torrid time. But then, totally against the run of play Bury equalised. Fowler tried to do too much on the ball and lost it to O'Neill, who set up Porter for a 15-yard shot inside the left-hand post.

United needed to get back in front quickly, and that's exactly what they did only 50 seconds after the restart. Craig Taylor and Williamson kept up the pressure on a Russell corner, and the ball finally dropped for Kuffour to finish with an opportunist volley from close-range.

Williamson, Kuffour and Russell all went close after that, and the third goal eventually came six minutes from time. Kuffour turned Lee Duxbury on the half-way line, burst away on the break and passed to Russel, who steadied himself and struck a cool left-foot shot across Garner and inside the right-hand post.

Result.......Result.......Result.

TORQUAY ....(1) **3** **BURY** ....(1) **1**
Graham 26 Porter 38
Kuffour 46
Russell 85

Att 2,732
Referee: M Warren

Stats......Stats.......Stats......Stats

TORQUAY						BURY
1st	**2nd**	**Total**		**Total**	**2nd**	**1st**
7	5	12	**Corners**	4	2	2
6	8	14	**Fouls**	18	13	5
0	0	0	**Yellow cards**	3	2	1
0	0	0	**Red cards**	1	1	0
2	2	4	**Caught Offside**	2	1	1
6	4	10	**Shots on target**	2	1	1
4	7	11	**Shots off target**	3	0	3
0	0	0	**Hit woodwork**	1	1	0
52	56	54%	**Possession**	46%	44	48

I'M not worried about anybody else giving us credit for anything. Success is relative, and we're trying to achieve as much as we can with the resources we've got.

Leroy Rosenior

AT the interval I thought we were just starting to build up a bit of momentum after getting a foothold in the game.

Andy Preece

Other Div 3 Results

Boston Utd 1 Oxford Utd 1, Cheltenham 3 Yeovil 1, Doncaster 5 Bristol Rovers 1, Kidderminster 2 Carlisle 1, Leyton Orient 2 Macclesfield 0, Mansfield 3 Darlington 1, Northampton 1 Hull 5, Rochdale 2 Scunthorpe 0, Southend 1 Huddersfield 2, York 2 Cambridge Utd 0

TORQUAY [1] 3 Bury [1] 1

Goalkeeper Stats: Arjan Van Heusden Crosses: Catch 2

Torquay Player Stats

No.	Player	Half	Shots on target L/R/H/Oth	Shots off target L/R/H/Oth	Caught offside	Fouls conceded	Free-kicks won	Corners taken	Clearances	Defensive blocks
5	Craig Taylor	1st	-/-/1/-	-/-/-/-	-	1	-	-	2	-
		2nd	-/-/1/-	-/-/1/-	-	1	1	-	1	-
28	Michael Williamson	1st	-/-/-/-	-/-/-/-	-	1	1	-	1	-
		2nd	-/-/-/-	-/-/1/-	-	1	1	-	-	-
18	Steve Woods	1st	-/-/1/-	-/-/-/-	-	-	-	-	1	-
		2nd	-/-/-/-	-/-/-/-	1	-	1	-	-	-
6	Alex Russell	1st	-/-/-/-	-/-/1/-	-	-	-	6	-	-
		2nd	1/-/-/-	-/1/-/-	-	3	2	5	-	-
11	Kevin Hill	1st	-/1/-/-	1/-/-/-	2	1	-	-	1	-
		2nd	-/-/-/-	-/-/-/-	-	2	-	-	-	-
10	David Graham	1st	-/-/-/-	-/2/-/-	-	2	2	1	-	-
		2nd	-/-/-/-	-/2/-/-	-	-	4	-	-	-
14	Matthew Hockley	1st	-/-/-/-	-/-/-/-	-	-	-	-	-	-
		2nd	-/-/-/-	-/2/-/-	-	-	2	-	-	-
8	Jason Fowler	1st	-/1/-/-	-/-/-/-	-	-	-	-	-	-
		2nd	-/-/-/-	-/-/-/-	-	-	-	-	2	-
12	Jo Kuffour	1st	1/1/-/-	-/-/-/-	-	1	2	-	-	-
		2nd	-/2/-/-	-/-/-/-	-	-	2	-	-	-
17	Brian McGlinchey	1st	-/-/-/-	-/-/-/-	-	-	-	-	-	-
		2nd	-/-/-/-	-/-/-/-	1	1	-	-	-	-

Subs not used: Dearden, Wills, Benefield, Camara, Broad. - **Formation: 4-4-2**

Goalkeeper Stats: Glyn Garner Saves: Tip Over 2, Block 2, Catch 2, Feet 4, Crosses: Tip Over 2, Catch 2 □ 6

No.	Player Stats	Shots on target	Shots off target	Caught offside	Fouls conceded	Free-kicks won	Corners taken	Clearances	Defensive blocks
16	Simon Whaley ▲ 78	-/-/-/-	-/-/-/-	-	-	1	-	-	-
6	Lee Unsworth ■ 75	-/-/-/-	-/-/-/-	-	3	1	-	1	1
3	Colin Woodthorpe □ 21	-/-/-/-	-/-/-/-	-	5	-	-	1	-
21	Lee Connell	-/-/-/-	-/-/-/-	-	2	-	-	-	-
22	Harpal Singh	-/-/-/-	-/-/-/-	-	-	-	1	1	1
17	Terry Dunfield ▼ 36	-/-/-/-	-/-/-/-	-	-	-	-	-	-
24	Glenn Whelan	-/-/-/-	-/-/-/-	-	1	3	3	3	-
12	Chris Porter	-/1/-/-	-/1/-/-	1	1	4	-	2	-
10	Joe O'Neill ▲ 36	-/-/-/-	-/-/-/-	-	2	-	-	-	-
19	Gareth Seddon ▼ 78 □ 64	-/1/-/-	-/2/-/-	1	3	3	-	-	-
5	Lee Duxbury	-/-/-/-	-/-/-/-	-	1	-	-	2	-
15	Steve Gunby	-/-/-/-	-/-/-/-	-	-	1	-	1	-

Subs not used: Kennedy, Preece, Cartledge. - **Formation: 5-3-2**

Torquay Played: 12 **Won** 6 **Drawn** 3 **Lost** 3 **For** 17 **Against** 13 **Pos** 5

Huddersfield [0] 1 TORQUAY [0] 0

11th October

It's doubtful if even Huddersfield Town's great old ground, now just a flattened memory in the shadow of the soaring Alfred McAlpine Stadium saw many better goals than the one which finished off Torquay in this game.

Tony Carss will be able to dine out on the first-time 25-yard volley which screamed into the top left-hand corner of Torquay United's net in the 80th minute on Saturday.

Instead of floating yet another high ball into the goalmouth, Andrew Holdsworth stood over a right-wing corner and spotted Carss pulling away unmarked outside the area. Allowing the ball to drift across his body and without letting it drop, Carss smashed the ball goal-wards with his cultured left foot.

United had two defenders and goalkeeper Kevin Dearden on the goalline, but even Dearden's despairing dive and Alex Russell's outstretched neck were mere gestures as Carss' volley flew past them.

Even though their defence kept Huddersfield at bay for so long, United could have few complaints about the result. For their attack was lightweight against a powerful home defence led by Nigerian centre-back Efe Sodje.

Yet Jo Kuffour with a header and Brian McGlinchey with a shot from a Kevin Hill nod-down both could have done better on half-chances.

At the other end Taylor & Co were put under relentless pressure, even if Huddersfield resorted to a stream of high balls, from crosses, free-kicks and the long throws of Clarke, all aimed at the heads of Booth and Stead.

Williamson, Woods and Taylor kept winning their headers. And McGlinchey was always alert on the cover. Then, just when it seemed as if United had survived the worst and Huddersfield could come up with nothing new to beat them, the Holdsworth-Carss corner move brought the house down.

And but for a terrific goalline clearance by McGlinchey from Julian Worthington in the 84th minute, it would have been 2-0.

Result.......Result.......Result.

HUDDERSFIELD..(0) **1** **TORQUAY** ......(0) **0**
Carss 80

Att 9,117
Referee: C Boyeson

Stats......Stats.......Stats......Stats

HUDDERSFIELD				TORQUAY		
1st	**2nd**	**Total**		**Total**	**2nd**	**1st**
2	3	5	**Corners**	2	1	1
12	5	17	**Fouls**	12	5	7
2	0	2	**Yellow cards**	2	2	0
0	0	0	**Red cards**	0	0	0
0	2	2	**Caught Offside**	4	1	3
7	9	16	**Shots on target**	0	0	0
4	2	6	**Shots off target**	6	4	2
0	0	0	**Hit woodwork**	0	0	0
46	52	49%	**Possession**	51%	48	54

THE scoreline didn't tell the whole story. I thought it was a terrific game of football and our performance was outstanding at the back, in midfield and up-front.

Peter Jackson

WE were beaten by a tremendous goal, totally out of the ordinary, but I do not believe my players deserved that and I am gutted for them.

Leroy Rosenior

Other Div 3 Results

Boston Utd 3 Cheltenham 1, Cambridge Utd 1 Bury 2, Darlington 0 Bristol Rovers 4, Kidderminster 1 Southend 2, Leyton Orient 1 Swansea 2, Macclesfield 1 Doncaster 3, Mansfield 2 York 0, Oxford Utd 1 Yeovil 0, Rochdale 1 Northampton 1

Huddersfield [0] 1 TORQUAY [0] 0

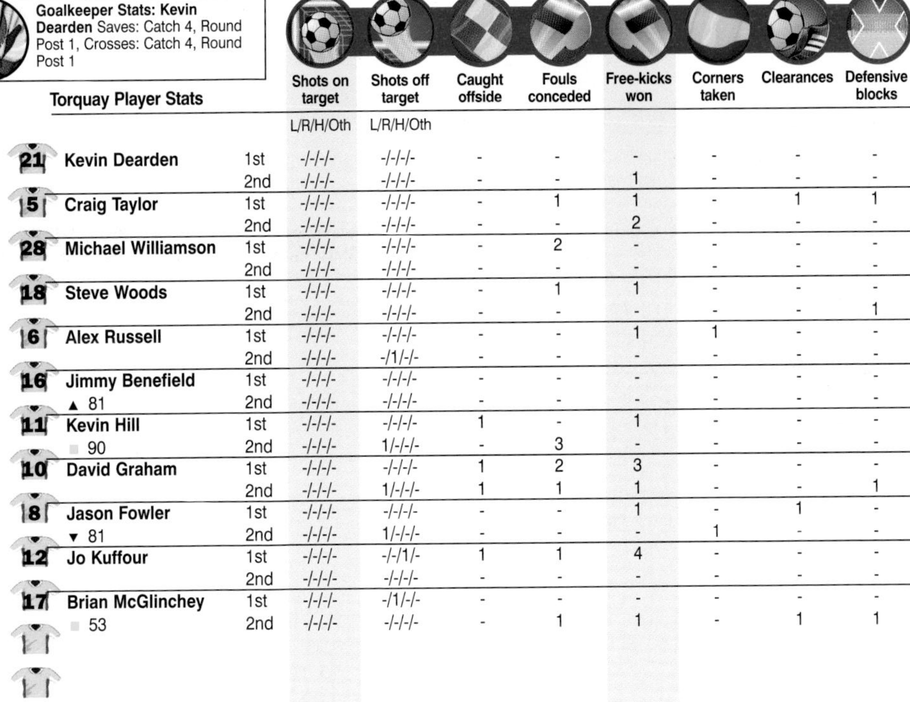

Goalkeeper Stats: Kevin Dearden Saves: Catch 4, Round Post 1, Crosses: Catch 4, Round Post 1

Torquay Player Stats

No.	Player	Half	Shots on target L/R/H/Oth	Shots off target L/R/H/Oth	Caught offside	Fouls conceded	Free-kicks won	Corners taken	Clearances	Defensive blocks
21	Kevin Dearden	1st	-/-/-/-	-/-/-/-	-	-	-	-	-	-
		2nd	-/-/-/-	-/-/-/-	-	-	1	-	-	-
5	Craig Taylor	1st	-/-/-/-	-/-/-/-	-	1	1	-	1	1
		2nd	-/-/-/-	-/-/-/-	-	-	2	-	-	-
28	Michael Williamson	1st	-/-/-/-	-/-/-/-	-	2	-	-	-	-
		2nd	-/-/-/-	-/-/-/-	-	-	-	-	-	-
18	Steve Woods	1st	-/-/-/-	-/-/-/-	-	1	1	-	-	-
		2nd	-/-/-/-	-/-/-/-	-	-	-	-	-	1
6	Alex Russell	1st	-/-/-/-	-/-/-/-	-	-	1	1	-	-
		2nd	-/-/-/-	-/1/-/-	-	-	-	-	-	-
16	Jimmy Benefield	1st	-/-/-/-	-/-/-/-	-	-	-	-	-	-
	▲ 81	2nd	-/-/-/-	-/-/-/-	-	-	-	-	-	-
11	Kevin Hill	1st	-/-/-/-	-/-/-/-	1	-	1	-	-	-
	■ 90	2nd	-/-/-/-	1/-/-/-	-	3	-	-	-	-
10	David Graham	1st	-/-/-/-	-/-/-/-	1	2	3	-	-	-
		2nd	-/-/-/-	1/-/-/-	1	1	1	-	-	1
8	Jason Fowler	1st	-/-/-/-	-/-/-/-	-	-	1	-	1	-
	▼ 81	2nd	-/-/-/-	1/-/-/-	-	-	-	1	-	-
12	Jo Kuffour	1st	-/-/-/-	-/-/1/-	1	1	4	-	-	-
		2nd	-/-/-/-	-/-/-/-	-	-	-	-	-	-
17	Brian McGlinchey	1st	-/-/-/-	-/1/-/-	-	-	-	-	-	-
	■ 53	2nd	-/-/-/-	-/-/-/-	-	1	1	-	1	1

Subs not used: Wills, Broad, Camara, Bond. - **Formation: 4-4-2**

Goalkeeper Stats: Ian Gray Crosses: Catch 1

Player Stats

No.	Player	Shots on target	Shots off target	Caught offside	Fouls conceded	Free-kicks won	Corners taken	Clearances	Defensive blocks
16	Efetobore Sodje	-/-/-/-	-/-/-/-	-	2	3	-	1	-
9	Jonathan Stead	-/2/1/-	-/1/2/-	-	3	2	-	-	1
4	Lee Fowler	-/2/-/-	-/-/-/-	-	1	-	-	-	-
18	Jonathan Worthington	-/3/-/-	-/-/-/-	-	-	2	-	-	-
23	Andy Booth	-/-/1/-	1/-/-/-	2	2	1	-	1	-
21	Andy Holdsworth ■ 36	-/-/-/-	-/-/-/-	-	2	1	1	-	-
11	Danny Schofield	1/-/-/-	-/-/-/-	-	1	1	-	-	-
15	Nathan Clarke	-/-/2/-	-/-/-/-	-	2	1	-	1	-
5	Steve Yates ■ 30	-/-/-/-	-/-/-/-	-	4	1	1	-	-
8	Anthony Carss	3/1/-/-	2/-/-/-	-	-	-	3	-	-

Subs not used: Newby, Senior, Scott, Holland, Mattis. - **Formation: 3-5-2**

Torquay Played: 13 **Won** 6 **Drawn** 3 **Lost** 4 **For** 17 **Against** 14 **Pos** 7

Peterborough [2] 3 TORQUAY [2] 2 — 14th October

All too often the LDV Vans Trophy is a sub-standard affair that has captured the imagination of next to no-one.

But two sides with vastly different agendas produced a 105-minute feast of football in this game. Twice Torquay hauled themselves back level in the first half after falling behind to their Second Division opponents before finally being killed off by David Farrell's 97th minute 'silver goal'.

Curtis Woodhouse fizzed an 11th minute free-kick a couple of feet over Kevin Dearden's bar. Gulls were relatively untroubled until Craig Taylor's needless but blatant shove on Posh striker Calum Willock resulted in a penalty. Captain Sagi Burton gleefully tucked away.

The power, pace and passing ability of Tony Bedeau provided a constant menace and his dashing 29th minute run and cross allowed Wills to smash the ball past Mark Tyler from a tough angle.

Posh only needed 90 seconds to restore their lead when a deep right-wing Willock cross was touched back into the path of Andy Clarke by Farrell and the 36-year-old front man fired past Dearden.

Eight minutes before the break Torquay levelled again when Taylor nodded a Jason Fowler cross back across the face of goal and Benefield stooped to head home from close range.

Even when Dearden was beaten with four minutes to go, Steve Woods spared Torquay with a goal-line clearance from Clarke while Posh boss Fry was adamant his team should have had a penalty after Mike Williamson appeared to handle in the area seconds later.

Despite the glut of chances at both ends, the game went into extra-time and, after Matthew Gill had seen a spectacular shot on the turn plucked from the air by Dearden, Farrell delivered the knockout blow.

The winger was in the right place to slot home into an empty net after Dearden had inadvertently pushed a stinging Clarke shot into his path.

Result.......Result.......Result.

PETERBORO ......(2) **3** **TORQUAY** ......(2) **2**

Burton 18(p) — Wills 29
Clarke 31 — Benefield 38
Farrell 97

Att 1,980
Referee: K Friend

Stats......Stats.......Stats......Stats

PETERBOROUGH				TORQUAY		
1st	2nd	Total		Total	2nd	1st
3	4	7	**Corners**	2	0	2
8	7	15	**Fouls**	11	4	7
0	2	2	**Yellow cards**	2	2	0
0	0	0	**Red cards**	0	0	0
1	2	3	**Caught Offside**	4	3	1
3	3	6	**Shots on target**	4	3	1
3	2	5	**Shots off target**	5	3	2
0	1	1	**Hit woodwork**	0	0	0
53	58	56%	**Possession**	44%	42	47

> **IT** was a real cracker of a game and it's great to finally get a result at home. We did it in some style although the defending was very poor at times.
>
> **Barry Fry**

> **OVERALL**, I was quite pleased by the performance. We were in charge for most of the match and they had no answer to our passing game.
>
> **Leroy Rosenior**

Other LDV Trophy South Results

Barnet 2 Brentford 2, Cheltenham 1 Colchester 3, QPR 2 Kidderminster 0, Southend 1 Bristol Rovers 1, Stevenage 0 Luton 1, Wycombe 1 Cambridge Utd 0, Yeovil 2 Bournemouth 0

14th October

Peterborough [2] 3 TORQUAY [2] 2

Goalkeeper Stats: Kevin Dearden
Saves: Catch 2, Parry 1, Crosses: Catch 4, Parry 1

Torquay Player Stats		Shots on target	Shots off target	Caught offside	Fouls conceded	Free-kicks won	Corners taken	Clearances	Defensive blocks
		L/R/H/Oth	L/R/H/Oth						
7 Tony Bedeau	1st	-/-/-/-	-/-/-/-	-	1	2	-	1	-
▼ 45	2nd	-/-/-/-	-/-/-/-	-	-	-	-	-	-
5 Craig Taylor	1st	-/-/-/-	-/-/-/-	-	2	-	-	1	-
■ 81	2nd	-/-/-/-	-/-/-/-	1	2	1	-	3	-
28 Michael Williamson	1st	-/-/-/-	-/-/-/-	1	-	1	-	1	-
■ 87	2nd	-/-/-/-	-/-/-/-	-	1	1	-	-	-
18 Steve Woods	1st	-/-/-/-	-/-/-/-	-	-	-	-	-	-
	2nd	-/-/-/-	-/-/-/-	-	1	-	-	3	-
6 Alex Russell	1st	-/-/-/-	-/-/-/-	-	1	-	1	-	-
	2nd	-/1/-/-	-/-/-/-	-	-	1	-	-	-
16 Jimmy Benefield	1st	-/1/-/-	-/1/-/-	-	-	2	-	-	-
	2nd	-/1/-/-	-/2/-/-	1	-	1	-	1	-
29 Joe Broad	1st	-/-/-/-	-/-/-/-	-	-	1	-	-	-
	2nd	-/-/-/-	-/-/-/-	-	-	1	-	-	-
15 Kevin Wills	1st	-/-/-/-	1/-/-/-	-	1	2	-	-	-
▼ 65	2nd	-/-/-/-	1/-/-/-	-	-	-	-	-	-
10 David Graham	1st	-/-/-/-	-/-/-/-	-	-	-	-	-	-
▲ 65	2nd	-/1/-/-	-/1/-/-	-	1	1	-	-	-
14 Matthew Hockley	1st	-/-/-/-	-/-/-/-	-	-	-	-	-	-
	2nd	-/-/-/-	-/-/-/-	-	-	-	-	1	-
8 Jason Fowler	1st	-/-/-/-	-/-/-/-	-	2	-	1	1	-
▼ 74	2nd	-/-/-/-	-/-/-/-	-	-	-	-	-	-
12 Jo Kuffour	1st	-/-/-/-	-/-/-/-	-	-	-	-	-	-
▲ 45	2nd	1/1/-/-	-/-/-/-	2	-	-	-	-	-
19 Graham Killoughery	1st	-/-/-/-	-/-/-/-	-	-	-	-	-	-
▲ 74	2nd	-/-/-/-	-/-/-/-	-	-	-	-	-	-

Subs not used: Orchard, Camara. - **Formation: 4-4-2**

Goalkeeper Stats: Mark Tyler Saves: Catch 4

	Player Stats	Shots on target	Shots off target	Caught offside	Fouls conceded	Free-kicks won	Corners taken	Clearances	Defensive blocks
7	David Farrell	1/-/-/-	1/1/-/-	-	3	1	1	1	-
16	Andrew Fotiadis ▲ 70	-/-/-/-	-/-/-/-	2	-	1	-	-	-
30	Calum Willock ▼ 70	-/1/-/-	1/-/-/-	-	-	5	-	-	-
17	Curtis Woodhouse ▼ 70	1/-/-/-	2/-/-/-	-	-	-	1	-	-
15	Christopher Kanu ■ 65	-/1/-/-	-/-/-/-	-	2	-	-	-	-
19	Gareth Jelleyman	-/-/-/-	-/-/-/-	-	1	-	-	-	-
29	Steven Thomson	-/-/-/-	-/1/-/-	1	1	1	4	-	-
11	Adam Newton	1/-/-/-	-/-/-/-	-	-	1	-	1	-
21	Sagi Burton ■ 88	-/-/-/-	-/-/-/-	-	5	-	-	1	1
9	Andy Clarke	1/1/-/-	-/-/-/-	2	1	1	-	-	-
2	Mathew Gill ▲ 70	1/-/-/-	-/-/-/-	-	-	1	3	-	-
12	Sean St. Ledger	-/-/-/-	-/-/-/-	-	2	1	-	3	2

Subs not used: Scott, Shields, Coulson. - **Formation: 4-4-2**

Torquay [1] 1 HULL [0] 1

18th October

Torquay United played Third Division favourites Hull City off the park at Plainmoor but were held to a draw. And United's recurring tendency to concede goals late in games was keeping them on the fringe of the promotion race instead of in the thick of it.

In the seventh minute Matt Hockley drove a pass at the heart of the Hull defence and Justin Whittle's tackle on Jo Kuffour popped the ball loose. Graham saw his chance, took one touch and then, spotting Paul Musselwhite slightly out of position, clipped a sublime 25-yard right-foot shot into the top left-hand corner.

Then in the 13th minute Russell won a tackle, hit Graham on the move, another touch, a fierce shot and Musselwhite pulled off a fine save and Kuffour also headed against the right-hand post from a Russell corner.

Instead of going for the kill, United started the second half disappointingly, giving possession away too cheaply, until the 57th minute when Graham beat the offside trap, cut in from the right and set up Kuffour who blazed wide on his weaker left foot.

It seemed only a matter of whether United could score the second goal that would have finished it and Peter Taylor had seen enough; making a double-substitution that was to pay off handsomely.

United continued to miss chances, with Russel and Kuffour both going close. And in the 77th minute Graham beat two defenders on Russell's pass and then, apparently trying to burst the net from 12 yards, lashed the ball over with only Musselwhite to beat.

Torquay must have felt like they might live to regret that chance, and only a minute after, it happened.

Hull substitute Jamie Forrester supplied the pass for Elliott to drill a left-foot shot into the top right-hand corner from 15 yards. It was the first time that Hull had looked like scoring since the first half.

Result.......Result.......Result.

TORQUAY ....(1) **1** **HULL** ....(0) **1**
Graham 7 Elliott 78

Att 3,720
Referee: T Parkes

Stats......Stats.......Stats......Stats

TORQUAY				HULL		
1st	2nd	Total		Total	2nd	1st
4	2	6	Corners	3	3	0
3	5	8	Fouls	11	8	3
0	0	0	Yellow cards	1	0	1
0	0	0	Red cards	0	0	0
2	4	6	Caught Offside	2	1	1
4	4	8	Shots on target	7	5	2
1	9	10	Shots off target	2	0	2
1	0	1	Hit woodwork	0	0	0
62	59	60%	Possession	40%	41	38

NO disrespect to Hull but we were the better side by a country mile. Our performance was terrific but it's all about winning.

Leroy Rosenoir

WE got away with murder. Torquay played much better than us and if they had scored two or three goals they would have deserved them.

Peter Taylor

Other Div 3 Results

Bristol Rovers 0 Cambridge Utd 2, Bury 0 Oxford Utd 4, Carlisle 0 Macclesfield 1, Cheltenham 0 Rochdale 2, Doncaster 4 Mansfield 2, Southend 1 Leyton Orient 2, Swansea 0 Kidderminster 0, Yeovil 1 Darlington 0, York 1 Boston Utd 1

TORQUAY [1] 1 Hull [0] 1

Goalkeeper Stats: Kevin Dearden Saves: Block 2, Catch 8, Crosses: Catch 4

Torquay Player Stats		Shots on target L/R/H/Oth	Shots off target L/R/H/Oth	Caught offside	Fouls conceded	Free-kicks won	Corners taken	Clearances	Defensive blocks
7 Tony Bedeau	1st	-/1/-/-	-/-/-/-	-	1	-	-	-	-
▼ 63	2nd	-/-/-/-	-/1/-/-	-	-	1	-	-	-
5 Craig Taylor	1st	-/-/-/-	-/-/-/-	-	-	-	-	-	-
	2nd	-/-/-/-	-/-/-/-	-	-	1	-	-	-
28 Michael Williamson	1st	-/-/-/-	-/-/-/-	-	-	-	-	-	-
	2nd	-/-/-/-	-/-/1/-	-	-	-	-	1	-
18 Steve Woods	1st	-/-/-/-	-/-/-/-	-	1	-	-	-	-
	2nd	-/1/-/-	-/1/-/-	-	1	1	-	1	-
6 Alex Russell	1st	-/-/-/-	-/1/-/-	-	-	-	4	-	-
	2nd	-/1/-/-	-/1/-/-	-	-	1	2	-	-
29 Joe Broad	1st	-/-/-/-	-/-/-/-	-	-	-	-	-	-
▲ 89	2nd	-/-/-/-	-/-/-/-	-	-	-	-	-	-
11 Kevin Hill	1st	-/-/-/-	-/-/-/-	-	-	-	-	-	-
▲ 63	2nd	-/-/-/-	-/-/-/-	3	-	-	-	-	-
10 David Graham	1st	-/2/-/-	-/-/-/-	2	-	1	-	-	-
▼ 89	2nd	1/-/-/-	2/1/-/-	1	2	1	-	-	-
15 Kevin Wills	1st	-/-/-/-	-/-/-/-	-	-	-	-	-	-
▲ 74	2nd	-/-/-/-	-/1/-/-	-	-	2	-	-	-
14 Matthew Hockley	1st	-/-/-/-	-/-/-/-	-	-	-	-	-	-
	2nd	-/-/-/-	-/-/-/-	-	2	-	-	-	-
8 Jason Fowler	1st	-/-/-/-	-/-/-/-	-	-	1	-	-	-
	2nd	-/-/-/-	-/-/-/-	-	-	-	-	-	-
12 Jo Kuffour	1st	-/-/1/-	-/-/-/-	-	1	1	-	-	-
▼ 74	2nd	-/1/-/-	1/-/-/-	-	-	-	-	-	-
17 Brian McGlinchey	1st	-/-/-/-	-/-/-/-	-	-	-	-	-	-
	2nd	-/-/-/-	-/-/-/-	-	-	1	-	1	-

Subs not used: Van Heusden, Killoughery. - **Formation: 4-4-2**

Goalkeeper Stats: Paul Musselwhite Saves: Catch 2, Parry 4, Crosses: Catch 4

	Player Stats	Shots on target	Shots off target	Caught offside	Fouls conceded	Free-kicks won	Corners taken	Clearances	Defensive blocks
16	Damien Delaney	-/-/-/-	-/-/-/-	-	2	-	-	3	-
9	Ben Burgess	-/-/1/-	-/1/-/-	-	-	2	-	-	-
7	Stuart Elliott	3/-/-/-	-/-/-/-	1	2	1	-	1	-
4	Ian Ashbee ■ 17	-/-/-/-	-/-/-/-	-	1	-	-	-	-
8	Jamie Forrester ▲ 70	-/-/-/-	-/-/-/-	-	-	1	-	-	-
14	Stuart Green ▼ 70	-/1/-/-	-/-/-/-	-	-	-	1	-	-
10	Danny Allsopp ▼ 70	-/2/-/-	-/1/-/-	1	2	1	-	-	-
24	Andrew Holt ▲ 70	-/-/-/-	-/-/-/-	-	1	-	-	-	-
29	Ryan France ▲ 61	-/-/-/-	-/-/-/-	-	-	-	-	1	-
3	Andrew Dawson	-/-/-/-	-/-/-/-	-	-	-	2	-	-
18	Jason Price ▼ 61	-/-/-/-	-/-/-/-	-	1	-	-	1	-
15	Justin Whittle	-/-/-/-	-/-/-/-	-	2	3	-	3	-
2	Alton Thelwell	-/-/-/-	-/-/-/-	-	-	-	-	1	-

Subs not used: Fettis, Hinds. - **Formation: 4-4-2**

Torquay Played: 14 **Won** 6 **Drawn** 4 **Lost** 4 **For** 18 **Against** 15 **Pos** 8

Torquay [1] 1 MANSFIELD [0] 0 — 21st October

Torquay United answered head coach Leroy Rosenior's pre-match call for a clean-sheet, and that was the key to a hard-fought victory over promotion rivals Mansfield Town.

Matt Hockley's 35th minute winner warmed the Gulls faithful who shivered in the first chill of winter, and it was no more than United's dogged midfielder deserved.

On a night when substance counted for much more than style, Hockley's tackling, work rate and sensible passing were tailor-made for the job. But without a resolute defence, again outstandingly led by skipper Craig Taylor, free-scoring Mansfield might well have snatched at least a point.

As it was, Hockley's goal was one of only two efforts they had on target all night, a miserly return by their normal standards. Mansfield started brightly but around the half-hour, after defenders Steve Woods, Mike Williamson and Taylor had all come up with important tackles, United started to find their range.

Alex Russell, who struggled to find a yellow shirt early on, and Jason Fowler combined to send Graham clear in the 31st minute, only for the Scot to blast over from 15 yards with keeper Kevin Pilkington to beat.

Then the breakthrough came. Fowler flicked the ball back to Williamson on the right. His long cross was knocked back into the goalmouth by Hill and Hockley was there to drive home a first-time left-foot shot from 10 yards.

After the break, United restarted slowly and Gulls fans had to endure a tense last half an hour when Mansfield really should have equalised in the 86th minute when Larkin was left clear on the left, inside the area, only to pull his shot wide.

But this time United rode their luck, got the three points and slotted back into contention for a promotion spot.

Result.......Result.......Result.

TORQUAY ....(1) **1** **MANSFIELD** ..(0) **0**
Hockley 35

Att 2,773
Referee: D Crick

Stats......Stats.......Stats......Stats

TORQUAY				MANSFIELD		
1st	**2nd**	**Total**		**Total**	**2nd**	**1st**
2	5	7	**Corners**	4	2	2
4	5	9	**Fouls**	16	8	8
2	0	2	**Yellow cards**	1	0	1
0	0	0	**Red cards**	0	0	0
0	1	1	**Caught Offside**	3	2	1
2	1	3	**Shots on target**	6	3	3
2	5	7	**Shots off target**	7	5	2
0	0	0	**Hit woodwork**	0	0	0
47	49	48%	**Possession**	52%	51	53

> **I'M** delighted that Matt Hockley scored the winner - he's worked extremely hard at his game and his confidence is now much higher than it used to be.
>
> **Leroy Rosenior**

> **WE** can't believe we are coming away with a defeat. You can count the number of times they got in our box on one hand - it was minimal.
>
> **John Gannon**

Other Div 3 Results

Bristol Rovers 1 Leyton Orient 1, Bury 0 Hull 0, Carlisle 1 Scunthorpe 4, Cheltenham 2 Darlington 1, Doncaster 2 Rochdale 1, Northampton 0 Kidderminster 1, Southend 0 Boston Utd 2, Swansea 0 Cambridge Utd 2, Yeovil 2 Huddersfield 1, York 2 Oxford Utd 2

TORQUAY [1] 1 Mansfield [0] 0

Goalkeeper Stats: Kevin Dearden Saves: Catch 6, Crosses: Catch 6 ■ 45

Torquay Player Stats		Shots on target L/R/H/Oth	Shots off target L/R/H/Oth	Caught offside	Fouls conceded	Free-kicks won	Corners taken	Clearances	Defensive blocks
7 Tony Bedeau	1st	-/-/-/-	-/-/-/-	-	1	3	-	1	-
▼ 33	2nd	-/-/-/-	-/-/-/-	-	-	-	-	-	-
5 Craig Taylor	1st	-/-/-/-	-/-/-/-	-	1	-	-	-	-
	2nd	-/-/-/-	-/-/-/-	-	1	1	-	2	-
28 Michael Williamson	1st	-/-/-/-	-/-/-/-	-	-	-	-	-	-
	2nd	-/-/-/-	-/-/-/-	-	-	2	-	3	-
18 Steve Woods	1st	-/-/-/-	-/-/-/-	-	-	-	-	-	-
	2nd	-/-/-/-	-/-/-/-	-	1	-	-	1	-
6 Alex Russell	1st	-/-/-/-	-/-/-/-	-	-	1	2	1	-
	2nd	-/-/-/-	-/-/-/-	-	-	1	5	-	-
16 Jimmy Benefield	1st	-/-/-/-	-/-/-/-	-	-	-	-	-	-
▲ 90	2nd	-/-/-/-	-/-/-/-	-	-	-	-	-	-
29 Joe Broad	1st	-/-/-/-	-/-/-/-	-	-	-	-	-	-
▲ 83	2nd	-/-/-/-	-/-/-/-	-	-	-	-	-	-
11 Kevin Hill	1st	-/-/-/-	-/-/-/-	-	-	1	-	-	-
▲ 33	2nd	-/-/-/-	-/-/-/-	-	2	2	-	1	-
10 David Graham	1st	1/-/-/-	-/1/-/-	-	-	1	-	-	-
▼ 90	2nd	-/1/-/-	1/2/-/-	-	1	1	-	-	-
14 Matthew Hockley	1st	1/-/-/-	-/-/-/-	-	1	1	-	-	-
	2nd	-/-/-/-	-/2/-/-	-	-	-	-	-	-
8 Jason Fowler	1st	-/-/-/-	-/1/-/-	-	-	-	-	-	-
▼ 83	2nd	-/-/-/-	-/-/-/-	-	-	-	-	-	-
12 Jo Kuffour	1st	-/-/-/-	-/-/-/-	-	-	1	-	-	-
	2nd	-/-/-/-	-/-/-/-	1	-	1	-	-	-
17 Brian McGlinchey	1st	-/-/-/-	-/-/-/-	-	1	-	-	1	-
■ 33	2nd	-/-/-/-	-/-/-/-	-	-	-	-	1	-

Subs not used: Wills, Killoughery. - **Formation: 4-4-2**

Goalkeeper Stats: Kevin Pilkington Saves: Catch 4, Crosses: Catch 4

	Player Stats	Shots on target	Shots off target	Caught offside	Fouls conceded	Free-kicks won	Corners taken	Clearances	Defensive blocks
2	Jamie Clarke	-/-/-/-	1/-/-/-	-	3	2	-	3	-
8	Craig Disley ▲ 78	-/-/-/-	-/-/1/-	-	-	-	-	-	-
4	Tom Curtis ▼ 78	-/-/1/-	-/1/-/-	-	1	1	-	2	-
20	Junior Mendes	1/2/-/-	-/-/-/-	2	-	-	-	-	-
21	Luke Dimech ■ 38	-/-/-/-	-/-/-/-	-	2	-	-	1	-
6	Tony Vaughan	-/-/-/-	-/1/-/-	-	-	1	-	-	-
7	Liam Lawrence	-/1/-/-	-/1/-/-	1	-	2	3	-	-
25	David Artell	-/-/-/-	-/-/1/-	-	2	-	-	6	-
22	Iyseden Christie ▼ 79	-/-/-/-	-/-/-/-	-	2	3	-	1	-
24	Lee Williamson	-/-/-/-	-/-/-/-	-	4	-	-	2	-
19	Andy White ▲ 79	-/-/-/-	-/-/-/-	-	1	-	-	-	-
9	Colin Larkin ▲ 61	-/-/1/-	1/-/-/-	-	-	-	-	1	-
11	Wayne Corden ▼ 61	-/-/-/-	-/-/-/-	-	1	-	1	-	-

Subs not used: J White, Day. - **Formation: 4-4-2**

Boston Utd [1] 4 TORQUAY [0] 0

25th October

None of the so-called big teams - Hull, Oxford, Huddersfield, Mansfield, Yeovil, Northampton - have come remotely close to doing what unconsidered Boston United did to the Gulls at windy York Street.

The Pilgrims, on a six game roll, had been impressive at home since they came into the League but they were not that good that they should have handed out this sort of thrashing.

Torquay were behind in the game before they had a chance to draw breath. When a Taylor header from a long clearance by Boston goalkeeper Paul Bastock dropped into midfield, United were not quick enough to the second ball. Redfearn, who has plied his trade with distinction in all four divisions over the last 20 years, took a touch and belted a right-foot shot from more than 25 yards into the top right-hand corner.

United went on to dominate the next half-hour but no-one really looked like scoring. Kuffour missed with a good heading chance when Kevin Hill beat right-back Chris Hogg and crossed invitingly in the eighth minute.

Then in the 28th minute Graham picked up the ball in midfield, skinned two defenders and with Bastock to beat, pulled a left-foot shot just wide when he should have scored. And in the 44th minute Graham spotted Bastock off his line, let fly with a 25-yard volley and the ball bounced off the top of the bar.

It looked as if Torquay almost expected the equaliser would come. They were wrong.

In the 61st minute Boston midfielder Lee Thompson shot from just outside the area, Woods tried to block it but the ball looped off his shoulder, over the stranded Dearden and into the net. Then in the last ten minutes the home side helped themselves to two more goals.

On eighty minutes Dearden couldn't hold a Thompson shot that bounced just in front of him and Duffield stabbed home the rebound. And in the Eighty ninth a Weatherstone through-ball beat reshuffled United's offside trap and Duffield nipped clear to tuck No.4 past Dearden.

Result.......Result.......Result.

BOSTON UTD ......(1) **4** **TORQUAY** ......(0) **0**
Redfearn 4
Thompson 61
Duffield 81, 90

Att 2,431
Referee: K Hill

Stats......Stats.......Stats......Stats

BOSTON UTD				TORQUAY		
1st	2nd	Total		Total	2nd	1st
1	3	4	Corners	3	1	2
9	6	15	Fouls	12	6	6
0	2	2	Yellow cards	4	3	1
0	0	0	Red cards	0	0	0
0	1	1	Caught Offside	8	3	5
3	4	7	Shots on target	3	1	2
3	2	5	Shots off target	4	1	3
0	0	0	Hit woodwork	1	0	1
38	38	38%	Possession	62%	62	62

> IT wasn't particularly pretty but it was certainly effective. We knew Torquay would play the ball around and we had to compete and combat that.
>
> **Neil Thompson**

> I feel deeply disappointed for the supporters who travelled up to watch us. We gave a poor performance and got what we deserved - nothing.
>
> **Leroy Rosenior**

Other Div 3 Results

Cambridge Utd 1 Yeovil 4, Darlington 1 Bury 3, Huddersfield 2 Carlisle 1, Kidderminster 0 Doncaster 2, Leyton Orient 1 Northampton 1, Macclesfield 1 Southend 2, Mansfield 4 Cheltenham 0, Oxford Utd 0 Bristol Rovers 0, Rochdale 0 Swansea 1, Scunthorpe 0 York 0

Boston Utd [1] 4 TORQUAY [0] 0

Goalkeeper Stats: Kevin Dearden Saves: Catch 1, Crosses: Catch 3

#	Torquay Player Stats		Shots on target L/R/H/Oth	Shots off target L/R/H/Oth	Caught offside	Fouls conceded	Free-kicks won	Corners taken	Clearances	Defensive blocks
5	Craig Taylor	1st	-/-/-/-	-/-/-/-	-	1	2	-	-	1
		2nd	-/-/-/-	-/-/-/-	1	-	-	-	-	-
28	Michael Williamson	1st	-/-/-/-	-/-/-/-	-	-	-	-	-	-
		2nd	-/-/-/-	-/-/-/-	-	1	-	-	-	-
18	Steve Woods	1st	-/-/-/-	-/-/-/-	-	1	1	-	-	-
	■ 23	2nd	-/-/-/-	-/-/-/-	-	1	-	-	-	-
6	Alex Russell	1st	-/-/-/-	-/-/-/-	-	-	-	2	-	-
	▼ 86	2nd	-/-/-/-	-/-/-/-	-	-	1	-	-	-
16	Jimmy Benefield	1st	-/-/-/-	-/-/-/-	-	-	-	-	-	-
	▲ 67	2nd	-/-/-/-	-/-/-/-	-	-	-	-	-	-
29	Joe Broad	1st	-/-/-/-	-/-/-/-	-	-	-	-	-	-
	▲ 87	2nd	-/-/-/-	-/-/-/-	-	-	-	-	-	-
23	Kain Bond	1st	-/-/-/-	-/-/-/-	-	-	-	-	-	-
	▲ 86	2nd	-/-/-/-	-/-/-/-	-	-	-	-	-	-
11	Kevin Hill	1st	-/1/-/-	-/-/-/-	2	-	2	-	-	-
	■ 63	2nd	-/-/-/-	-/-/-/-	-	1	2	-	1	-
10	David Graham	1st	-/-/-/-	1/1/-/-	1	1	2	-	-	-
	▼ 87 ■ 54	2nd	-/1/-/-	-/-/-/-	2	1	1	-	-	-
14	Matthew Hockley	1st	-/-/-/-	-/-/-/-	-	1	2	-	-	-
		2nd	-/-/-/-	-/-/-/-	-	-	-	-	-	-
8	Jason Fowler	1st	-/-/-/-	-/1/-/-	1	-	-	-	-	-
	▼ 67 ■ 58	2nd	-/-/-/-	-/-/-/-	-	1	-	-	-	-
12	Jo Kuffour	1st	-/1/-/-	-/-/-/-	-	-	-	-	-	-
		2nd	-/-/-/-	-/1/-/-	-	-	1	-	-	-
17	Brian McGlinchey	1st	-/-/-/-	-/-/-/-	1	2	-	-	-	-
		2nd	-/-/-/-	-/-/-/-	-	1	1	1	-	-

Subs not used: Wills, Camara. - **Formation: 4-4-2**

Goalkeeper Stats: Paul Bastock Saves: Fumble 1, Catch 2, Crosses: Catch 4

#	Player Stats	Shots on target	Shots off target	Caught offside	Fouls conceded	Free-kicks won	Corners taken	Clearances	Defensive blocks
6	Mark Greaves	-/-/-/-	-/-/-/-	-	3	-	-	-	-
8	Graeme Jones ▼ 74	-/-/-/-	-/-/-/-	-	3	2	-	-	-
25	Adebayo Akinfenwa ▼ 85	-/-/-/-	-/-/-/-	1	-	3	-	-	-
20	Lee Beevers	-/-/-/-	-/-/-/-	-	2	-	-	-	-
17	Stuart Douglas ▲ 85	-/-/-/-	-/-/-/-	-	-	1	-	-	-
9	Peter Duffield ▲ 74	1/1/-/-	-/-/1/-	-	-	-	-	-	-
4	Paul Ellender ■ 90	-/-/1/-	-/-/-/-	-	4	2	-	-	-
5	Stuart Balmer	-/-/-/-	-/-/-/-	-	-	-	-	1	-
24	Chris Hogg	-/-/-/-	-/-/-/-	-	-	-	-	-	-
18	Lee Thompson	1/-/-/-	-/1/-/-	-	-	2	-	-	-
10	Simon Weatherstone	1/-/-/-	-/1/-/-	-	-	-	-	-	-
15	Neil Redfearn ■ 60	-/2/-/-	-/2/-/-	-	3	2	4	-	-

Subs not used: Clarke, Croudson, Rusk. - **Formation: 4-4-2**

Torquay Played: 16 **Won** 7 **Drawn** 4 **Lost** 5 **For** 19 **Against** 19 **Pos** 8

...October Team Stats.....Team Stats......Team Stats......Team S

League table at the end of October

		HOME					AWAY						
	P	W	D	L	F	A	W	D	L	F	A	Pts	Df
Hull	16	7	1	0	24	9	3	4	1	12	5	35	22
Doncaster	16	5	2	1	16	6	4	2	2	15	9	31	16
Oxford Utd	16	6	2	0	13	2	2	5	1	10	7	31	14
Swansea	16	5	2	1	18	7	4	1	3	11	13	30	9
Yeovil	16	6	0	2	13	5	4	0	4	11	12	30	7
Mansfield	16	6	1	1	23	8	3	1	4	13	14	29	14
Huddersfield	16	6	1	1	14	5	1	3	4	9	14	25	4
Torquay	**16**	**5**	**2**	**1**	**13**	**9**	**2**	**2**	**4**	**6**	**10**	**25**	**0**
Lincoln City	16	3	4	1	10	5	3	2	3	10	10	24	5
York	16	4	3	1	12	7	2	2	4	3	11	23	-3
Bristol Rovers	16	3	3	2	9	8	3	1	4	12	12	22	1
Scunthorpe	16	2	4	2	13	12	3	3	2	12	13	22	0
Cambridge U	16	1	3	4	10	15	4	3	1	13	7	21	1
Rochdale	16	2	3	3	11	12	3	2	3	12	10	20	1
Boston Utd	16	4	3	1	14	7	1	2	5	4	13	20	-2
Bury	16	3	2	3	10	13	3	0	5	13	16	20	-6
Leyton Orient	16	2	3	3	10	12	2	3	3	7	10	18	-5
Cheltenham	16	4	1	3	14	15	1	2	5	11	21	18	-11
Northampton	16	3	2	3	6	8	1	3	4	7	13	17	-8
Macclesfield	16	2	4	2	10	9	1	2	5	8	16	15	-7
Darlington	16	4	1	3	10	11	0	2	6	8	18	15	-11
Southend	16	2	1	5	7	13	2	2	4	7	12	15	-11
Kidderminster	16	2	1	5	7	13	2	2	4	6	11	15	-11
Carlisle	16	1	1	6	6	14	0	1	7	5	16	5	-19

October matches table

	P	W	D	L	F	A	Pts
Doncaster	5	5	0	0	16	5	15
Oxford Utd	6	3	3	0	9	3	12
Hull	5	3	2	0	11	3	11
Boston Utd	5	3	2	0	11	3	11
Lincoln City	5	3	1	1	11	9	10
Mansfield	5	3	0	2	11	6	9
Yeovil	5	3	0	2	8	6	9
Huddersfield	5	3	0	2	7	7	9
Leyton Orient	5	2	2	1	7	5	8
Swansea	5	2	2	1	5	5	8
Rochdale	5	2	1	2	6	4	7
Bury	5	2	1	2	6	9	7
Torquay	**6**	**2**	**1**	**3**	**5**	**8**	**7**
Kidderminster	5	2	1	2	4	5	7
Southend	5	2	0	3	6	8	6
Cambridge Utd	5	2	0	3	6	8	6
Cheltenham	5	2	0	3	6	11	6
York	5	1	3	1	5	5	6
Scunthorpe	5	1	2	2	6	7	5
Bristol Rovers	5	1	2	2	6	8	5
Macclesfield	5	1	0	4	5	10	3
Northampton	5	0	3	2	4	9	3
Carlisle	5	0	0	5	4	11	0
Darlington	5	0	0	5	3	13	0

October team stats details

Club Name	Ply	Shots On	Shots Off	Corners	Hit W'work	Caught Offside	Offside Trap	Fouls	Yellow Cards	Red Cards	Pens Awarded	Pens Con
Boston Utd	5	28	24	20	0	27	19	73	9	1	- (-)	-
Bristol Rovers	5	20	20	19	2	24	13	64	9	2	- (-)	1
Bury	5	22	19	32	1	15	12	82	13	1	- (-)	-
Cambridge U	5	23	31	27	2	23	22	54	6	0	- (-)	-
Carlisle	5	27	26	30	2	20	6	72	14	2	- (-)	-
Cheltenham	5	25	35	29	0	25	31	50	6	1	- (-)	2
Darlington	5	16	14	20	0	27	33	74	9	1	1 (-)	2
Doncaster	5	37	35	44	1	16	30	61	8	0	3 (3)	1
Huddersfield	5	46	36	23	2	11	21	81	12	1	1 (-)	1
Hull	5	40	21	27	2	22	32	58	5	1	1 (-)	1
Kidderminster	5	27	24	37	0	9	18	60	10	0	- (-)	-
Leyton Orient	5	26	24	28	0	12	25	74	10	2	- (-)	-
Lincoln City	5	44	18	19	1	20	15	66	10	2	1 (1)	1
Macclesfield	5	29	19	31	1	16	6	65	9	3	- (-)	-
Mansfield	5	43	29	38	2	18	13	66	1	0	2 (2)	1
Northampton	5	21	18	28	3	18	16	75	10	1	- (-)	-
Oxford Utd	6	37	32	29	2	8	16	88	10	0	- (-)	-
Rochdale	5	37	17	30	0	25	20	62	7	0	1 (1)	-
Scunthorpe	5	51	22	40	1	17	19	67	17	2	1 (1)	2
Southend	5	34	29	32	1	12	15	65	6	0	1 (1)	1
Swansea	5	21	20	21	1	20	20	53	9	0	- (-)	-
Torquay	**6**	**27**	**41**	**34**	**2**	**27**	**11**	**66**	**11**	**0**	**- (-)**	**-**
Yeovil	5	29	22	30	1	31	18	66	4	0	1 (1)	-
York	5	36	13	18	4	14	26	56	8	1	- (-)	-

...October Player Stats..... Player Stats...... Player Stats......Pla

Monthly Top scorers

Chris Brown (Doncaster)	4
Gregg Blundell (Doncaster)	3
Matthew Tipton (Macclesfield)	3
Dave Kitson (Cambridge Utd)	3
Kevin Townson (Rochdale)	3
Gary Alexander (Leyton Orient)	3
Andy Booth (Huddersfield)	3
Steve Basham (Oxford Utd)	3
Francis Tierney (Doncaster)	2
David Graham (Torquay)	2

Penalties scored

3 M McIndoe (Doncaster), 2 L Lawrence (Mansfield), 1 P Mayo (Lincoln City), J Smith (Southend)

Assists

Danny Allsopp (Hull)	3
Danny Boxall (Bristol Rovers)	2
Mark Gower (Southend)	2
Danny Whitaker (Macclesfield)	2
Anthony Carss (Huddersfield)	2
Gavin Williams (Yeovil)	2
Stuart Bimson (Cambridge Utd)	2

Quickest goals

0:24 mins - Dave Kitson (Swansea vs Cambridge Utd)

1:21 mins - Francis Tierney (Doncaster vs Rochdale)

3:01 mins - Martin Devaney (Cheltenham vs Yeovil)

3:11 mins - Kevin Townson (Doncaster vs Rochdale)

3:24 mins - Terry Skiverton (Yeovil vs Huddersfield)

Top Keeper

	Mins	Gls
Andy Woodman (Oxford U)	580	3
Paul Musselwhite (Hull)	478	3
Paul Bastock (Boston Utd)	478	3
Neil Edwards (Rochdale)	483	4
G Thompson (Northampton)	117	1
Lee Harrison (Leyton O)	487	5
Mark Ovendale (York)	480	5
Roger Freestone (Swansea)	478	5

Shots on target

Jonathan Stead (Huddersfield)	11
Danny Allsopp (Hull)	10
Steven MacLean (Scunthorpe)	10
Andy Booth (Huddersfield)	10
Steve Torpey (Scunthorpe)	9
Grant McCann (Cheltenham)	9
Steve Basham (Oxford Utd)	9
Dave Kitson (Cambridge Utd)	9
Matthew Tipton (Macclesfield)	9
John Melligan (Kidderminster)	9

Shots off target

David Graham (Torquay)	15
Jonathan Stead (Huddersfield)	12
Danny Allsopp (Hull)	8
Dean Whitehead (Oxford Utd)	7
Ben Burgess (Hull)	7
Steve Basham (Oxford Utd)	7
John Doolan (Doncaster)	7
Lee Johnson (Yeovil)	7
Grant McCann (Cheltenham)	7
Bob Taylor (Cheltenham)	7

Caught offside

Kevin Gall (Yeovil)	14
Paul Brayson (Cheltenham)	12
Martin Carruthers (Macclesfield)	10
Richie Foran (Carlisle)	10
David Graham (Torquay)	9
Simon Weatherstone (Yeovil)	9
Kevin Hill (Torquay)	8
Danny Allsopp (Hull)	8
John Taylor (Cambridge Utd)	8

Free-kicks won

David Graham (Torquay)	24
John Melligan (Kidderminster)	16
Steve Torpey (Scunthorpe)	16
Duncan Jupp (Southend)	15
Chris Brown (Doncaster)	15
Richie Foran (Carlisle)	14
Ijah Anderson (Bristol Rovers)	13
Liam Lawrence (Mansfield)	13
Dave Kitson (Cambridge Utd)	13

Torquay v Hull

Fouls conceded

Chris Brown (Doncaster)	19
Paul Tait (Bristol Rovers)	15
Julian Alsop (Oxford Utd)	15
Richie Foran (Carlisle)	14
Kevin Nugent (Swansea)	13
Danny Swailes (Bury)	13
Graeme Jones (Boston Utd)	13
Kevin Hill (Torquay)	12
David Graham (Torquay)	12

Fouls without a card

Andy Booth (Huddersfield)	12
Paul Trollope (Northampton)	11
Martin Carruthers (Macclesfield)	11
Colin Pluck (Yeovil)	11
Ben Burgess (Hull)	10
Nathan Clarke (Huddersfield)	10
Jake Edwards (Yeovil)	10
Mickael Antoine-Curier (Grimsby)	9
Jon Ashton (Oxford Utd)	9

Alex Russel tussles with a Huddersfield player.
Torquay v Huddersfield
HPL01360_TNA_098

Kevin Hill attempts to take the ball past Oxford's David Waterman.
Torquay v Oxford
HPL01492_TNA_036

Doncaster [1] 1 TORQUAY [0] 0 — 1st November

It was a wonder that lackluster Torquay United didn't lose to in-form Doncaster Rovers more heavily at Belle Vue.

And the Gulls' away form was starting to cause real concern. Their failure to score for the fourth successive away game condemned them to another defeat, but not even the most blinkered traveling fan would claim that they deserved anything more from this game.

All United's best players were in defence. Skipper Craig Taylor took the eye, but they never really recovered from a ragged start. They were lucky that Doncaster didn't kill them off in the opening part of the game.

As it was the Rovers had to wait until the 21st minute for what turned out to be their winner. For once, there were question marks about United's defence as midfielder Green was not picked up and ran through unopposed on John Doolan's pass to flick the ball past the advancing Kevin Dearden.

United head coach Leroy Rosenior expressed his faith in his players and he duly stuck to the same starting eleven which had lost 0-4 at Boston seven days before.

But the only Torquay forward who looked as if he might score was leading marksman David Graham, but the Scotsman had no support and even poorer service.

Matt Hockley and Jo Kuffour both missed rare but great chances before half-time. Hockley's finish from Wills' pass was weak and Kuffour missed the ball completely from 12 yards out after Graham had set him up.

Four minutes into the second half Rosenior took Kuffour off and sent on Jimmy Benefield in an effort to spark some improvement in attack. He did his best, but it was not enough in a low-key second half which seldom entertained the 6,863 crowd.

They seldom threatened to upset Doncaster's impressive run, which had seen them rise from 17th place to second, while Torquay had slipped to 10th.

Result.......Result.......Result.

DONCASTER ......(1) **1** **TORQUAY** ......(0) **0**
Green 21

Att 6,863
Referee: R Pearson

Stats......Stats.......Stats......Stats

DONCASTER				TORQUAY		
1st	**2nd**	**Total**		**Total**	**2nd**	**1st**
6	5	11	**Corners**	2	2	0
4	5	9	**Fouls**	13	7	6
1	0	1	**Yellow cards**	3	2	1
0	0	0	**Red cards**	0	0	0
4	1	5	**Caught Offside**	6	5	1
6	3	9	**Shots on target**	12	7	5
1	1	2	**Shots off target**	2	2	0
0	0	0	**Hit woodwork**	0	0	0
61	59	60%	**Possession**	40%	41	39

"I was pleased to keep a clean sheet especially when they came back at us in the second half. We are certainly on a roll.

Dave Penney"

WE looked jaded and sloppy at the start. We had a couple of chances to nick a point but whether we deserved to or not is another matter.

Leroy Rosenior"

Other Div 3 Results

Bury 2 Yeovil 1, Cheltenham 1 York 1, Hull 2 Macclesfield 2, Kidderminster 2 Cambridge Utd 2, Leyton Orient 2 Rochdale 1, Mansfield 2 Boston Utd 1, Oxford Utd 3 Darlington 1, Scunthorpe 6 Huddersfield 2, Southend 0 Northampton 1, Swansea 0 Bristol Rovers 0

Doncaster [1] 1 TORQUAY [0] 0

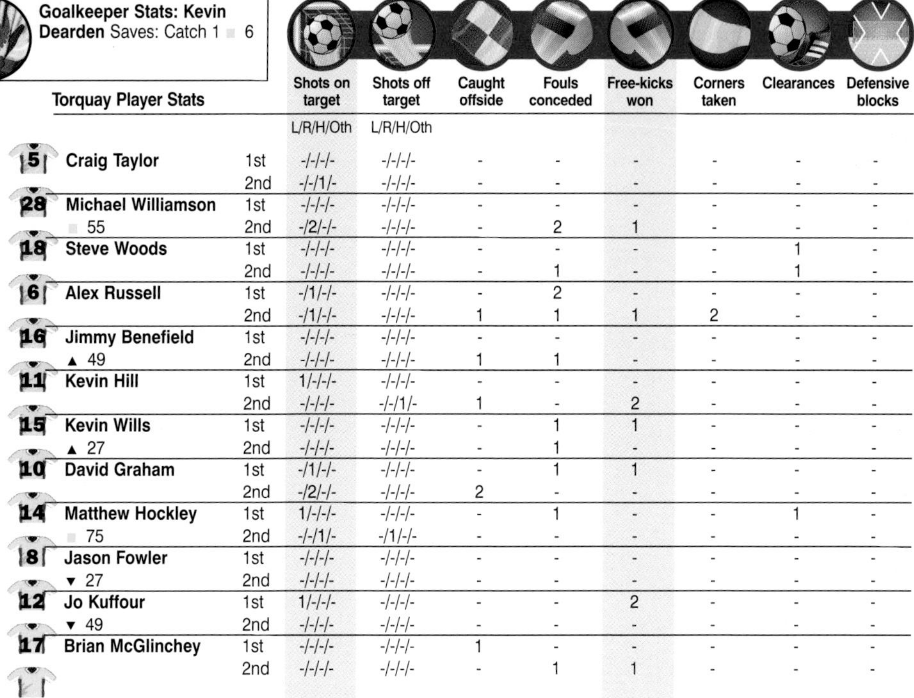

Goalkeeper Stats: Kevin Dearden Saves: Catch 1 ■ 6

No.	Torquay Player Stats		Shots on target L/R/H/Oth	Shots off target L/R/H/Oth	Caught offside	Fouls conceded	Free-kicks won	Corners taken	Clearances	Defensive blocks
5	Craig Taylor	1st	-/-/-/-	-/-/-/-	-	-	-	-	-	-
		2nd	-/-/1/-	-/-/-/-	-	-	-	-	-	-
28	Michael Williamson	1st	-/-/-/-	-/-/-/-	-	-	-	-	-	-
	■ 55	2nd	-/2/-/-	-/-/-/-	-	2	1	-	-	-
18	Steve Woods	1st	-/-/-/-	-/-/-/-	-	-	-	-	1	-
		2nd	-/-/-/-	-/-/-/-	-	1	-	-	1	-
6	Alex Russell	1st	-/1/-/-	-/-/-/-	-	2	-	-	-	-
		2nd	-/1/-/-	-/-/-/-	1	1	1	2	-	-
16	Jimmy Benefield	1st	-/-/-/-	-/-/-/-	-	-	-	-	-	-
	▲ 49	2nd	-/-/-/-	-/-/-/-	1	1	-	-	-	-
11	Kevin Hill	1st	1/-/-/-	-/-/-/-	-	-	-	-	-	-
		2nd	-/-/-/-	-/-/1/-	1	-	2	-	-	-
15	Kevin Wills	1st	-/-/-/-	-/-/-/-	-	1	1	-	-	-
	▲ 27	2nd	-/-/-/-	-/-/-/-	-	1	-	-	-	-
10	David Graham	1st	-/1/-/-	-/-/-/-	-	1	1	-	-	-
		2nd	-/2/-/-	-/-/-/-	2	-	-	-	-	-
14	Matthew Hockley	1st	1/-/-/-	-/-/-/-	-	1	-	-	1	-
	■ 75	2nd	-/-/1/-	-/1/-/-	-	-	-	-	-	-
8	Jason Fowler	1st	-/-/-/-	-/-/-/-	-	-	-	-	-	-
	▼ 27	2nd	-/-/-/-	-/-/-/-	-	-	-	-	-	-
12	Jo Kuffour	1st	1/-/-/-	-/-/-/-	-	-	2	-	-	-
	▼ 49	2nd	-/-/-/-	-/-/-/-	-	-	-	-	-	-
17	Brian McGlinchey	1st	-/-/-/-	-/-/-/-	1	-	-	-	-	-
		2nd	-/-/-/-	-/-/-/-	-	1	1	-	-	-

Subs not used: Van Heusden, Hazell, Camara. - **Formation: 4-4-2**

Goalkeeper Stats: Andy Warrington Saves: Catch 5

No.	Player Stats	Shots on target	Shots off target	Caught offside	Fouls conceded	Free-kicks won	Corners taken	Clearances	Defensive blocks
4	David Morley ▲ 90	-/-/-/-	-/-/-/-	-	-	-	-	-	-
26	Chris Brown ▼ 84	1/-/-/-	-/-/-/-	-	1	5	-	-	-
21	Michael McIndoe	1/1/1/-	-/-/-/-	-	1	2	6	-	-
14	Leo Fortune-West ▲ 85	-/-/-/-	-/-/-/-	-	-	-	-	-	-
20	Paul Green ▼ 85	-/1/-/-	-/-/-/-	-	-	1	-	-	-
3	Tim Ryan	-/-/-/-	-/1/-/-	1	-	2	-	-	-
6	Mark Albrighton	-/-/-/-	-/-/-/-	-	-	1	-	-	-
12	John McGrath	1/-/-/-	-/-/-/-	-	2	1	4	-	-
19	Ricky Ravenhill ▲ 84	-/-/-/-	-/-/-/-	-	-	-	-	-	-
18	Jamie Price	-/-/-/-	-/-/-/-	-	1	-	-	-	-
23	Stephen Foster	-/-/-/-	-/-/-/-	-	1	-	-	-	-
5	John Doolan ▼ 90	-/-/-/-	1/-/-/-	-	2	1	1	-	-
8	Gregg Blundell ■ 6	1/2/-/-	-/-/-/-	3	1	-	-	-	-

Subs not used: Richardson, Barnes. - **Formation: 4-4-2**

Torquay Played: 17 **Won** 7 **Drawn** 4 **Lost** 6 **For** 19 **Against** 20 **Pos** 10

Torquay [0] 1 BURTON ALBION [1] 2 — 8th November

Disrupted by injuries and riddled with self-doubt, Torquay United needed an FA Cup-tie against determined underdogs like a hole in the head. Burton Albion sensed it and duly seized their chance as winter came to Plainmoor.

The one thing that any League side must do against so-called minnows is to give them no encouragement early on but United did just the opposite.

After only ten minutes Burton winger Colkin crossed from the left. Lone striker Dale Anderson pressured a moment of uncertainty and Steve Woods miskicked his clearance over Arjan Van Heusden and into his own net.

From then it was one-way traffic, with David Graham, Tony Bedeau, Taylor, Matt Hockley and Jimmy Benefield all going close.

Moments after Hockley headed just over from a great cross by Alex Russell, United equalised. Hazell dashed past the stumbling Glenn Kirkwood on the left, Graham stepped over his low cross and Benefield scored with a first-time right-foot from ten yards.

It seemed like United would surely go on to win. But just when everybody expected Burton to fall back even further and settle for a replay, they put together their most adventurous spell of the match.

Even then, it was hard to see Burton scoring, yet in the 70th minute they snatched what turned out to be the winner. Albion forced their first corner of the match, United only half-cleared it and the ball eventually dropped out to Clough.

Burton's 38-year-old player-manager, whose brain leaves his legs well behind these days, chipped the ball back into the area, the pass sprung United's advancing offside-trap and left substitute Robbie Talbot clear. He drove the ball past Arjan Van Heusden from ten yards.

Graham, Hill and Taylor all went close as United tried desperately to save themselves in the closing stages. But fortune favours the brave and Burton hung on for the victory.

Result.......Result.......Result.

TORQUAY..............(0) **1** **BURTON A**......(1) **2**
Benefield 55 — Woods 10 (og)
Att 2,790 — Talbot 71
Referee: L Probert

Stats......Stats.......Stats......Stats

TORQUAY				BURTON ALBION		
1st	2nd	Total		Total	2nd	1st
3	9	12	Corners	3	3	0
4	3	7	Fouls	6	2	4
0	0	0	Yellow cards	1	1	0
0	0	0	Red cards	0	0	0
1	3	4	Caught Offside	2	1	1
5	4	9	Shots on target	3	2	1
7	6	13	Shots off target	1	0	1
0	0	0	Hit woodwork	0	0	0
67	73	70%	Possession	30%	27	33

"**OF** course I am massively disappointed for everybody in the club When things are going like this you just have to keep going and keep playing.

Leroy Rosenior"

"**WE'VE** been close to beating a league side in the last few years and to win it without a replay is a lovely feeling.

Nigel Clough"

Other FA Cup Round 1 Results

Barnet 2 Stalybridge 2, Blackpool 4 Boreham W 0, Bournemouth 1 Bristol R 0, Brentford 7 Gainsboro 1, Bury 1 Rochdale 2, Cheltenham 3 Hull 1, Chester 0 Gravesend 1, Colchester 1 Oxford Utd 0, Farnborough 0 Weston-S-M 1, Grantham 1 Leyton Orient 2, Grays A 1 Aldershot 2, Grimsby 1 QPR 0, Hartlepool 4 Whitby 0, Kidderminster 2 Northwich 1, Lancaster 1 Cambridge U 2, Macclesfield 3 Boston U 0, Mansfield 6 B Stortford 0, Northampton 3 Plymouth 2, Oldham 3 Carlisle 0, Peterborough 2 Hereford 0, Port Vale 2 Ford Utd 2, Scarborough 1 Doncaster 0, Scunthorpe 2 Shrewsbury 1, Southend P Canvey I P, Stevenage 2 Stockport 1, Swansea 3 Rushden & D's 0, Telford 3 Crawley T 2, Tranmere 3 Chesterfield 2, Woking 3 Histon 1, Wycombe 4 Swindon 1, Yeovil 4 Wrexham 1

TORQUAY [0] 1 Burton Albion [1] 2

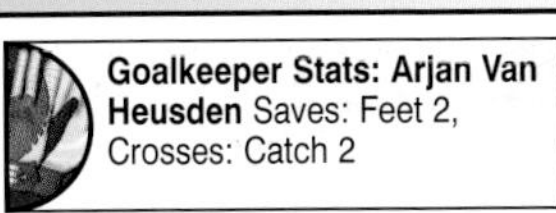

Goalkeeper Stats: Arjan Van Heusden Saves: Feet 2, Crosses: Catch 2

#	Torquay Player Stats		Shots on target L/R/H/Oth	Shots off target L/R/H/Oth	Caught offside	Fouls conceded	Free-kicks won	Corners taken	Clearances	Defensive blocks
10	David Graham	1st	1/-/-/-	-/2/-/-	1	-	2	-	-	-
		2nd	-/-/-/-	-/2/-/-	3	-	-	-	-	-
7	Tony Bedeau	1st	-/1/-/-	-/-/-/-	-	-	-	-	-	-
		2nd	-/-/-/-	-/-/-/-	-	2	-	-	-	-
15	Kevin Wills	1st	-/-/-/-	-/-/-/-	-	-	-	-	-	-
	▲ 74	2nd	-/-/-/-	-/2/-/-	-	-	-	-	-	-
2	Reuben Hazell	1st	-/-/-/-	-/-/-/-	-	2	1	-	-	-
		2nd	-/-/-/-	-/-/-/-	-	-	-	-	-	-
5	Craig Taylor	1st	-/-/1/-	-/-/-/-	-	-	-	-	-	-
		2nd	-/-/-/-	-/-/-/-	-	-	-	-	1	-
14	Matthew Hockley	1st	-/1/-/-	-/1/-/-	-	-	-	-	-	-
	▼ 74	2nd	-/-/-/-	-/-/1/-	-	-	-	-	-	-
8	Jason Fowler	1st	-/-/-/-	-/-/-/-	-	-	-	-	-	-
	▼ 63	2nd	-/-/-/-	-/-/-/-	-	-	-	-	-	-
4	Lee Canoville	1st	-/-/-/-	-/-/-/-	-	-	1	-	-	-
		2nd	-/-/-/-	-/-/-/-	-	-	-	-	-	-
18	Steve Woods	1st	-/-/-/-	-/-/-/-	-	1	-	-	-	-
		2nd	-/-/-/-	-/-/-/-	-	-	-	-	1	-
6	Alex Russell	1st	-/1/-/-	-/1/-/-	-	-	-	3	-	-
		2nd	-/1/-/-	-/1/-/-	-	-	2	9	-	-
16	Jimmy Benefield	1st	-/-/-/-	1/-/2/-	-	1	-	-	-	-
		2nd	-/1/-/-	-/-/-/-	-	1	-	-	-	-
11	Kevin Hill	1st	-/-/-/-	-/-/-/-	-	-	-	-	-	-
	▲ 63	2nd	-/2/-/-	-/-/-/-	-	-	-	-	-	-

Subs not used: Dearden, Bond, Stevens. - **Formation: 4-4-2**

Goalkeeper Stats: Matt Duke Saves: Catch 6, Crosses: Catch 6

#	Player Stats	Shots on target	Shots off target	Caught offside	Fouls conceded	Free-kicks won	Corners taken	Clearances	Defensive blocks
8	Jonathan Howard	-/-/-/-	-/-/-/-	1	1	-	-	-	-
16	Dale Anderson	1/-/-/-	-/-/-/-	-	-	3	-	-	-
21	Steve Chettle ▼ 59	-/-/-/-	-/-/-/-	-	-	-	-	2	1
11	Andrew Ducros	-/-/-/-	-/-/-/-	-	-	1	2	-	-
20	Nigel Clough	-/1/-/-	-/-/-/-	-	-	-	-	-	-
18	Robert Talbot ▲ 25	-/1/-/-	-/-/-/-	-	1	1	-	-	-
14	Aaron Webster	-/-/-/-	1/-/-/-	-	-	2	1	3	-
23	Gary Crosby ▲ 59	-/-/-/-	-/-/-/-	-	-	-	-	2	-
12	Glenn Kirkwood	-/-/-/-	-/-/-/-	-	2	-	-	5	1
3	Lee Colkin ▼ 25	-/-/-/-	-/-/-/-	-	-	-	-	-	-
7	Darren Stride	-/-/-/-	-/-/-/-	1	2	-	-	3	1
24	Adam Willis ■ 77	-/-/-/-	-/-/-/-	-	-	-	-	2	-

Subs not used: Williams, Robinson, Sinton. - **Formation: 4-5-1**

Torquay [0] 3 CHELTENHAM [0] 1

15th November

David Graham showed just why he's worth every penny that the Gulls were paying him. United played well to a point, without finishing the job, in the first half. It clearly needed somebody to produce something extra to break the deadlock.

Cue Graham after 55 minutes. Brian McGlinchey and Kevin Hill combined to set him away down the left, Graham beat Robins defender John Brough on the turn, cut in and, as keeper Shane Higgs spread himself, drove the ball over him and into the far corner. The pace of the shot gave Higgs no chance.

But United have still not taken the self-destruct button out of their system, and only five minutes later they let Cheltenham back into the game. Higgs belted the ball to the edge of United's area, where Paul Brayson laid it back for Damien Spencer to crack a 20-year left-foot shot past Kevin Dearden's outstretched right hand.

Skipper Craig Taylor went close with two headers before Graham struck again in the 68th minute. And what a strike. There seemed no danger of him scoring when he chased a long ball by Steve Woods down the right. But from just inside the are, on an acute angle, he unleashed an outrageous lob-volley over the startled Higgs and just inside the far post.

In the 74th minute only a full-length save by Higgs denied Grahm his hat-trick, even though referee Alan Butler somehow awarded a goal-kick. And three minutes later Graham headed a Russell corner against the bar.

It took United until the 86th minute to put the result beyond doubt. This time Graham turned provider, pulling back an inviting low cross from the right for Russell to drive home his second goal of the season.

Result.......Result.......Result.

TORQUAY ....(0) **3** **CHELTENHAM**(0) **1**
Graham 51, 68 Spencer 56
Russell 86

Att 2,653
Referee: Alan Butler

Stats......Stats.......Stats......Stats

TORQUAY				CHELTENHAM		
1st	2nd	Total		Total	2nd	1st
5	7	12	Corners	3	2	1
4	5	9	Fouls	15	5	10
0	0	0	Yellow cards	0	0	0
0	0	0	Red cards	0	0	0
0	1	1	Caught Offside	4	3	1
4	9	13	Shots on target	9	7	2
2	2	4	Shots off target	1	1	0
0	1	1	Hit woodwork	0	0	0
64	58	61%	Possession	39%	42	36

AT half-time I told the players to keep playing, pass the ball and not worry about making mistakes. They did that and scored the goals to go with it.

Leroy Rosenior

I thought Torquay deserved to win in the end. David Graham is an excellent player and he can finish off the moves which Torquay's passing create.

John Ward

Other Div 3 Results

Boston Utd 3 Leyton Orient 0, Bristol Rovers 1 Bury 2, Cambridge Utd 1 Oxford Utd 1, Carlisle 0 Mansfield 2, Huddersfield 3 Hull 1, Macclesfield 2 Scunthorpe 2, Rochdale 0 Kidderminster 1, Yeovil 4 Southend 0, York 1 Doncaster 0

TORQUAY [0] 3 Cheltenham [0] 1

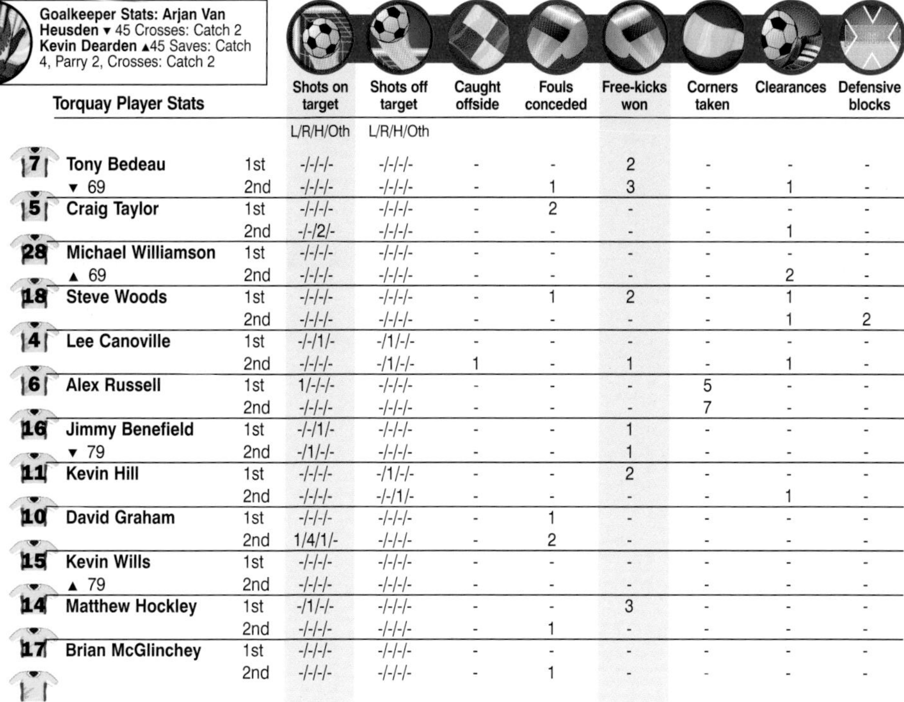

Goalkeeper Stats: Arjan Van Heusden ▼ 45 Crosses: Catch 2 **Kevin Dearden** ▲45 Saves: Catch 4, Parry 2, Crosses: Catch 2

Torquay Player Stats

No.	Player	Half	Shots on target L/R/H/Oth	Shots off target L/R/H/Oth	Caught offside	Fouls conceded	Free-kicks won	Corners taken	Clearances	Defensive blocks
7	Tony Bedeau	1st	-/-/-/-	-/-/-/-	-	-	2	-	-	-
	▼ 69	2nd	-/-/-/-	-/-/-/-	-	1	3	-	1	-
5	Craig Taylor	1st	-/-/-/-	-/-/-/-	-	2	-	-	-	-
		2nd	-/-/2/-	-/-/-/-	-	-	-	-	1	-
28	Michael Williamson	1st	-/-/-/-	-/-/-/-	-	-	-	-	-	-
	▲ 69	2nd	-/-/-/-	-/-/-/-	-	-	-	-	2	-
18	Steve Woods	1st	-/-/-/-	-/-/-/-	-	1	2	-	1	-
		2nd	-/-/-/-	-/-/-/-	-	-	-	-	1	2
4	Lee Canoville	1st	-/-/1/-	-/1/-/-	-	-	-	-	-	-
		2nd	-/-/-/-	-/1/-/-	1	-	1	-	1	-
6	Alex Russell	1st	1/-/-/-	-/-/-/-	-	-	-	5	-	-
		2nd	-/-/-/-	-/-/-/-	-	-	-	7	-	-
16	Jimmy Benefield	1st	-/-/1/-	-/-/-/-	-	-	1	-	-	-
	▼ 79	2nd	-/1/-/-	-/-/-/-	-	-	1	-	-	-
11	Kevin Hill	1st	-/-/-/-	-/1/-/-	-	-	2	-	-	-
		2nd	-/-/-/-	-/-/1/-	-	-	-	-	1	-
10	David Graham	1st	-/-/-/-	-/-/-/-	-	1	-	-	-	-
		2nd	1/4/1/-	-/-/-/-	-	2	-	-	-	-
15	Kevin Wills	1st	-/-/-/-	-/-/-/-	-	-	-	-	-	-
	▲ 79	2nd	-/-/-/-	-/-/-/-	-	-	-	-	-	-
14	Matthew Hockley	1st	-/1/-/-	-/-/-/-	-	-	3	-	-	-
		2nd	-/-/-/-	-/-/-/-	-	1	-	-	-	-
17	Brian McGlinchey	1st	-/-/-/-	-/-/-/-	-	-	-	-	-	-
		2nd	-/-/-/-	-/-/-/-	-	1	-	-	-	-

Subs not used: Camara, Bond. - **Formation: 4-4-2**

Goalkeeper Stats: Shane Higgs Saves: Catch 4, Crosses: Catch 10

No.	Player Stats	Shots on target	Shots off target	Caught offside	Fouls conceded	Free-kicks won	Corners taken	Clearances	Defensive blocks
6	Michael Duff	-/1/-/-	-/-/-/-	-	-	2	1	3	-
9	Paul Brayson	-/2/-/-	-/1/-/-	1	-	1	-	-	-
21	Ben Cleverley ▼ 65	-/-/-/-	-/-/-/-	-	-	2	-	1	-
14	David Bird	-/-/-/-	-/-/-/-	-	-	-	-	1	-
8	Mark Yates	-/-/-/-	-/-/-/-	-	2	1	-	1	-
28	John Finnigan ▼ 86	-/1/-/-	-/-/-/-	-	4	-	-	1	1
10	Damian Spencer	1/2/-/-	-/-/-/-	3	3	3	-	1	-
11	Grant McCann	2/-/-/-	-/-/-/-	-	3	-	-	3	-
7	Lee Howells ▼ 72	-/-/-/-	-/-/-/-	-	1	-	1	4	-
4	Richard Forsyth ▲ 65	-/-/-/-	-/-/-/-	-	1	-	1	-	-
5	John Brough	-/-/-/-	-/-/-/-	-	1	-	-	2	3
26	Bob Taylor ▲ 86	-/-/-/-	-/-/-/-	-	-	-	-	-	-
16	Martin Devaney ▲ 72	-/-/-/-	-/-/-/-	-	-	-	-	-	-

Subs not used: Book, Jones. - **Formation: 4-4-2**

Torquay Played: 18 **Won** 8 **Drawn** 4 **Lost** 6 **For** 22 **Against** 21 **Pos** 9

Kidderminster [1] 1 TORQUAY [1] 2

22nd November

Whether or not they were inspired by the great deeds done in Sydney that morning, United's players produced exactly the sort of tigerish effort and determination after half-time which had been missing from too many of their away performances.

Gulls supporters had seen their side squander leads too often, but this time their tackling, work-rate and alertness made certain of an important away win. Yet United had to overcome a distinctly shaky first half-hour before they looked the part.

When United took the lead after seven minutes, it was against the run of play. Kevin Hill lobbed the ball into the Harriers penalty-area, Graham beat two defenders to flick the ball on and Wills, who had started the move and then supported, chested it down to score with a right-foot shot from 12 yards.

But the Harriers were giving United's defence major problems, and they equalised only five minutes later. Andy White cut inside past Brian McGlinchey and Taylor, laid the ball back to midfielder Danny Williams and he gave Van Heusden no chance with a cracking right-foot sidefoot shot from the edge of the area.

Woods did well to block a goalbound header by Harriers skipper Wayne Hatswell, and in the 39th minute Bo Henriksen played a one-two with White and fired just wide from 18 yards.

But United began to get a grip just before half-time, and their second-half performance was much improved. Wills went close, set up by Russell, before a breathtaking piece of play by Graham created the second goal in the 58th minute.

Taking a Canoville pass on his chest, with his back to Hatswell, Graham flicked the ball over the defender's head, left him for dead on the turn and ran at the retreating Harriers defence.

Checking back from the right past two challenges, Graham spotted Wills just onside, found him with a perfect reverse pass and Wills was left clear to score with a right-foot shot from 15 yards.

Result.......Result.......Result.

KIDDERMINST ....(1) **1** **TORQUAY** ......(1) **2**
D Williams 12 — Wills 7, 58

Att 2,725
Referee: M Thorpe

Stats......Stats.......Stats......Stats

KIDDERMINSTER				TORQUAY		
1st	**2nd**	**Total**		**Total**	**2nd**	**1st**
5	5	10	**Corners**	3	2	1
6	4	10	**Fouls**	13	7	6
0	1	1	**Yellow cards**	1	1	0
0	0	0	**Red cards**	0	0	0
1	1	2	**Caught Offside**	3	1	2
3	1	4	**Shots on target**	5	2	3
4	2	6	**Shots off target**	1	0	1
0	0	0	**Hit woodwork**	1	0	1
44	52	48%	**Possession**	52%	48	56

WE just have to dig in again. Right from the word go the players were never on top of their game and we were beaten by a better team.

Jan Molby

THE second goal I think it killed them off. Our attitude away from home had to get better than it was and it was excellent in the second half.

Leroy Rosenior

Other Div 3 Results

Bury 1 Northampton 0, Cheltenham 2 Carlisle 1, Doncaster 3 Boston Utd 0, Hull 0 Yeovil 0, Leyton Orient 2 York 2, Mansfield 3 Huddersfield 3, Oxford Utd 3 Macclesfield 1, Scunthorpe 4 Cambridge Utd 0, Southend 4 Rochdale 0, Swansea 1 Darlington 0

Kidderminster [1] 1 TORQUAY [1] 2

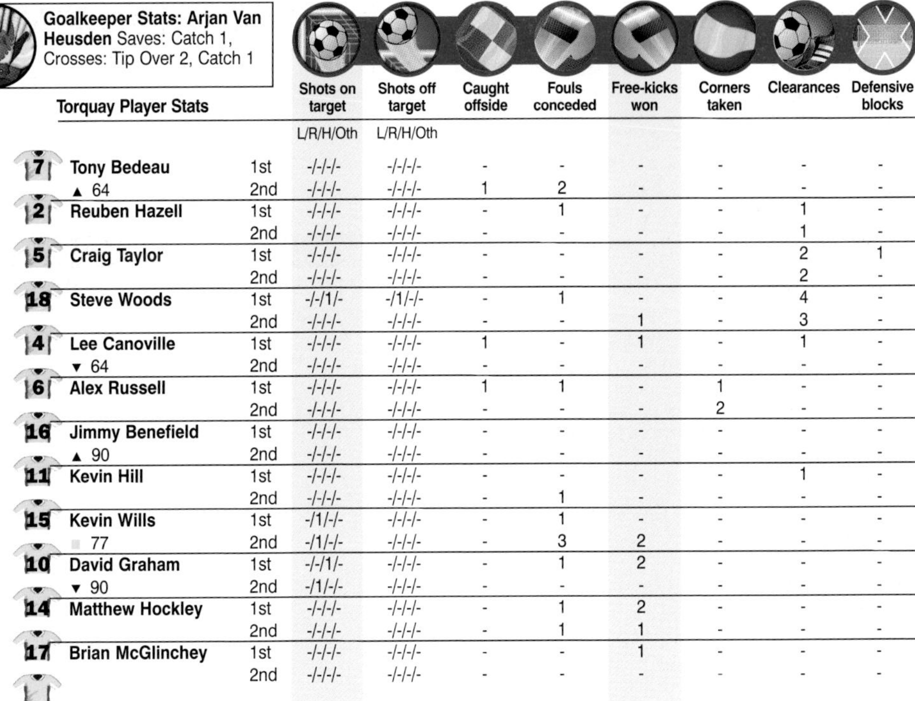

Goalkeeper Stats: Arjan Van Heusden Saves: Catch 1, Crosses: Tip Over 2, Catch 1

Torquay Player Stats		Shots on target L/R/H/Oth	Shots off target L/R/H/Oth	Caught offside	Fouls conceded	Free-kicks won	Corners taken	Clearances	Defensive blocks
7 Tony Bedeau	1st	-/-/-/-	-/-/-/-	-	-	-	-	-	-
▲ 64	2nd	-/-/-/-	-/-/-/-	1	2	-	-	-	-
2 Reuben Hazell	1st	-/-/-/-	-/-/-/-	-	1	-	-	1	-
	2nd	-/-/-/-	-/-/-/-	-	-	-	-	1	-
5 Craig Taylor	1st	-/-/-/-	-/-/-/-	-	-	-	-	2	1
	2nd	-/-/-/-	-/-/-/-	-	-	-	-	2	-
18 Steve Woods	1st	-/-/1/-	-/1/-/-	-	1	-	-	4	-
	2nd	-/-/-/-	-/-/-/-	-	-	1	-	3	-
4 Lee Canoville	1st	-/-/-/-	-/-/-/-	1	-	1	-	1	-
▼ 64	2nd	-/-/-/-	-/-/-/-	-	-	-	-	-	-
6 Alex Russell	1st	-/-/-/-	-/-/-/-	1	1	-	1	-	-
	2nd	-/-/-/-	-/-/-/-	-	-	-	2	-	-
16 Jimmy Benefield	1st	-/-/-/-	-/-/-/-	-	-	-	-	-	-
▲ 90	2nd	-/-/-/-	-/-/-/-	-	-	-	-	-	-
11 Kevin Hill	1st	-/-/-/-	-/-/-/-	-	-	-	-	1	-
	2nd	-/-/-/-	-/-/-/-	-	1	-	-	-	-
15 Kevin Wills	1st	-/1/-/-	-/-/-/-	-	1	-	-	-	-
■ 77	2nd	-/1/-/-	-/-/-/-	-	3	2	-	-	-
10 David Graham	1st	-/-/1/-	-/-/-/-	-	1	2	-	-	-
▼ 90	2nd	-/1/-/-	-/-/-/-	-	-	-	-	-	-
14 Matthew Hockley	1st	-/-/-/-	-/-/-/-	-	1	2	-	-	-
	2nd	-/-/-/-	-/-/-/-	-	1	1	-	-	-
17 Brian McGlinchey	1st	-/-/-/-	-/-/-/-	-	-	1	-	-	-
	2nd	-/-/-/-	-/-/-/-	-	-	-	-	-	-

Subs not used: Dearden, Bernard, Broad. - **Formation: 3-5-2**

Goalkeeper Stats: Stuart Brock Saves: Catch 1, Crosses: Catch 3

	Player Stats	Shots on target	Shots off target	Caught offside	Fouls conceded	Free-kicks won	Corners taken	Clearances	Defensive blocks
14	Sean Parrish	-/-/-/-	-/-/-/-	-	1	1	-	-	-
24	Robert Betts ▲ 57	-/-/-/-	-/-/-/-	-	-	-	-	-	-
23	Steve Burton	-/-/-/-	1/-/-/-	-	1	1	10	1	-
9	John Williams ▼ 57	-/-/-/-	-/1/-/-	-	1	-	-	-	-
6	Matthew Gadsby ▲ 34	-/-/-/-	-/-/-/-	-	1	-	-	-	-
5	Craig Hinton	-/-/-/-	-/-/-/-	-	-	2	-	-	-
7	Dean Bennett	-/-/-/-	-/-/-/-	-	-	1	-	-	-
2	Adie Smith ▼ 34	-/-/-/-	-/-/-/-	-	1	-	-	-	-
22	Wayne Hatswell	-/-/2/-	-/1/1/-	-	1	5	-	2	1
12	Bo Henriksen	-/1/-/-	1/-/-/-	1	1	1	-	-	-
17	Matt Lewis ▲ 80	-/-/-/-	-/-/-/-	-	-	-	-	-	-
4	Danny Williams	-/1/-/-	-/-/-/-	-	1	-	-	-	-
25	Andy White ▼ 80 ■ 69	-/-/-/-	-/1/-/-	1	2	2	-	2	-

Subs not used: Danby, Ayres. - **Formation: 4-3-3**

Torquay Played: 19 **Won** 9 **Drawn** 4 **Lost** 6 **For** 24 **Against** 22 **Pos** 8

Torquay [1] 3 SOUTHEND [0] 0

29th November

After Torquay had taken the lead in a nervous first-half, a large improvement was needed in the second. Two goals in two minutes did the trick, with Matt Hockley and David Graham adding the finishing touches.

They were lucky that Southend didn't score at least three times in the opening minutes. Lewis Hunt's volleyed just over, Drewe Broughton should have buried a header and Bramble's 14th minute free-kick hit the foot of Arjan Van Heusden's right-hand post from 25 yards.

United's normal accuracy in passing was missing and things looked worrying. All they could do was hang on. Luckily, in the likes of skipper Craig Taylor, Steve Woods and Brian McGlinchey at the back, they had the men to do it.

It still took them 40 minutes to register their first shot on target, through Kevin Hill, but that effort sparked a dramatic improvement. In what remained of the first half, Alex Russell went close from 20 yards, Graham hit the post, had two more shots saved on the line. Then Bedeau scored.

Nearly two minutes into stoppage-time, a Graham-Russell move down the left set up a cross by the United midfielder, Graham flicked the ball on at the near-post and Bedeau stooped to nod home at the far-post.

Then, as the rain swept in, Torquay settled the contest. Hockley set Bedeau away on the right, his cross to the far-post was knocked back in by Hill and Hockley was there to stab the ball home from two yards.

Two minutes later Graham forced a corner on the left. Russell took it and Graham's header, a deflection made certain it beat keeper Darryl Flahavan, gave him his 12th goal of the season.

Result.......Result.......Result.

TORQUAY ....(1) **3** **SOUTHEND**....(0) **0**
Bedeau 45
Hockley 52
Graham 54

Att 2,631
Referee: S Tanner

Stats......Stats.......Stats......Stats

TORQUAY				SOUTHEND		
1st	2nd	Total		Total	2nd	1st
5	4	9	**Corners**	2	1	1
10	4	14	**Fouls**	16	6	10
1	0	1	**Yellow cards**	2	0	2
0	0	0	**Red cards**	0	0	0
0	0	0	**Caught Offside**	3	2	1
6	5	11	**Shots on target**	2	1	1
2	2	4	**Shots off target**	9	6	3
1	1	2	**Hit woodwork**	1	0	1
47	54	51%	**Possession**	49%	46	53

AFTER the two goals early in the second half we didn't do anything stupid and played with a lot of professionalism and experience.

Leroy Rosenior

WE dominated the first 40 minutes of the match but didn't score. Conceding a goal on the stroke of half-time proved a turning point.

Steve Tilson

Other Div 3 Results

Boston Utd 2 Kidderminster 2, Bristol Rovers 2 Hull 1, Cambridge Utd 1 Leyton Orient 4, Carlisle 0 Doncaster 1, Darlington 2 Scunthorpe 2, Huddersfield 0 Cheltenham 0, Macclesfield 1 Bury 0, Northampton 0 Mansfield 3, Rochdale 1 Oxford Utd 2, York 0 Swansea 0

29th November

TORQUAY [1] 3 Southend [0] 0

Goalkeeper Stats: Arjan Van Heusden Crosses: Catch 1

Torquay Player Stats

No.	Player	Half	Shots on target L/R/H/Oth	Shots off target L/R/H/Oth	Caught offside	Fouls conceded	Free-kicks won	Corners taken	Clearances	Defensive blocks
7	Tony Bedeau	1st	-/-/1/-	-/-/-/-	-	-	1	-	-	-
		2nd	-/1/-/-	-/-/-/-	-	-	-	1	-	-
5	Craig Taylor	1st	-/-/-/-	-/-/-/-	-	1	-	-	1	-
		2nd	-/-/-/-	-/-/-/-	-	2	-	-	-	-
2	Reuben Hazell	1st	-/-/-/-	-/-/-/-	-	1	-	-	-	-
	▲ 18	2nd	-/1/-/-	-/-/-/-	-	-	-	-	1	-
18	Steve Woods	1st	-/-/-/-	-/-/-/-	-	1	1	-	2	-
		2nd	-/-/-/-	-/-/-/-	-	1	-	-	1	-
4	Lee Canoville	1st	-/-/-/-	-/-/-/-	-	-	-	-	-	-
	▼ 18	2nd	-/-/-/-	-/-/-/-	-	-	-	-	-	-
16	Jimmy Benefield	1st	-/-/-/-	-/-/-/-	-	-	-	-	-	-
	▲ 85	2nd	-/-/-/-	-/-/-/-	-	-	1	-	-	-
6	Alex Russell	1st	1/-/-/-	-/-/-/-	-	1	1	5	-	-
	▼ 77	2nd	-/-/-/-	-/-/-/-	-	-	1	3	-	-
29	Joe Broad	1st	-/-/-/-	-/-/-/-	-	-	-	-	-	-
	▲ 77	2nd	-/-/-/-	-/-/-/-	-	-	-	-	-	-
11	Kevin Hill	1st	1/-/-/-	-/-/-/-	-	-	2	-	-	-
	■ 37	2nd	-/-/-/-	-/-/-/-	-	-	-	-	1	-
10	David Graham	1st	2/-/1/-	-/1/1/-	-	1	2	-	-	-
	▼ 85	2nd	-/1/1/-	1/1/-/-	-	-	3	-	-	-
15	Kevin Wills	1st	-/-/-/-	-/-/-/-	-	4	2	-	-	-
		2nd	-/-/-/-	-/-/-/-	-	1	-	-	-	-
14	Matthew Hockley	1st	-/-/-/-	-/-/-/-	-	1	-	-	-	-
		2nd	-/1/-/-	-/-/-/-	-	-	1	-	-	-
17	Brian McGlinchey	1st	-/-/-/-	-/-/-/-	-	-	1	-	2	-
		2nd	-/-/-/-	-/-/-/-	-	-	-	-	-	-

Subs not used: Dearden, Bernard. - **Formation: 4-4-2**

Goalkeeper Stats: Darryl Flahavan Saves: Catch 2, Parry 2, Crosses: Parry 1, Punch 1

No.	Player Stats	Shots on target	Shots off target	Caught offside	Fouls conceded	Free-kicks won	Corners taken	Clearances	Defensive blocks
12	Steven Clark ▲ 56	-/-/-/-	-/-/-/-	-	-	-	-	-	-
23	Lewis Hunt ■ 20	-/-/-/-	1/-/-/-	-	4	1	-	1	-
24	Leon Constantine ▼ 82	-/1/-/-	-/1/-/-	1	1	-	-	3	-
4	Leon Cort	-/-/-/-	-/-/-/-	-	2	3	-	4	-
9	Tesfaye Bramble	-/1/-/-	-/-/-/-	-	1	3	-	-	-
6	David McSweeney	-/-/-/-	-/-/-/-	-	-	1	-	1	-
22	Jay Smith	-/-/-/-	-/2/-/-	-	-	1	-	-	-
8	Kevin Maher	-/-/-/-	-/1/-/-	-	3	1	1	-	-
15	Michael Husbands ▲ 76	-/-/-/-	-/1/-/-	-	1	-	-	-	-
14	Che Wilson ■ 33	-/-/-/-	-/-/-/-	-	2	-	-	1	-
7	Mark Gower ▼ 56	-/-/-/-	-/1/-/-	-	-	-	1	-	-
10	Drewe Broughton ▼ 76	-/-/-/-	-/-/1/-	2	2	3	-	1	-
21	Michael Kightly ▲ 82	-/-/-/-	1/-/-/-	-	-	-	-	-	-

Subs not used: Emberson, Tilson. - **Formation: 4-4-2**

Torquay Played: 20 **Won** 10 **Drawn** 4 **Lost** 6 **For** 27 **Against** 22 **Pos** 7

...November Team Stats.....Team Stats......Team Stats......Team S

League table at the end of November

		HOME					AWAY						
	P	W	D	L	F	A	W	D	L	F	A	Pts	Df
Oxford Utd	20	8	2	0	19	4	3	6	1	13	9	41	19
Doncaster	20	7	2	1	20	6	5	2	3	16	10	40	20
Mansfield	20	7	2	1	28	12	5	1	4	18	14	39	20
Hull	20	7	3	0	26	11	3	4	3	14	10	37	19
Yeovil	20	8	0	2	20	6	4	1	5	12	14	37	12
Swansea	20	6	3	1	19	7	4	2	4	12	15	35	9
Torquay	**20**	**7**	**2**	**1**	**19**	**10**	**3**	**2**	**5**	**8**	**12**	**34**	**5**
Lincoln City	20	5	4	1	15	6	3	3	4	11	13	31	7
Scunthorpe	20	4	4	2	23	14	3	5	2	16	17	30	8
Huddersfield	20	7	2	1	17	6	1	4	5	14	23	30	2
York	20	5	4	1	13	7	2	4	4	6	14	29	-2
Bury	20	5	2	3	13	14	4	0	6	15	18	29	-4
Bristol Rovers	20	4	3	3	12	11	3	2	5	13	15	26	-1
Leyton Orient	20	3	4	3	14	15	3	3	4	11	14	25	-4
Boston Utd	20	5	4	1	19	9	1	2	7	5	18	24	-3
Cambridge U	20	1	4	5	12	20	4	4	2	15	13	23	-6
Northampton	20	4	2	4	8	12	2	3	5	8	14	23	-10
Cheltenham	20	5	2	3	17	17	1	3	6	12	24	23	-12
Rochdale	20	2	3	5	12	15	3	2	5	13	16	20	-6
Macclesfield	20	3	5	2	13	11	1	3	6	11	21	20	-8
Kidderminster	20	2	2	6	10	17	3	3	4	9	13	20	-11
Southend	20	3	1	6	11	14	2	2	6	7	19	18	-15
Darlington	20	4	3	3	12	13	0	2	8	9	22	17	-14
Carlisle	20	1	1	8	6	17	0	1	9	6	20	5	-25

November matches table

	P	W	D	L	F	A	Pts
Mansfield	4	3	1	0	10	4	10
Oxford Utd	4	3	1	0	9	4	10
Torquay	**4**	**3**	**0**	**1**	**8**	**3**	**9**
Doncaster	4	3	0	1	5	1	9
Bury	4	3	0	1	5	3	9
Scunthorpe	4	2	2	0	14	6	8
Yeovil	4	2	1	1	8	3	7
Leyton Orient	4	2	1	1	8	7	7
Lincoln City	4	2	1	1	6	4	7
York	4	1	3	0	4	3	6
Northampton	4	2	0	2	3	5	6
Huddersfield	4	1	2	1	8	10	5
Kidderminster	4	1	2	1	6	6	5
Macclesfield	4	1	2	1	6	7	5
Cheltenham	4	1	2	1	4	5	5
Swansea	4	1	2	1	2	2	5
Boston Utd	4	1	1	2	6	7	4
Bristol Rovers	4	1	1	2	4	6	4
Southend	4	1	0	3	4	8	3
Hull	4	0	2	2	4	7	2
Cambridge Utd	4	0	2	2	4	11	2
Darlington	4	0	2	2	3	6	2
Rochdale	4	0	0	4	2	9	0
Carlisle	4	0	0	4	1	7	0

November team stats details

Club Name	Ply	Shots On	Shots Off	Corners	Hit W'work	Caught Offside	Offside Trap	Fouls	Yellow Cards	Red Cards	Pens Awarded	Pens Con
Boston Utd	4	18	17	17	2	27	4	64	9	0	- (-)	-
Bristol Rovers	4	23	11	30	0	29	18	61	4	0	- (-)	-
Bury	4	16	16	13	0	13	7	56	10	0	- (-)	-
Cambridge U	4	18	11	21	1	20	11	30	5	1	- (-)	-
Carlisle	4	16	12	16	0	13	19	49	5	1	- (-)	-
Cheltenham	4	36	15	17	1	13	12	61	3	0	- (-)	-
Darlington	4	13	15	14	0	14	10	65	11	4	- (-)	-
Doncaster	4	33	12	28	0	16	20	52	7	0	- (-)	1
Huddersfield	4	29	20	22	4	7	11	50	8	1	- (-)	-
Hull	4	20	22	23	0	7	19	55	5	0	- (-)	-
Kidderminster	4	27	19	32	0	18	26	46	3	0	1 (1)	1
Leyton Orient	4	26	12	29	2	10	18	63	9	0	1 (1)	-
Lincoln City	4	39	12	17	2	19	19	38	8	0	- (-)	1
Macclesfield	4	23	28	19	1	11	6	39	5	1	- (-)	-
Mansfield	4	33	16	25	1	9	14	34	4	0	1 (1)	1
Northampton	4	19	20	20	0	8	15	53	5	0	- (-)	1
Oxford Utd	4	28	15	29	0	10	8	52	5	0	- (-)	-
Rochdale	4	25	8	30	0	25	30	62	9	1	2 (1)	4
Scunthorpe	4	31	27	32	0	10	20	71	11	0	1 (1)	1
Southend	4	28	25	17	1	15	10	52	8	2	2 (1)	1
Swansea	4	27	16	23	0	13	22	39	7	1	- (-)	-
Torquay	**4**	**41**	**11**	**26**	**4**	**10**	**14**	**49**	**5**	**0**	**- (-)**	**-**
Yeovil	4	22	24	27	2	19	9	52	5	1	2 (1)	-
York	4	26	12	21	0	14	8	46	9	1	1 (1)	-

 Monthly Match Details: Games 48 **Home Wins** 25 **Away Wins** 9 **Draws** 14

NOVEMBER STATS

...November Player Stats..... Player Stats...... Player Stats......Pla

Monthly Top scorers

Player	
Steven MacLean (Scunthorpe)	7
Jonathan Stead (Huddersfield)	3
Simon Yeo (Lincoln City)	3
David Graham (Torquay)	3
Junior Mendes (Mansfield)	3
Andy Booth (Huddersfield)	3
Wayne Purser (Leyton Orient)	2
Joe O'Neill (Bury)	2
Chris Brown (Doncaster)	2
Danny Schofield (Huddersfield)	2

Penalties scored

4 D Dunning (York), C Hinton (Kidderminster), L McEvilly (Rochdale), L Johnson (Yeovil)

Assists

Player	
Danny Schofield (Huddersfield)	3
Liam Lawrence (Mansfield)	3
Peter Beagrie (Scunthorpe)	3
Dean Whitehead (Oxford Utd)	3
Gary Fletcher (Lincoln City)	2
Ryan Williams (Bristol Rovers)	2
Leon Cort (Southend)	2

Quickest goals

2:06 mins - Justin Miller (Leyton Orient vs York)

3:46 mins - Chris Priest (Oxford Utd vs Macclesfield)

4:17 mins - Ben Burgess (Bristol Rovers vs Hull)

4:35 mins - Iyseden Christie (Northampton vs Mansfield)

5:33 mins - Martin Carruthers (Hull vs Macclesfield)

Top Keeper

	Mins	Gls
A Warrington (Doncaster)	387	1
Roger Freestone (Swansea)	379	2
Kevin Dearden (Torquay)	146	1
Chris Weale (Yeovil)	382	3
Glyn Garner (Bury)	380	3
Mark Ovendale (York)	378	3
A Van Heusden (Torquay)	235	2
Andy Woodman (Oxford U)	383	4

Shots on target

Player	
David Graham (Torquay)	16
Jonathan Stead (Huddersfield)	11
Steven MacLean (Scunthorpe)	11
Lewis Haldane (Bristol Rovers)	10
Michael McIndoe (Doncaster)	9
Junior Mendes (Mansfield)	8
Simon Yeo (Lincoln City)	8
Lee Trundle (Swansea)	8
Paul Simpson (Carlisle)	7
Andy Booth (Huddersfield)	7

Shots off target

Player	
Neil Redfearn (Boston Utd)	12
Damian Spencer (Cheltenham)	7
Jason Price (Hull)	6
Gareth Williams (Cambridge Utd)	5
Matthew Tipton (Macclesfield)	5
Paul Simpson (Carlisle)	5
John Miles (Macclesfield)	5
Danny Schofield (Huddersfield)	5
Steven MacLean (Scunthorpe)	5
Chris Priest (Macclesfield)	5

Caught offside

Player	
Lewis Haldane (Bristol Rovers)	12
Graeme Jones (Boston Utd)	9
Kevin Townson (Rochdale)	9
Gregg Blundell (Doncaster)	8
Adam Boyd (Boston Utd)	8
Simon Yeo (Lincoln City)	8
Andy White (Kidderminster)	8
Chris Shuker (Rochdale)	7
Steven MacLean (Scunthorpe)	7

Free-kicks won

Player	
Tesfaye Bramble (Southend)	23
Andy White (Kidderminster)	12
Chris Brass (York)	12
Lewis Haldane (Bristol Rovers)	12
Gary Fletcher (Lincoln City)	11
Lee Nogan (York)	11
Leon Britton (Swansea)	11
Chris Brown (Doncaster)	11
Martin Carruthers (Macclesfield)	11

Bedeau with Hazell

Fouls conceded

Player	
Steven MacLean (Scunthorpe)	15
Sonny Parker (Bristol Rovers)	14
Paul Ellender (Boston Utd)	13
Graeme Jones (Boston Utd)	12
Barry Conlon (Darlington)	12
Kevin Wills (Torquay)	11
Andy Butler (Scunthorpe)	11
Wayne Hatswell (Kidderminster)	10
Gareth Griffiths (Rochdale)	10

Fouls without a card

Player	
Mark Yates (Cheltenham)	10
Bob Taylor (Cheltenham)	9
Ben Burgess (Hull)	9
Mark Peters (Leyton Orient)	9
Damian Spencer (Cheltenham)	9
Chris Hargreaves (Northampton)	8
Christian Edwards (Bristol R)	8
Matthew Sparrow (Scunthorpe)	8
Gary Alexander (Leyton Orient)	8

GOAL, GOAL, GOAL, Tony Bedeau scores the first.
Torquay v Southend
HPL01191_TNA_004

Bedeau celebrates his goal with Reuben Hazell.
Torquay v Southend
HPL01191_TNA_016

Torquay [0] 1 YORK [0] 1

The sight of Martin Gritton warming up with the rest of the squad before kick-off cheered Torquay United fans far more than most of what followed at a wet and windy Plainmoor.

The only real consolation in the cold light of day was that United played so poorly and still didn't lose. United looked as if they were in the mood for handing out presents in the first half.

Still, they should have taken the lead in the tenth minute when Graham, perhaps surprised that an Alex Russell free-kick had missed Taylor's forehead, shot tamely from six yards and the best chance of the first half was gone.

United had a real escape in the 43rd minute when Lee Bullock hit the side-netting after a pinball session in the goalmouth. And York took the lead only two minutes into the second half. Taylor's headed backpass was read by York striker Lee Nogan. He nipped in and flicked the ball over the advancing Van Heusden.

Matt Hockley went close from 25 yards and York defender Chris Smith had to come up with a great covering tackle to deny Graham before the equaliser came.

Russel passed to Hockley in a forward position on the right, he helped the ball on to Broad, whose volleyed cross took keeper Ovendale out of the game and, with Tony Bedeau all over him, Jon Parkin could only knock the ball over his own line from point-blank range.

That equaliser should have sparked an Alamo-job in the last half-hour, but United could find no higher gears.

They plugged away, and Kuffour did liven an attack which functioned more on hope than expectation all afternoon. Canoville had a deflected shot saved and Russell's frustrating afternoon was epitomised when he skied a chance from 25 yards with the keeper off his line and beaten in the 85th minute.

Result.......Result.......Result.

TORQUAY ....(0) **1** **YORK** ....(0) **1**
Parkin 57 (og) — Nogan 47

Att 2,564
Referee: K Friend

Stats......Stats.......Stats......Stats

TORQUAY						YORK
1st	**2nd**	**Total**		**Total**	**2nd**	**1st**
1	3	4	**Corners**	10	3	7
4	7	11	**Fouls**	14	6	8
0	0	0	**Yellow cards**	2	2	0
0	0	0	**Red cards**	0	0	0
4	0	4	**Caught Offside**	2	0	2
1	2	3	**Shots on target**	8	2	6
0	4	4	**Shots off target**	6	3	3
0	0	0	**Hit woodwork**	0	0	0
38	45	41%	**Possession**	59%	55	62

"**THEY** played 3-5-2 that caught us by surprise really. I'll give Chris Brass credit for that because that caught us on the back foot and we never got off the back foot.

Leroy Rosenior"

"**WE** were winning a lot of balls in their third of the pitch rather than in the middle third and that was pleasing because we had been working on that.

Chris Brass"

Other Div 3 Results

Boston Utd 1 Northampton 1, Bristol Rovers 0 Yeovil 1, Bury 1 Rochdale 2, Cambridge Utd 1 Darlington 0, Cheltenham 1 Doncaster 3, Kidderminster 2 Leyton Orient 1, Macclesfield 4 Huddersfield 0, Oxford Utd 2 Carlisle 1, Scunthorpe 1 Hull 1, Swansea 2 Southend 3

TORQUAY [0] 1 York [0] 1

Goalkeeper Stats: Arjan Van Heusden Saves: Catch 6, Parry 2, Crosses: Catch 6, Parry 2

Torquay Player Stats		Shots on target L/R/H/Oth	Shots off target L/R/H/Oth	Caught offside	Fouls conceded	Free-kicks won	Corners taken	Clearances	Defensive blocks
7 Tony Bedeau	1st	-/-/-/-	-/-/-/-	-	1	-	-	-	-
	2nd	-/-/-/-	-/1/1/-	-	3	2	-	-	-
5 Craig Taylor	1st	-/-/-/-	-/-/-/-	-	-	-	-	1	-
	2nd	-/-/-/-	-/-/-/-	-	2	-	-	-	-
18 Steve Woods	1st	-/-/-/-	-/-/-/-	-	1	1	-	1	-
	2nd	-/-/-/-	-/-/-/-	-	1	-	-	2	-
4 Lee Canoville	1st	-/-/-/-	-/-/-/-	-	-	-	-	1	-
▼ 82	2nd	1/-/-/-	-/-/-/-	-	-	-	-	3	-
6 Alex Russell	1st	-/-/-/-	-/-/-/-	-	-	-	1	-	-
	2nd	-/1/-/-	-/-/-/-	-	-	1	3	-	-
16 Jimmy Benefield	1st	-/-/-/-	-/-/-/-	-	-	2	-	2	-
▼ 45	2nd	-/-/-/-	-/-/-/-	-	-	-	-	-	-
25 Narada Bernard	1st	-/-/-/-	-/-/-/-	-	-	-	-	-	-
▲ 82	2nd	-/-/-/-	-/-/-/-	-	-	-	-	-	-
29 Joe Broad	1st	-/-/-/-	-/-/-/-	-	-	-	-	-	-
▲ 45	2nd	-/-/-/-	-/-/-/-	-	-	-	-	-	-
15 Kevin Wills	1st	-/-/-/-	-/-/-/-	3	-	2	-	-	-
▼ 45	2nd	-/-/-/-	-/-/-/-	-	-	-	-	-	-
10 David Graham	1st	-/1/-/-	-/-/-/-	1	2	3	-	-	-
	2nd	-/-/-/-	1/-/-/-	-	1	-	-	-	-
14 Matthew Hockley	1st	-/-/-/-	-/-/-/-	-	-	-	-	-	-
	2nd	-/-/-/-	-/1/-/-	-	-	-	-	-	-
12 Jo Kuffour	1st	-/-/-/-	-/-/-/-	-	-	-	-	-	-
▲ 45	2nd	-/-/-/-	-/-/-/-	-	-	3	-	-	-
17 Brian McGlinchey	1st	-/-/-/-	-/-/-/-	-	-	-	-	1	-
	2nd	-/-/-/-	-/-/-/-	-	-	-	-	-	-

Subs not used: Dearden, Camara. - **Formation: 4-4-2**

Goalkeeper Stats: Mark Ovendale Saves: Catch 4, Crosses: Catch 2

	Player Stats	Shots on target	Shots off target	Caught offside	Fouls conceded	Free-kicks won	Corners taken	Clearances	Defensive blocks
28	Gary Browne ▲ 79	-/-/-/-	-/-/-/-	-	-	1	-	-	-
24	Dave Merris	-/-/-/-	-/-/-/-	-	-	1	-	-	-
8	Lee Bullock	-/-/-/-	-/1/1/-	-	3	1	-	2	-
2	Darren Edmondson ■ 63	-/2/-/-	-/-/-/-	-	1	-	-	1	-
7	Chris Brass	-/-/-/-	-/-/-/-	-	-	-	-	1	-
4	Richard Cooper	-/1/-/-	-/1/1/-	-	2	1	-	-	-
5	Jonathan Parkin ■ 60	-/-/-/-	-/-/-/-	-	3	1	-	3	-
9	Lee Nogan ▼ 79	-/1/-/-	-/-/-/-	1	2	1	-	-	-
29	Jon Shaw	1/2/1/-	-/-/-/-	1	1	1	-	-	-
6	Chris Smith	-/-/-/-	1/-/-/-	-	2	3	-	-	-
22	Darren Dunning	-/-/-/-	1/-/-/-	-	-	1	10	-	-

Subs not used: Brackstone, Fox, Porter, Law. - **Formation: 3-5-2**

Torquay Played: 21 **Won** 10 **Drawn** 5 **Lost** 6 **For** 28 **Against** 23 **Pos** 7

Carlisle [1] 2 TORQUAY [0] 0

20th December

It was a bad day at the office for Torquay against a Carlisle team languishing at the bottom of the league. After 12 successive league defeats, Carlisle simply got stuck in everywhere that United went missing and made it Lucky 13 with only their second win in 22 games this season.

Safety-first seemed to be the order of the day on an already heavy, greasy pitch. Yet within a few minutes United were making problems for themselves, putting Arjan Van Heusden's suspect kicking under unnecessary pressure and inviting Carlisle on to them.

The key man for the Cumbrians was 36-year-old debutant Andy Preece. In the air and on the ground wily old pro Preece gave Craig Taylor a torrid time.

But despite United's second-gear start, they should either have scored or been playing against ten men after only ten minutes. David Graham nipped round Kevin Gray on a long clearance and was going clear when the Carlisle defender clearly pulled him back.

Graham would have been in on goal. But referee Mike Jones did not even award a free-kick.

Six minutes later Carlisle were gifted the lead. A pass from midfield should have been cleared by Torquay, but Preece suddenly realised he was in with a chance and galloped on to slip the ball past Van Heusden.

United needed to galvanise themselves early in the second half, but instead they effectively waved goodbye to the points. Fryatt forced Van Heusden to a good low save after a mistake by Woods, and in the 53rd minute Carlisle scored again.

Right-back Paul Arnison received a square free kick, tried a speculative shot from 35 yards and the ball flew over a surprised Van Heusden and into the top right-hand corner.

United did improve a little in the rest of the second half, after Jo Kuffour replaced Joe Broad. But the fact was that they failed to register a single shot or header of any consequence after half-time.

Result.......Result.......Result.

CARLISLE ....(1) **2** **TORQUAY** ......(0) **0**
Preece 16
Arnison 53

Att 3,600
Referee: M Jones

Stats......Stats.......Stats......Stats

CARLISLE						TORQUAY
1st	**2nd**	**Total**		**Total**	**2nd**	**1st**
6	4	10	**Corners**	4	1	3
10	5	15	**Fouls**	15	10	5
1	0	1	**Yellow cards**	4	3	1
0	0	0	**Red cards**	1	1	0
1	1	2	**Caught Offside**	7	4	3
5	4	9	**Shots on target**	7	2	5
4	1	5	**Shots off target**	1	0	1
0	0	0	**Hit woodwork**	0	0	0
50	52	51%	**Possession**	49%	48	50

"**ANDY** Preece led the line fantastically well. After hearing about his sacking [by Bury] I didn't want to allow him to play anywhere else.

Paul Simpson"

"**THREE** big decisions went against us. The ref gave some shocking decisions - he wasn't up to scratch but saying that we didn't perform.

Leroy Rosenior"

Other Div 3 Results

Darlington 0 Macclesfield 1, Huddersfield 1 Oxford Utd 1, Hull 0 Mansfield 1, Leyton Orient 2 Bury 0, Rochdale 1 Boston Utd 0, Southend 0 Bristol Rovers 1, Yeovil 2 Scunthorpe 1

Carlisle [1] 2 TORQUAY [0] 0

Goalkeeper Stats: Arjan Van Heusden Saves: Catch 2, Round Post 1, Crosses: Catch 1, Punch 1, Parry 1, Round Post 1

#	Torquay Player Stats		Shots on target L/R/H/Oth	Shots off target L/R/H/Oth	Caught offside	Fouls conceded	Free-kicks won	Corners taken	Clearances	Defensive blocks
7	Tony Bedeau	1st	-/-/-/-	-/-/-/-	-	1	1	-	2	-
	□ 23 ■ 71	2nd	-/-/-/-	-/-/-/-	1	1	1	-	-	-
5	Craig Taylor	1st	-/-/-/-	1/-/-/-	-	-	-	-	1	-
		2nd	-/-/-/-	-/-/-/-	1	2	-	-	1	-
9	Martin Gritton	1st	-/-/-/-	-/-/-/-	-	1	1	-	-	-
	▲ 36 □ 60	2nd	-/-/-/-	-/-/-/-	2	-	1	-	-	-
18	Steve Woods	1st	-/-/1/-	-/-/-/-	-	1	-	-	1	1
		2nd	-/-/1/-	-/-/-/-	-	-	1	-	-	1
4	Lee Canoville	1st	-/-/-/-	-/-/-/-	-	-	-	-	-	-
	□ 6	2nd	-/-/-/-	-/-/-/-	-	1	-	-	1	-
6	Alex Russell	1st	-/-/-/-	-/-/-/-	-	-	2	3	-	-
		2nd	-/-/-/-	-/-/-/-	-	2	-	1	-	-
11	Kevin Hill	1st	-/-/-/-	-/-/-/-	-	-	-	-	1	-
	□ 79	2nd	-/-/-/-	-/-/-/-	-	2	-	-	-	-
29	Joe Broad	1st	1/1/-/-	-/-/-/-	-	1	1	-	-	-
	▼ 62	2nd	-/-/-/-	-/-/-/-	-	-	-	-	-	-
15	Kevin Wills	1st	-/-/-/-	-/-/-/-	2	1	1	-	-	-
	▼ 36	2nd	-/-/-/-	-/-/-/-	-	-	-	-	-	-
10	David Graham	1st	-/2/-/-	-/-/-/-	1	-	3	-	-	-
		2nd	-/-/-/-	-/-/-/-	-	1	2	-	-	-
14	Matthew Hockley	1st	-/-/-/-	-/-/-/-	-	-	-	-	-	-
		2nd	-/1/-/-	-/-/-/-	-	1	-	-	3	-
12	Jo Kuffour	1st	-/-/-/-	-/-/-/-	-	-	-	-	-	-
	▲ 62	2nd	-/-/-/-	-/-/-/-	-	-	-	-	-	-

Subs not used: Fowler, Benefield, Dearden. - **Formation: 4-4-2**

Goalkeeper Stats: Matthew Glennon Saves: Catch 4, Round Post 1, Crosses: Catch 2, Punch 1, Round Post 1

#	Player Stats	Shots on target	Shots off target	Caught offside	Fouls conceded	Free-kicks won	Corners taken	Clearances	Defensive blocks
13	William McDonagh	-/1/-/-	-/-/-/-	-	1	-	-	-	-
14	Kevin Gray	-/-/-/-	-/-/1/-	-	6	-	-	1	-
30	Matt Fryatt ▼ 86	2/-/-/-	-/-/-/-	2	2	-	-	-	-
31	Andy Preece	1/-/-/-	1/-/-/-	-	1	4	-	-	-
20	Brendan McGill	-/-/1/-	-/-/-/-	-	-	-	5	-	-
23	Kevin Henderson ▲ 86	-/-/-/-	-/-/-/-	-	-	1	-	-	-
8	Chris Billy	1/1/-/-	-/1/-/-	-	1	-	-	1	-
3	Tom Cowan	-/-/-/-	-/1/-/-	-	1	5	-	-	-
12	Lee Andrews ▲ 73	-/-/-/-	-/-/-/-	-	-	-	-	-	-
26	Paul Simpson ▼ 73	-/-/-/-	1/-/-/-	-	-	1	4	-	-
2	Paul Arnison □ 45	-/1/-/-	-/-/-/-	-	3	1	1	1	-
4	Paul Raven	-/-/1/-	-/-/-/-	-	-	2	-	1	-

Subs not used: Rundle, Farrell, Keen. - **Formation: 4-4-2**

Torquay Played: 22 **Won** 10 **Drawn** 5 **Lost** 7 **For** 28 **Against** 25 **Pos** 7

Torquay [0] 0 SWANSEA [0] 0

26th December

In some of the worst conditions ever seen at Plainmoor, Torquay United finally had to settle for an eventful goalless draw against Play-Off rivals Swansea City yesterday.

It was the first stalemate that the Gulls have been involved in for 37 league and cup games but both sides did their best to entertain the biggest crowd of the season so far (4,447).Only two desperate goal-line clearances in the last five minutes ensured that the points were shared.

Swansea, who were without their suspended leading scorer Lee Trundle, had won only three times in 12 league games, but they still had quality players on show.

It took a brilliant save early on by Arjan Van Heusden to deny Richard Duffy's volley after a Karl Connolly corner hit Gritton and dropped to the Swansea full-back in the 14th minute.

It was a long time before United created a real chance, Bedeau firing just over from 30 yards in the 37th minute when David Graham supplied the pass and asked for the return.

Gritton glanced an Alex Russell cross wide in the 41st minute, but Swansea could point to near-misses for James Thomas twice, Connolly and Robinson before half-time, and United were probably happy with 0-0 at the interval.

Torquay gradually upped the pace in the second-half, but Swansea were always dangerous on the counter. And as the weather worsened in the closing stages, both sides gathered themselves in a final bid for victory.

In the 85th minute Taylor came up with an exceptional goalline clearance from Swansea sub Kevin Nugent after Bedeau had nervously allowed Robinson to beat him on the edge of the area.

Hockley went agonisingly close with a 25-yarder seconds later, and in injury time Van Heusden dashed a long way out of his area to whack the ball away from Thomas on the break.

Result.......Result.......Result.

TORQUAY ....(0) **0** **SWANSEA**......(0) **0**
Att 4,447
Referee: A Penn

Stats......Stats.......Stats......Stats

TORQUAY						SWANSEA
1st	2nd	Total		Total	2nd	1st
1	6	7	**Corners**	13	4	9
6	6	12	**Fouls**	8	3	5
1	1	2	**Yellow cards**	1	1	0
0	0	0	**Red cards**	0	0	0
2	3	5	**Caught Offside**	5	3	2
2	3	5	**Shots on target**	4	1	3
2	2	4	**Shots off target**	5	3	2
0	0	0	**Hit woodwork**	0	0	0
41	47	44%	**Possession**	56%	53	59

“ I guess on another day we might have won but - given the conditions - I am happy with a point, but once again decisions that might have gone our way haven't.

Leroy Rosenior ”

“ **THEY** defended well and we had to in the second half especially because we knew they would come at us - which they did.

Brian Flynn ”

Other Div 3 Results

Bristol Rovers 1 Northampton 2, Bury 1 Carlisle 3, Cambridge Utd 0 Southend 1, Cheltenham 3 Macclesfield 2, Darlington 0 Huddersfield 1, Doncaster 1 Scunthorpe 0, Mansfield 1 Rochdale 0, Oxford Utd 2 Leyton Orient 1, Yeovil 1 Kidderminster 2, York 0 Hull 2

26th December

TORQUAY [0] 0 Swansea [0] 0

Goalkeeper Stats: Arjan Van Heusden Saves: Catch 4, Crosses: Catch 4

	Torquay Player Stats		Shots on target L/R/H/Oth	Shots off target L/R/H/Oth	Caught offside	Fouls conceded	Free-kicks won	Corners taken	Clearances	Defensive blocks
7	Tony Bedeau	1st	-/-/-/-	-/1/-/-	-	1	2	-	1	-
		2nd	-/-/-/-	-/-/-/-	-	-	1	-	1	-
5	Craig Taylor	1st	-/-/-/-	-/-/-/-	-	-	1	-	4	-
	■ 50	2nd	-/-/1/-	-/-/-/-	-	1	-	-	2	-
9	Martin Gritton	1st	1/-/-/-	-/-/1/-	-	1	-	-	-	-
	▼ 62	2nd	-/-/-/-	-/-/-/-	1	1	-	-	-	-
18	Steve Woods	1st	-/-/-/-	-/-/-/-	-	-	-	-	1	1
		2nd	-/-/-/-	-/-/-/-	-	1	-	-	1	-
4	Lee Canoville	1st	-/-/-/-	-/-/-/-	-	-	-	-	1	-
		2nd	-/-/-/-	-/-/-/-	-	1	-	-	1	-
6	Alex Russell	1st	-/-/-/-	-/-/-/-	-	1	1	1	-	-
		2nd	-/1/-/-	-/1/-/-	-	-	-	6	-	-
11	Kevin Hill	1st	-/-/-/-	-/-/-/-	-	-	-	-	1	-
		2nd	-/-/-/-	-/-/-/-	-	1	-	-	1	-
10	David Graham	1st	-/1/-/-	-/-/-/-	2	2	-	-	-	-
	■ 7	2nd	-/-/-/-	-/1/-/-	2	1	-	-	-	-
15	Kevin Wills	1st	-/-/-/-	-/-/-/-	-	-	-	-	-	-
	▲ 62	2nd	-/-/-/-	-/-/-/-	-	-	-	-	-	-
14	Matthew Hockley	1st	-/-/-/-	-/-/-/-	-	-	-	-	-	-
	▲ 67	2nd	-/1/-/-	-/-/-/-	-	-	-	-	-	-
8	Jason Fowler	1st	-/-/-/-	-/-/-/-	-	1	1	-	-	-
	▼ 67	2nd	-/-/-/-	-/-/-/-	-	-	-	-	-	-
12	Jo Kuffour	1st	-/-/-/-	-/-/-/-	-	-	-	-	-	-
		2nd	-/-/-/-	-/-/-/-	-	-	2	-	-	-

Subs not used: Dearden, Benefield, Broad. - **Formation: 4-4-2**

Goalkeeper Stats: Roger Freestone Saves: Catch 2, Crosses: Catch 2

	Player Stats	Shots on target	Shots off target	Caught offside	Fouls conceded	Free-kicks won	Corners taken	Clearances	Defensive blocks
7	Leon Britton	-/-/-/-	-/-/-/-	-	1	-	2	-	-
14	Bradley Maylett	-/-/-/-	-/-/-/-	1	1	2	1	-	-
18	Andy Robinson	-/1/-/-	2/-/-/-	-	1	3	2	1	-
3	Michael Howard	-/-/-/-	-/-/-/-	-	1	-	-	3	1
16	Karl Connolly ▼ 63	1/-/-/-	-/-/-/-	1	-	-	8	-	-
27	Alan Tate	-/-/-/-	-/-/-/-	-	1	2	-	3	1
19	Richard Duffy	1/-/-/-	-/-/-/-	-	-	-	-	3	-
9	James Thomas	1/-/-/-	-/1/1/-	3	1	2	-	1	-
22	Izzy Iriekpen	-/-/-/-	-/-/-/-	-	1	2	-	2	-
11	Lenny Johnrose	-/-/-/-	-/-/-/-	-	1	1	-	3	-
8	Kevin Nugent ▲ 63 ■ 82	-/-/-/-	1/-/-/-	-	-	-	-	-	-

Subs not used: O'Leary, Coates, Durkan, Murphy. - **Formation: 4-4-2**

Torquay Played: 23 **Won** 10 **Drawn** 6 **Lost** 7 **For** 28 **Against** 25 **Pos** 8

Leyton Orient [0] 0 TORQUAY [0] 0 — 28th December

After going 33 games without a goalless draw, Torquay United registered their second blank scoreline in succession against Leyton Orient.

United had started so many away games poorly that it was nice to see them having a go from the start in this game. Rosenior picked a new pairing up front, with Tony Bedeau partnering David Graham in a livewire attack.

And they started as if they had something to prove. With the wind behind him, Hockley tried a long-range shot from the kick-off. Orient keeper Glenn Morris dealt with that effort, and in the eleventh minute he had to come up with a fine effort to deny Bedeau.

Woozley's free-kick from the left picked out his teammate, but Bedeau's close-range header at the far-post carried no real power and Morris parried it. Then Graham slipped Broad in on the right, but he crossed the ball instead of shooting on an angle and another chance was gone.

It took Orient nearly a quarter of an hour to threaten, but it was a good effort, Arjan Van Heusden pushing Gary Alexander's 20-yarder round the post. And when United only half-cleared the corner, Mark Peters headed against the bar and over.

Orient gradually took territorial control but the Gulls then slipped into counter-attacking mode and they made and missed a glorious chance in the 38th minute when Graham flicked Bedeau through, only for his first touch to take the ball too close to Morris, who dashed out and blocked.

With the wind behind them in the second period, United continued to take the fight to their opponents. Skipper Craig Taylor had a headed goal disallowed in the 57th minute, then Russell fired just wide from 25 yards.

Then three minutes from time Orient 'keepr Morris clinched a point for his side with a desperate tip-over save after Bedeau cut in from the left and let fly from long range.

Result.......Result.......Result.

LEYTON ORIENT..(0) **0** **TORQUAY** ......(0) **0**
Att 4,288
Referee: A Marriner

Stats......Stats.......Stats......Stats

LEYTON ORIENT				TORQUAY		
1st	2nd	Total		Total	2nd	1st
3	3	6	Corners	2	1	1
7	7	14	Fouls	13	6	7
0	0	0	Yellow cards	1	1	0
0	0	0	Red cards	0	0	0
2	2	4	Caught Offside	10	7	3
4	3	7	Shots on target	5	2	3
4	3	7	Shots off target	6	3	3
1	0	1	Hit woodwork	0	0	0
39	49	44%	Possession	56%	51	61

TO be totally honest, I thought overall they were slightly the better side and would probably say it was two points dropped for them rather than us

Martin Ling

WE were hanging on a bit, not desperately, but I thought they could break through us more easily than we could break through them.

Leroy Rosenior

Other Div 3 Results

Carlisle 1 Darlington 1, Huddersfield 1 Bury 0, Hull 3 Doncaster 1, Kidderminster 1 Bristol Rovers 0, Macclesfield 1 Mansfield 1, Northampton 1 Cheltenham 0, Rochdale 1 York 2, Scunthorpe 0 Boston Utd 1, Southend 0 Oxford Utd 1, Swansea 3 Yeovil 2

28th December

Leyton Orient [0] 0 TORQUAY [0] 0

Goalkeeper Stats: Arjan Van Heusden Saves: Catch 1, Parry 2, Crosses: Catch 6, Parry 2

No.	Torquay Player Stats		Shots on target L/R/H/Oth	Shots off target L/R/H/Oth	Caught offside	Fouls conceded	Free-kicks won	Corners taken	Clearances	Defensive blocks
10	David Graham	1st	-/-/-/-	-/2/-/-	2	1	1	-	-	-
		2nd	-/-/-/-	-/-/-/-	1	-	2	-	-	-
7	Tony Bedeau	1st	-/1/1/-	-/-/-/-	1	1	1	-	-	-
		2nd	-/1/-/-	-/-/-/-	5	1	1	-	-	-
2	Reuben Hazell	1st	-/-/-/-	-/-/-/-	-	-	-	-	1	-
		2nd	-/-/-/-	-/-/-/-	-	-	-	-	-	-
3	David Woozley	1st	-/-/-/-	-/-/-/-	-	2	-	-	1	-
		2nd	-/-/-/-	1/-/-/-	-	1	-	-	2	-
5	Craig Taylor	1st	-/-/-/-	1/-/-/-	-	-	-	-	1	-
		2nd	-/-/-/-	-/-/-/-	-	-	-	-	1	-
14	Matthew Hockley	1st	-/1/-/-	-/-/-/-	-	1	1	-	-	-
		2nd	-/-/-/-	-/1/-/-	-	1	1	-	1	-
18	Steve Woods	1st	-/-/-/-	-/-/-/-	-	-	1	-	3	-
		2nd	-/-/-/-	-/-/-/-	-	1	1	-	2	-
12	Jo Kuffour	1st	-/-/-/-	-/-/-/-	-	-	-	-	-	-
	▲ 56	2nd	1/-/-/-	-/-/-/-	-	2	-	-	-	-
4	Lee Canoville	1st	-/-/-/-	-/-/-/-	-	1	1	-	-	-
	▼ 56	2nd	-/-/-/-	-/-/-/-	-	-	-	-	-	-
6	Alex Russell	1st	-/-/-/-	-/-/-/-	-	-	-	-	-	-
	▲ 60 ■ 80	2nd	-/-/-/-	-/1/-/-	-	-	-	1	-	-
11	Kevin Hill	1st	-/-/-/-	-/-/-/-	-	1	-	-	1	-
		2nd	-/-/-/-	-/-/-/-	1	-	1	-	2	-
29	Joe Broad	1st	-/-/-/-	-/-/-/-	-	-	2	1	-	-
	▼ 60	2nd	-/-/-/-	-/-/-/-	-	-	1	-	-	-

Subs not used: Fowler, Wills, Dearden. - **Formation: 4-4-2**

Goalkeeper Stats: Glenn Morris Saves: Catch 1, Round Post 1, Parry 1, Crosses: Catch 3, Parry 1

No.	Player Stats	Shots on target	Shots off target	Caught offside	Fouls conceded	Free-kicks won	Corners taken	Clearances	Defensive blocks
7	Justin Miller	-/-/-/-	-/2/-/-	-	2	1	-	2	-
20	Donny Barnard ▲ 60	-/-/-/-	-/-/-/-	-	-	-	-	-	-
2	Matthew Joseph	-/-/-/-	-/-/-/-	-	-	1	-	-	-
16	Wayne Purser	-/-/2/-	-/-/-/-	-	2	3	-	-	-
11	Ciaran Toner ▼ 60	-/-/-/-	-/-/-/-	-	2	1	-	-	-
19	David Hunt	-/-/-/-	1/-/-/-	-	1	-	2	1	-
9	Gary Alexander	-/1/1/-	-/-/-/-	1	3	1	-	-	-
15	Chris Tate ▲ 71	-/-/-/-	-/-/-/-	-	-	-	-	-	-
23	Tom Newey ▼ 76	-/-/-/-	-/-/-/-	-	-	1	-	-	-
22	Boniek Forbes ▲ 76	1/-/-/-	-/-/-/-	-	-	1	-	1	-
17	Jabo Ibehre ▼ 71	-/-/1/-	-/-/2/-	3	-	1	-	-	-
3	Matthew Lockwood	1/-/-/-	1/-/-/-	-	-	1	4	-	-
18	Mark Peters	-/-/-/-	-/-/1/-	-	4	2	-	-	-

Subs not used: Harrison, Jones. - **Formation: 4-4-2**

Torquay Played: 24 **Won** 10 **Drawn** 7 **Lost** 7 **For** 28 **Against** 25 **Pos** 8

...December Team Stats.....Team Stats......Team Stats......Team S

League table at the end of December

		HOME					AWAY						
	P	W	D	L	F	A	W	D	L	F	A	Pts	Df
Oxford Utd	24	10	2	0	23	6	4	7	1	15	10	51	22
Doncaster	24	9	2	1	24	7	6	2	4	20	14	49	23
Hull	25	9	3	1	31	13	4	5	3	17	11	47	24
Mansfield	24	8	2	2	30	14	6	2	4	20	15	46	21
Yeovil	24	9	0	3	23	9	5	1	6	15	17	43	12
Swansea	24	7	3	2	24	12	4	3	5	13	18	39	7
Lincoln City	23	5	5	1	17	8	5	3	4	14	14	38	9
Torquay	**24**	**7**	**4**	**1**	**20**	**11**	**3**	**3**	**6**	**8**	**14**	**37**	**3**
Huddersfield	24	8	3	1	19	7	2	4	6	15	27	37	0
York	25	6	4	2	14	9	3	5	5	9	19	36	-5
Scunthorpe	24	4	5	3	24	16	3	5	4	17	20	31	5
Cambridge U	24	2	4	6	13	21	5	5	2	19	16	30	-5
Northampton	24	5	2	5	10	14	3	4	5	11	16	30	-9
Bristol Rovers	24	4	3	5	13	14	4	2	6	14	16	29	-3
Leyton Orient	24	4	5	3	16	15	3	3	6	13	18	29	-4
Kidderminster	24	4	2	6	13	18	4	3	5	11	15	29	-9
Bury	25	5	2	5	15	19	4	0	9	15	23	29	-12
Boston Utd	24	5	5	2	20	11	2	2	8	6	19	28	-4
Macclesfield	24	4	6	2	18	12	2	3	7	14	24	27	-4
Rochdale	24	3	3	6	14	17	4	2	6	15	18	26	-6
Cheltenham	23	6	2	4	21	22	1	3	7	12	25	26	-14
Southend	24	3	1	8	11	16	4	2	6	11	21	24	-15
Darlington	25	5	3	5	15	15	0	3	9	10	24	21	-14
Carlisle	24	2	2	8	9	18	1	1	10	10	23	12	-22

December matches table

	P	W	D	L	F	A	Pts
Hull	5	3	1	1	8	3	10
Oxford Utd	4	3	1	0	6	3	10
Doncaster	4	3	0	1	8	5	9
Kidderminster	4	3	0	1	5	3	9
Macclesfield	4	2	1	1	8	4	7
Carlisle	4	2	1	1	7	4	7
Lincoln City	3	2	1	0	5	3	7
Northampton	4	2	1	1	5	4	7
Cambridge Utd	4	2	1	1	5	4	7
Mansfield	4	2	1	1	4	3	7
York	5	2	1	2	4	7	7
Huddersfield	4	2	1	1	3	5	7
Yeovil	4	2	0	2	6	6	6
Rochdale	4	2	0	2	4	4	6
Southend	4	2	0	2	4	4	6
Swansea	4	1	1	2	6	8	4
Leyton Orient	4	1	1	2	4	4	4
Darlington	5	1	1	3	4	4	4
Boston Utd	4	1	1	2	2	3	4
Cheltenham	3	1	0	2	4	6	3
Bristol Rovers	4	1	0	3	2	4	3
Torquay	**4**	**0**	**3**	**1**	**1**	**3**	**3**
Scunthorpe	4	0	1	3	2	5	1
Bury	5	0	0	5	2	10	0

December team stats details

Club Name	Ply	Shots On	Shots Off	Corners	Hit W'work	Caught Offside	Offside Trap	Fouls	Yellow Cards	Red Cards	Pens Awarded	Pens Con
Boston Utd	4	15	22	15	1	14	13	53	10	2	- (-)	-
Bristol Rovers	4	18	7	19	1	16	6	61	5	1	1 (1)	2
Bury	5	17	17	23	0	17	7	64	7	0	1 (1)	-
Cambridge Utd	4	30	19	22	0	14	11	56	6	0	3 (2)	2
Carlisle	4	31	18	29	2	8	20	59	4	0	1 (1)	3
Cheltenham	3	20	26	21	1	11	7	28	3	0	- (-)	-
Darlington	5	31	23	35	1	13	11	63	6	0	- (-)	1
Doncaster	4	27	8	23	1	25	16	74	7	0	2 (2)	1
Huddersfield	4	14	30	19	0	3	9	53	7	2	- (-)	1
Hull	5	32	34	27	2	22	27	60	6	0	1 (1)	2
Kidderminster	4	25	18	38	0	13	11	55	7	0	- (-)	-
Leyton Orient	4	17	22	20	3	6	19	57	4	1	- (-)	1
Lincoln City	3	18	10	16	0	9	14	45	3	0	1 (1)	2
Macclesfield	4	25	19	21	3	20	7	29	6	0	1 (1)	-
Mansfield	4	23	14	24	0	10	24	48	8	0	1 (1)	-
Northampton	4	30	25	23	2	10	14	53	2	1	- (-)	1
Oxford Utd	4	21	19	17	0	19	6	57	9	1	2 (2)	-
Rochdale	4	21	20	33	0	13	7	38	9	0	1 (1)	-
Scunthorpe	4	20	22	28	0	10	20	49	7	0	2 (2)	1
Southend	4	24	27	20	1	10	22	57	6	4	2 (-)	-
Swansea	4	27	31	39	0	11	18	31	9	0	1 (1)	1
Torquay	**4**	**20**	**15**	**17**	**0**	**26**	**13**	**51**	**7**	**1**	**- (-)**	**-**
Yeovil	4	22	15	25	1	16	5	62	10	1	- (-)	1
York	5	20	29	20	0	11	20	59	10	0	- (-)	1

Monthly Match Details: Games 49 **Home Wins** 21 **Away Wins** 19 **Draws** 9

...December Player Stats..... Player Stats...... Player Stats......Pla

Monthly Top scorers

Jason Price (Hull)	4
Lee Nogan (York)	3
Matthew Tipton (Macclesfield)	2
James Thomas (Swansea)	2
Gregg Blundell (Doncaster)	2
Gary Fletcher (Lincoln City)	2
Gary Alexander (Leyton Orient)	2
Steve Brackenridge (Macclesfield)	2
Gabriel Zakuani (Leyton Orient)	2
Ben Burgess (Hull)	2

Penalties scored

2 P Beagrie (Scunthorpe), L Guttridge (Cambridge Utd), A Crosby (Scunthorpe), M McIndoe (Doncaster)

Assists

Andy Lindegaard (Yeovil)	3
Andy Preece (Carlisle)	3
Darren Dunning (York)	2
Kevin Gall (Yeovil)	2
Damian Spencer (Cheltenham)	2
Barry Conlon (Darlington)	2
Martin Smith (Northampton)	2

Quickest goals

2:21 mins - Matthew Robinson (Oxford Utd vs Carlisle)

2:21 mins - Richard Butcher (Mansfield vs Lincoln City)

2:55 mins - Jason Price (Hull vs Doncaster)

6:02 mins - Gabriel Zakuani (Kidderminster vs Leyton Orient)

8:28 mins - Gary Fletcher (Lincoln City vs Cambridge Utd)

Top Keeper

	Mins	Gls
Paul Musselwhite (Hull)	283	1
Stuart Brock (Kidderminster)	387	3
Andy Woodman (Oxford U)	384	3
Kevin Pilkington (Mansfield)	383	3
Paul Bastock (Boston Utd)	382	3
A Van Heusden (Torquay)	376	3
Michael Price (Darlington)	475	4
Lee Harrison (Leyton O)	193	2

Shots on target

Andy Robinson (Swansea)	10
Ben Burgess (Hull)	10
Junior Agogo (Bristol Rovers)	8
James Thomas (Swansea)	8
Jason Price (Hull)	7
Gregg Blundell (Doncaster)	7
Tesfaye Bramble (Southend)	7
Marc Richards (Northampton)	7
Barry Conlon (Darlington)	7
Ashley Nicholls (Darlington)	6

Shots off target

Andy Robinson (Swansea)	9
Stuart Elliott (Hull)	9
Steven MacLean (Scunthorpe)	7
Adam Boyd (Boston Utd)	7
Ben Burgess (Hull)	7
Grant McCann (Cheltenham)	7
Gareth Seddon (Bury)	6
Martin Smith (Northampton)	6
Richard Cooper (York)	6
Lee Matthews (Darlington)	6

Lee Canoville (v Swansea)

Caught offside

Gregg Blundell (Doncaster)	17
David Graham (Torquay)	9
Junior Agogo (Bristol Rovers)	8
Steve Basham (Oxford Utd)	8
Graeme Jones (Boston Utd)	8
Tony Bedeau (Torquay)	7
James Thomas (Swansea)	7
Julian Alsop (Oxford Utd)	7
Stuart Elliott (Hull)	7

Free-kicks won

Tom Cowan (Carlisle)	16
Stuart Elliott (Hull)	13
Tesfaye Bramble (Southend)	13
Andy Preece (Carlisle)	12
Lee Matthews (Darlington)	12
David Graham (Torquay)	11
Julian Alsop (Oxford Utd)	11
Jason Price (Hull)	11
Joe O'Neill (Bury)	10

Fouls conceded

Leo Fortune-West (Doncaster)	12
Ben Burgess (Hull)	12
Darren Dunning (York)	12
David Hunt (Leyton Orient)	12
Kevin Gray (Carlisle)	11
Danny Williams (Kidderminster)	10
Matthew Clarke (Darlington)	10
Mark Bailey (Lincoln City)	10
Daniel Webb (Cambridge Utd)	10

Fouls without a card

David Hunt (Leyton Orient)	12
Kevin Gray (Carlisle)	11
Mark Bailey (Lincoln City)	10
James Hunt (Oxford Utd)	9
Jonathan Stead (Huddersfield)	9
David Morley (Doncaster)	9
Michael McIndoe (Doncaster)	8
Stuart Elliott (Hull)	8
William McDonagh (Carlisle)	8

GOAL GOAL GOAL GOAL GOAL. Eyes wide shut...Tony Bedeau may not know it yet, but Jon Parkin definitely does. His own goal under pressure from Bedeau, gave Torquay a share of the spoils, deserved only for their second half performance after a woeful first 45 minutes.
Torquay v York.
HPL01222_TNA_019

Substitute Joe Broad whose performance along with other sub Jo Kuffour livened up a lacklustre Torquay side.
Torquay v York.
HPL01227_TNA_005

Torquay's Tony Bedeau and Swansea's Brad Maylett clash for the ball.
Torquay v Swansea
HPL01246_TNA_029

Jason Fowler chases Swansea's Karl Connolly.
Torquay v Swansea
HPL01246_TNA_025

Rochdale [1] 1 TORQUAY [0] 0

3rd January

A combination of wasteful finishing and plain bad luck saw Torquay United extend their goal-draught to more than eight hours.

Leroy Rosenior's side made and missed enough chances to have won a couple of games and the fact that Rochdale's winner on Saturday came from a penalty only made things worse.

Referee Martin Atkinson ruled that United left-back David Woozley had held Dale defender Gareth Griffiths down on a left-wing free-kick by Matt Doughty, and Kevin Townson put away the spot-kick in the 35th minute.

But United should really have been safe at that point. United repeatedly opened up the home defence in the first 20 minutes and Dale's veteran keeper Neil Edwards was in almost non-stop action.

Even he was helpless in the eighth minute when Martin Gritton missed an absolute sitter, hitting the bar with a free close-range header when it looked more difficult to miss than score.

Apart from the penalty, Rochdale's only real moment of joy came just after the Gritton miss, when Paul Connor turned the otherwise excellent Craig Taylor, raced away and then blazed his shot high and wide.

For a short spell after the interval, Rochdale did liven up and look dangerous, but Woods and Taylor were always solid at the back, and Fowler soon provided a good outlet on the right wing.

United always looked the better side, and in the closing stages it was almost like the Alamo in the Rochdale goalmouth. One dipping shot by Matt Hockley took an awkward bounce and took Edwards by surprise in the 85th minute, the keeper only just stopping the effort and then clawing it away.

And in stoppage time Hockley sent in another effort which Edwards could only parry. The ball could have gone anywhere, but it rebounded to Darryl Burgess, who hoofed it clear.

Result.......Result.......Result.

ROCHDALE..........(1) **1** **TORQUAY** ......(0) **0**
Townson 36(p)

Att 2,559
Referee: M Atkinson

Stats......Stats.......Stats......Stats

ROCHDALE				TORQUAY		
1st	**2nd**	**Total**		**Total**	**2nd**	**1st**
1	4	5	**Corners**	4	0	4
8	8	16	**Fouls**	14	6	8
1	0	1	**Yellow cards**	4	4	0
0	0	0	**Red cards**	0	0	0
2	2	4	**Caught Offside**	1	1	0
3	5	8	**Shots on target**	13	8	5
0	0	0	**Shots off target**	0	0	0
0	0	0	**Hit woodwork**	0	0	0
43	42	42%	**Possession**	58%	58	57

I knew it was going to be tough and we could have come in 3-1 down at half-time. Sometimes if you work hard you have a bit of luck.

Steve Parkin

I think we should have won the game. We bossed it for long periods and created more chances. They sat back when we were chasing the game.

Leroy Rosenior

Other Div 3 Results

Carlisle 2 Boston Utd 1, Huddersfield 3 Doncaster 1, Hull 2 Cambridge Utd 0, Leyton Orient 1 Darlington 0

Rochdale [1] 1 TORQUAY [0] 0

Goalkeeper Stats: Arjan Van Heusden Saves: Catch 2

Torquay Player Stats

No.	Player	Half	Shots on target L/R/H/Oth	Shots off target L/R/H/Oth	Caught offside	Fouls conceded	Free-kicks won	Corners taken	Clearances	Defensive blocks
5	Craig Taylor	1st	-/1/-/-	-/-/-/-	-	1	-	-	-	-
		2nd	-/-/-/-	-/-/-/-	-	-	2	-	-	-
3	David Woozley	1st	-/-/-/-	-/-/-/-	-	1	-	-	-	-
	▼ 45	2nd	-/-/-/-	-/-/-/-	-	-	-	-	-	-
2	Reuben Hazell	1st	-/-/-/-	-/-/-/-	-	-	-	1	-	-
	▼ 45	2nd	-/-/-/-	-/-/-/-	-	-	-	-	-	-
9	Martin Gritton	1st	1/-/1/-	-/-/-/-	-	1	2	-	-	-
	▼ 68	2nd	-/1/-/-	-/-/-/-	1	-	2	-	-	-
4	Lee Canoville	1st	-/-/-/-	-/-/-/-	-	1	-	-	-	-
	■ 87	2nd	-/-/-/-	-/-/-/-	-	1	1	-	-	-
18	Steve Woods	1st	-/-/-/-	-/-/-/-	-	-	-	-	-	-
	■ 82	2nd	-/-/-/-	-/-/-/-	-	1	-	-	-	-
6	Alex Russell	1st	-/1/-/-	-/-/-/-	-	1	1	3	1	-
		2nd	1/2/-/-	-/-/-/-	-	1	-	-	-	-
11	Kevin Hill	1st	1/-/-/-	-/-/-/-	-	-	3	-	-	-
	■ 53	2nd	2/-/-/-	-/-/-/-	-	1	1	-	1	-
10	David Graham	1st	-/-/-/-	-/-/-/-	-	1	2	-	-	-
		2nd	-/-/-/-	-/-/-/-	-	-	-	-	-	-
15	Kevin Wills	1st	-/-/-/-	-/-/-/-	-	-	-	-	-	-
	▲ 68	2nd	-/-/-/-	-/-/-/-	-	1	-	-	-	-
14	Matthew Hockley	1st	-/-/-/-	-/-/-/-	-	2	-	-	-	-
	■ 49	2nd	-/1/-/-	-/-/-/-	-	1	-	-	-	-
8	Jason Fowler	1st	-/-/-/-	-/-/-/-	-	-	-	-	-	-
	▲ 45	2nd	-/-/-/-	-/-/-/-	-	-	-	-	-	-
12	Jo Kuffour	1st	-/-/-/-	-/-/-/-	-	-	-	-	-	-
	▲ 45	2nd	-/1/-/-	-/-/-/-	-	-	2	-	-	-

Subs not used: Dearden, Broad. - **Formation: 3-5-2**

Goalkeeper Stats: Neil Edwards Saves: Catch 12, Crosses: Catch 2

No.	Player Stats	Shots on target	Shots off target	Caught offside	Fouls conceded	Free-kicks won	Corners taken	Clearances	Defensive blocks
2	Wayne Evans	-/-/-/-	-/-/-/-	-	3	-	-	1	-
5	Gareth Griffiths	-/-/-/-	-/-/-/-	-	1	2	-	1	-
3	Michael Simpkins	1/-/-/-	-/-/-/-	-	-	-	-	-	-
9	Andy Bishop ▲ 73	-/-/1/-	-/-/-/-	-	1	-	-	-	-
27	Paul Connor ▼ 73	-/2/-/-	-/-/-/-	3	3	2	-	-	-
8	Christopher Beech	-/-/-/-	-/-/-/-	-	1	1	-	-	-
12	Kevin Donovan ▲ 82	-/-/-/-	-/-/-/-	-	-	-	-	-	-
10	Matt Doughty ▼ 82	-/1/-/-	-/-/-/-	-	-	1	2	1	-
19	Kevin Townson	-/-/-/-	-/-/-/-	1	1	3	-	-	-
4	Sean McClare ■ 29	-/1/-/-	-/-/-/-	-	2	2	-	1	-
6	Daryl Burgess	-/-/-/-	-/-/-/-	-	3	1	-	1	-
7	Leo Bertos	1/-/-/-	-/-/-/-	-	1	2	3	-	-

Subs not used: Gilks, Warner, Grand. - **Formation: 4-4-2**

Torquay Played: 25 **Won** 10 **Drawn** 7 **Lost** 8 **For** 28 **Against** 26 **Pos** 9

Torquay [2] 3 NORTHAMPTON [0] 1

10th January

Back on song with a vengeance, Torquay United put their recent lean spell behind them to clinch three absolutely vital points against Northampton Town at a wet and windy Plainmoor.

Northampton were the biggest spenders of last summer and yet they were comprehensively outplayed and they could hardly have complained if they had lost by four or five goals.

United ripped into their opponents from the first minute. After only 75 seconds Russell crossed from the left and it took a brilliant save by Lee Harper to keep out Kuffour's close-range left-foot volley. United had to wait only 12 minutes for the breakthrough.

Kuffour laid the ball off to Russell in midfield, he made 20 yards of ground, unleashed a long-range shot which Harper could not hold and Kuffour was there to dispatch the rebound from eight yards.

Two minutes later Harper miskicked under pressure, the ball sailed to Hill nearly 40 yards out and his airborne first-time left-foot volley was heading for the top left-hand corner until Harper scrambled back across his goal to keep the ball out.

United badly needed a second goal after Northampton began to creep back into the contest. When it came, in the 39th minute, it was worth waiting for.

Cutting in from the right, Canoville made the most of the room conceded by a retreating defence and then let fly with his weaker left foot from 25 yards. He caught it perfectly...2-0 and a candidate for goal of the season.

It looked like a rout was on the cards, but instead Northampton were allowed back into the match.

In the 55th minute, Smith crossed and defender Ian Sampson headed home at the far-post. A draw would have been a travesty, given United's earlier command, but Gulls fans were just getting into Hang-On mode when the third goal finished the contest.

Russell and Hill took a short corner on the left, the Town defence managed to block Russell's cross, but Taylor seized on the loose ball to score with a left-foot volley from ten yards.

Result.......Result.......Result.

TORQUAY ....(2) **3** **NORTHAMPTN**(0) **1**
Kuffour 12 Sampson 55
Canoville 40
Taylor 78

Att 2,585
Referee: P Armstrong

Stats......Stats.......Stats......Stats

TORQUAY				NORTHAMPTON		
1st	2nd	Total		Total	2nd	1st
3	5	8	Corners	4	2	2
6	5	11	Fouls	16	9	7
0	0	0	Yellow cards	1	1	0
0	0	0	Red cards	0	0	0
3	4	7	Caught Offside	5	4	1
9	4	13	Shots on target	6	2	4
5	2	7	Shots off target	2	2	0
0	0	0	Hit woodwork	0	0	0
53	50	52%	Possession	48%	50	47

WE were tremendous in the first half - we created chance after chance, missing some easy ones and then scoring a scruffy goal.

Leroy Rosenior

THAT'S the first time that I don't think we have been competitive enough. We just weren't at it, and we deserved to get beat.

Colin Calderwood

Other Div 3 Results

Boston Utd 3 Macclesfield 1, Bristol Rovers 1 Scunthorpe 0, Bury 2 Swansea 0, Cambridge Utd 1 Huddersfield 2, Darlington 0 Hull 1, Doncaster 5 Leyton Orient 0, Mansfield 1 Kidderminster 0, Yeovil 1 Rochdale 0, York 2 Carlisle 0

10th January — TORQUAY [2] 3 Northampton [0] 1

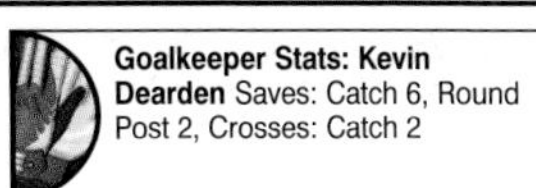

Goalkeeper Stats: Kevin Dearden Saves: Catch 6, Round Post 2, Crosses: Catch 2

Torquay Player Stats		Shots on target L/R/H/Oth	Shots off target L/R/H/Oth	Caught offside	Fouls conceded	Free-kicks won	Corners taken	Clearances	Defensive blocks
2 Reuben Hazell	1st	-/-/-/-	-/-/1/-	-	-	-	-	-	-
	2nd	-/-/-/-	-/-/-/-	-	-	2	-	-	-
5 Craig Taylor	1st	-/-/-/-	-/-/-/-	-	1	2	-	-	-
	2nd	1/1/-/-	-/-/-/-	-	-	-	-	-	-
9 Martin Gritton ▼ 74	1st	-/-/-/-	-/-/1/-	3	-	1	-	-	-
	2nd	-/-/-/-	-/-/-/-	1	-	1	-	-	-
18 Steve Woods	1st	-/1/-/-	-/-/-/-	-	1	-	-	2	-
	2nd	-/-/-/-	-/1/-/-	-	1	-	-	3	-
4 Lee Canoville	1st	1/-/-/-	-/-/-/-	-	-	-	-	1	-
	2nd	-/1/-/-	-/-/-/-	1	-	-	-	-	-
6 Alex Russell	1st	1/1/-/-	-/1/-/-	-	-	1	3	-	-
	2nd	-/-/-/-	-/-/-/-	-	-	1	5	-	-
11 Kevin Hill	1st	1/-/-/-	1/-/-/-	-	2	-	-	-	-
	2nd	-/-/-/-	-/-/-/-	2	1	-	-	-	-
29 Joe Broad ▲ 66	1st	-/-/-/-	-/-/-/-	-	-	-	-	-	-
	2nd	-/-/-/-	-/-/-/-	-	-	2	-	-	-
15 Kevin Wills ▲ 74	1st	-/-/-/-	-/-/-/-	-	-	-	-	-	-
	2nd	-/-/-/-	-/-/-/-	-	2	1	-	-	-
14 Matthew Hockley	1st	-/-/1/-	-/1/-/-	-	1	1	-	-	-
	2nd	-/-/-/-	-/-/-/-	-	-	-	-	-	-
8 Jason Fowler ▼ 66	1st	-/-/-/-	-/-/-/-	-	1	1	-	1	-
	2nd	1/-/-/-	-/-/-/-	-	1	-	-	-	-
12 Jo Kuffour	1st	1/2/-/-	-/-/-/-	-	-	1	-	-	-
	2nd	-/-/-/-	-/1/-/-	-	-	2	-	-	-

Subs not used: Bond, Woozley, Benefield. - **Formation: 4-4-2**

Goalkeeper Stats: Lee Harper Saves: Catch 6, Parry 4, Crosses: Catch 2, Round Post 2, Parry 2

	Player Stats	Shots on target	Shots off target	Caught offside	Fouls conceded	Free-kicks won	Corners taken	Clearances	Defensive blocks
19	Martin Smith	1/-/-/-	1/-/-/-	1	-	2	4	-	-
20	Chris Hargreaves	-/-/1/-	-/-/-/-	-	2	-	-	-	-
12	Mathew Sadler ▼ 45	-/-/-/-	-/-/-/-	-	-	-	-	-	-
4	Ashley Westwood	-/-/-/-	-/-/-/-	-	3	1	-	6	-
11	Paul Trollope ■ 77	-/-/-/-	-/-/-/-	-	3	-	-	-	-
9	Marc Richards ▲ 45	-/1/-/-	-/-/1/-	-	3	1	-	-	-
28	Richard Walker ▼ 45	-/-/-/-	-/-/-/-	1	2	2	-	-	1
17	Greg Lincoln ▲ 45	-/-/-/-	-/-/-/-	-	1	1	-	-	-
25	Derek Asamoah	-/1/-/-	-/-/-/-	3	1	-	-	-	-
6	Paul Reid	-/-/-/-	-/-/-/-	-	-	1	-	4	-
14	Ian Sampson	-/-/1/-	-/-/-/-	-	1	1	-	4	1
30	Des Lyttle ▼ 73	-/1/-/-	-/-/-/-	-	-	1	-	2	-
18	Paul Harsley ▲ 73	-/-/-/-	-/-/-/-	-	-	1	-	-	-

Subs not used: Thompson, Willmott. - **Formation: 3-5-2**

Torquay Played: 26 **Won** 11 **Drawn** 7 **Lost** 8 **For** 31 **Against** 27 **Pos** 9

Lincoln City [1] 1 TORQUAY [1] 3 — 17th January

Torquay United displayed all the qualities needed for promotion in this match as they matched grit with skill to come away with a vital 3 points.

Even into the wind, rain and hail which swept down at regular intervals, United went at Lincoln with a vengeance from the start. Good work by Kuffour on the left nearly set up an early breakthrough for Gritton, and by the tenth minute they were in front.

McGlinchey crossed from the left, Kuffour held off his defender in the middle, nudged the ball back and Fowler closed in to bury a perfectly-hit first-time right-foot volley from 15 yards.

It is a rarity to spend 90 minutes at Sincil Bank without coming under severe pressure and, with the weather behind them, Lincoln duly turned the screw before half-time, the pressure finally paying off in the 38th minute.

Ben Sedgemore took a corner from the left and Paul Mayo was not picked up on his run, leaving him to power home a header which gave Dearden no chance.

But after half-time it was Torquay who dominated. In the 46th minute Kuffour volleyed over the bar on the turn after Canoville had a shot blocked, and ten minutes later United were back in front.

Graham found Kuffour with a raking cross-field ball from right to left, Kuffour left Bailey for dead on the edge of the box, crossed low and Kevin Hill was prowling to turn in his long-awaited first goal of the season.

Then, in the 87th minute, came the coup de grace. Russell drilled a low ball to Graham and, while Lincoln were at sixes and sevens, his back-heeled pass left Kuffour clear to take one touch and drive a right-foot shot past the exposed Marriott.

Result.......Result.......Result.

LINCOLN CITY ....(1) **1** **TORQUAY** ......(1) **3**

Mayo 39 — Fowler 10, Hill 56, Kuffour 89

Att 3,873
Referee: A Bates

Stats......Stats.......Stats......Stats

LINCOLN CITY				TORQUAY		
1st	**2nd**	**Total**		**Total**	**2nd**	**1st**
6	3	9	**Corners**	1	1	0
8	4	12	**Fouls**	10	6	4
1	0	1	**Yellow cards**	1	0	1
0	0	0	**Red cards**	0	0	0
1	0	1	**Caught Offside**	3	1	2
4	1	5	**Shots on target**	5	3	2
1	4	5	**Shots off target**	2	1	1
0	0	0	**Hit woodwork**	0	0	0
49	56	52%	**Possession**	48%	44	51

> I thought Torquay played well. We conceded a sloppy goal which gave them the impetus. For the first 20 minutes we were not at the races.
>
> **Gary Simpson**

> **IN** the end we created good chances and got a comfortable win, but it wasn't comfortable for long periods of the game because Lincoln make it hard.
>
> **Leroy Rosenior**

Other Div 3 Results

Carlisle 2 Yeovil 0, Huddersfield 2 Boston Utd 0, Hull 4 Oxford Utd 2, Kidderminster 1 Darlington 1, Leyton Orient 3 Mansfield 1, Macclesfield 0 Cambridge Utd 1, Northampton 2 York 1, Rochdale 2 Bristol Rovers 2, Scunthorpe 0 Bury 0, Southend 0 Doncaster 2, Swansea 0 Cheltenham 0

17th January

Lincoln City [1] 1 TORQUAY [1] 3

Goalkeeper Stats: Kevin Dearden Saves: Tip Over 1, Catch 3

No.	Torquay Player Stats		Shots on target L/R/H/Oth	Shots off target L/R/H/Oth	Caught offside	Fouls conceded	Free-kicks won	Corners taken	Clearances	Defensive blocks
5	Craig Taylor	1st	-/-/-/-	-/-/-/-	-	1	-	-	-	-
		2nd	-/-/-/-	-/-/-/-	-	-	1	-	-	-
2	Reuben Hazell	1st	-/-/-/-	-/-/-/-	-	-	-	-	-	-
	▲ 82	2nd	-/-/-/-	-/-/-/-	-	1	-	-	-	-
9	Martin Gritton	1st	-/-/-/-	-/-/-/-	-	-	-	-	-	-
	▼ 54	2nd	-/-/-/-	-/-/-/-	1	1	-	-	-	-
18	Steve Woods	1st	-/-/-/-	-/-/-/-	-	1	-	-	-	-
		2nd	-/-/-/-	-/-/-/-	-	-	-	-	-	-
4	Lee Canoville	1st	-/-/-/-	-/-/-/-	-	-	-	-	-	-
		2nd	-/-/-/-	-/-/-/-	-	1	-	-	-	-
6	Alex Russell	1st	-/-/-/-	-/-/-/-	-	-	-	-	-	-
		2nd	-/-/-/-	-/-/-/-	-	2	-	1	1	-
11	Kevin Hill	1st	-/-/-/-	-/-/-/-	1	-	1	-	-	-
	■ 21	2nd	-/1/-/-	-/-/-/-	-	-	2	-	-	-
10	David Graham	1st	-/-/-/-	-/-/-/-	-	-	-	-	-	-
	▲ 54	2nd	-/-/-/-	-/-/-/-	-	-	-	-	-	-
14	Matthew Hockley	1st	-/1/-/-	-/-/-/-	-	1	2	-	2	-
		2nd	-/-/-/-	-/-/-/-	-	-	-	-	-	-
8	Jason Fowler	1st	-/1/-/-	-/-/-/-	-	1	4	-	-	-
	▼ 82	2nd	-/-/-/-	-/-/-/-	-	-	-	-	-	-
12	Jo Kuffour	1st	-/-/-/-	-/1/-/-	1	-	-	-	-	-
		2nd	-/2/-/-	-/1/-/-	-	1	1	-	-	-
17	Brian McGlinchey	1st	-/-/-/-	-/-/-/-	-	-	1	-	-	-
		2nd	-/-/-/-	-/-/-/-	-	-	-	-	-	-

Subs not used: Woozley, Wills, Broad. - **Formation: 4-4-2**

Goalkeeper Stats: Alan Marriott Saves: Catch 1, Round Post 1, Crosses: Catch 2

No.	Player Stats	Shots on target	Shots off target	Caught offside	Fouls conceded	Free-kicks won	Corners taken	Clearances	Defensive blocks
6	Ben Sedgemore	-/-/-/-	1/-/-/-	-	1	3	4	-	-
27	Gary Fletcher	-/-/-/-	-/-/1/-	-	-	2	-	-	-
15	Simon Weaver ▼ 75	-/-/-/-	-/-/1/-	-	-	-	-	-	-
25	Niall McNamara ▲ 35	-/-/-/-	-/1/-/-	-	-	-	-	-	-
2	Mark Bailey	-/1/-/-	-/-/-/-	-	3	1	-	-	-
9	Simon Yeo ▲ 75	-/-/-/-	-/-/-/-	-	-	1	-	-	-
5	Paul Morgan	-/-/-/-	-/-/-/-	-	1	-	-	-	-
4	Ben Futcher	-/1/-/-	-/-/-/-	-	2	1	-	-	-
30	Francis Green	-/-/-/-	-/-/-/-	-	-	1	-	-	-
10	Dene Cropper ▲ 67	-/-/-/-	-/-/-/-	-	-	1	-	-	-
3	Paul Mayo	2/-/1/-	1/-/-/-	-	3	-	5	-	-
28	Marcus Richardson ▼ 67	-/-/-/-	-/-/-/-	1	1	-	-	-	-
11	Peter Gain ▼ 35 ■ 6	-/-/-/-	-/-/-/-	-	1	-	-	-	-

Subs not used: Bloomer, Liburd. - **Formation: 3-5-2**

Torquay Played: 27 **Won** 12 **Drawn** 7 **Lost** 8 **For** 34 **Against** 28 **Pos** 8

Torquay [3] 4 MACCLESFIELD [1] 1 — 24th January

Without a goal of their own for more than eight hours over Christmas and New Year, Torquay United had now hit ten in their last three games.

If anybody summed up United's current form, it's Kevin Hill. The 300-game left-winger had to wait five months for his first goal of the season, and now he had two in two games.

His first was brilliant. Steve Woods flicked on Alex Russell's flag-kick and Hill, with his back to goal, took off and hit a first-time 'bicycle kick' over his head and into the roof of the net from ten yards.

Then in the 33rd minute David Graham, who had only just missed a great chance set up by Jo Kuffour, scored his 13th goal of the season and his first in seven games. Matt Hockley found Jason Fowler on the right and his cross left Graham with an easy cushion-header from close range.

Graham, again set up by the increasingly impressive Kuffour, went close again before Taylor made it 3-0 in the 41st minute.

Former Plymouth left-back Jon Beswetherick sliced a clearance back out to Russell after a corner, Russell crossed again to the far-post where Taylor brushed a defender aside before heading his third goal of the season.

Having taken complete charge, United then threw Macclesfield a lifeline on the stroke of half-time, allowing the lively John Miles to cross from the left for Colin Little to fire a left-foot shot in off Dearden's fingertips.

United then began to grab hold of the game. Graham allowed Karl Munroe to get back and foil him after a Taylor header had put him away in the 82nd minute.

Two minutes laterthey finished the job. Russell, on his third 'assist' of the afternoon, took a diagonal free-kick from the right and Gritton rose to glance home a header just inside the far post.

Result.......Result.......Result.

TORQUAY ....(3) **4** **M'CLESFIELD** (1) **1**

Hill 8 — Little 45
Graham 33
Taylor 41
Gritton 87

Att 2,770
Referee: L Cable

Stats......Stats.......Stats......Stats

TORQUAY				MACCLESFIELD		
1st	**2nd**	**Total**		**Total**	**2nd**	**1st**
7	2	9	**Corners**	7	2	5
7	6	13	**Fouls**	10	3	7
0	0	0	**Yellow cards**	2	1	1
0	0	0	**Red cards**	1	1	0
0	3	3	**Caught Offside**	6	3	3
2	4	6	**Shots on target**	7	3	4
4	1	5	**Shots off target**	6	4	2
0	0	0	**Hit woodwork**	0	0	0
53	67	60%	**Possession**	40%	33	47

"I don't think it was one of our best performances, but we put our chances away. We were very professional in the second half."

Leroy Rosenior

"**WE** were very poor indeed at the back, and if those guys want to carry on playing for this club, they will have to do much better than that."

John Askey

Other Div 3 Results

Bristol Rovers 1 Carlisle 0, Bury 0 Kidderminster 0, Cambridge Utd 0 Rochdale 0, Cheltenham 0 Hull 2, Darlington P Northampton P, Mansfield 1 Southend 0, Oxford Utd P Scunthorpe P, Yeovil 1 Leyton Orient 2, York P Huddersfield P

TORQUAY [3] 4 Macclesfield [1] 1

Goalkeeper Stats: Kevin Dearden Saves: Catch 3, Parry 1, Crosses: Catch 1

No.	Torquay Player Stats		Shots on target L/R/H/Oth	Shots off target L/R/H/Oth	Caught offside	Fouls conceded	Free-kicks won	Corners taken	Clearances	Defensive blocks
7	Tony Bedeau	1st	-/-/-/-	-/-/-/-	-	-	-	-	-	-
	▲ 75	2nd	-/-/-/-	-/-/-/-	-	-	-	-	2	-
2	Reuben Hazell	1st	-/-/-/-	-/-/-/-	-	1	1	-	1	-
		2nd	-/-/-/-	-/-/-/-	-	2	1	-	1	-
5	Craig Taylor	1st	-/-/-/-	-/-/-/-	-	1	-	-	-	-
		2nd	-/-/-/-	-/-/-/-	-	-	-	-	1	-
9	Martin Gritton	1st	-/-/-/-	-/-/-/-	-	-	-	-	-	-
	▲ 71	2nd	-/-/1/-	-/-/-/-	-	1	-	-	-	-
18	Steve Woods	1st	-/-/-/-	-/-/-/-	-	-	-	1	-	-
		2nd	-/-/-/-	-/-/-/-	-	-	-	-	1	-
6	Alex Russell	1st	-/1/-/-	-/-/-/-	-	1	-	5	1	-
		2nd	-/-/-/-	-/-/-/-	-	-	-	2	-	-
29	Joe Broad	1st	-/-/-/-	-/-/-/-	-	-	-	-	-	-
	▲ 86	2nd	-/-/-/-	-/-/-/-	-	-	-	-	-	-
11	Kevin Hill	1st	1/-/-/-	-/-/-/-	-	2	1	-	1	-
		2nd	-/2/-/-	-/-/-/-	-	1	-	-	-	-
10	David Graham	1st	-/-/-/-	1/1/-/-	-	1	2	-	-	-
	▼ 86	2nd	-/1/-/-	-/1/-/-	3	-	1	-	-	-
14	Matthew Hockley	1st	-/-/-/-	-/1/-/-	-	1	-	-	-	-
		2nd	-/-/-/-	-/-/-/-	-	-	1	-	-	-
8	Jason Fowler	1st	-/-/-/-	-/-/-/-	-	-	1	1	1	-
	▼ 75	2nd	-/-/-/-	-/-/-/-	-	2	-	-	-	-
12	Jo Kuffour	1st	-/-/-/-	-/1/-/-	-	-	2	-	-	-
	▼ 71	2nd	-/-/-/-	-/-/-/-	-	-	-	-	-	-
17	Brian McGlinchey	1st	-/-/-/-	-/-/-/-	-	-	-	-	1	-
		2nd	-/-/-/-	-/-/-/-	-	-	-	-	-	-

Subs not used: Van Heusden, Woozley. - **Formation: 4-4-2**

Goalkeeper Stats: Steve Wilson Saves: Catch 1, Parry 1, Crosses: Catch 2

No.	Player Stats	Shots on target	Shots off target	Caught offside	Fouls conceded	Free-kicks won	Corners taken	Clearances	Defensive blocks
8	Chris Priest	-/1/-/-	-/-/-/-	1	1	-	-	1	-
5	Karl Munroe	-/-/1/-	-/-/-/-	-	2	1	-	2	1
18	Colin Little	1/-/-/-	-/-/-/-	2	1	1	-	1	-
15	Michael Welch	-/-/-/-	-/-/-/-	1	1	2	-	-	-
21	Jon Beswetherick	-/-/-/-	1/-/-/-	-	-	2	3	5	-
9	Matthew Tipton ■ 4 ■ 85	1/1/-/-	-/1/-/-	-	2	1	-	-	-
26	Steve Brackenridge ▲ 86	-/-/-/-	-/-/-/-	-	-	-	-	-	-
12	Danny Whitaker	-/-/-/-	-/-/-/-	-	-	1	3	-	-
23	Matthew Carragher ■ 45	-/-/-/-	1/-/-/-	-	1	1	1	1	-
10	John Miles	-/1/-/-	-/2/-/-	2	-	2	-	-	-
27	Michael Carr ▼ 62	-/-/-/-	-/-/-/-	-	2	2	-	2	-
4	David Smith ▼ 86 ▲ 62	1/-/-/-	1/-/-/-	-	-	-	-	-	-

Subs not used: Miskelly, Carruthers, Vernon. - **Formation: 4-4-2**

Torquay Played: 28 **Won** 13 **Drawn** 7 **Lost** 8 **For** 38 **Against** 29 **Pos** 7

...January Team Stats.....Team Stats......Team Stats......Team S

League table at the end of January

	HOME						AWAY						
	P	**W**	**D**	**L**	**F**	**A**	**W**	**D**	**L**	**F**	**A**	**Pts**	**Df**
Hull	29	11	3	1	37	15	6	5	3	20	11	59	31
Doncaster	29	11	2	2	30	9	7	2	5	23	17	58	27
Oxford Utd	28	11	3	0	25	7	4	8	2	17	14	56	21
Mansfield	28	10	2	2	32	14	6	3	5	21	18	53	21
Huddersfield	28	10	3	1	24	8	4	4	6	19	28	49	7
Yeovil	28	10	1	4	27	13	5	1	7	15	19	47	10
Lincoln City	28	6	6	2	20	12	6	4	4	16	14	46	10
Torquay	**28**	**9**	**4**	**1**	**27**	**13**	**4**	**3**	**7**	**11**	**16**	**46**	**9**
Swansea	27	7	5	2	24	12	4	3	6	13	20	41	5
York	29	7	4	3	16	11	3	6	6	10	21	40	-6
Leyton Orient	29	6	5	3	20	16	4	3	8	15	25	38	-6
Bristol Rovers	28	6	3	5	15	14	4	3	7	17	20	36	-2
Cambridge U	28	2	5	7	14	23	6	5	3	20	18	34	-7
Bury	29	6	3	5	17	19	4	1	10	16	25	34	-11
Scunthorpe	27	4	7	3	24	16	3	5	5	17	21	33	4
Northampton	27	6	2	5	12	15	3	4	7	12	20	33	-11
Cheltenham	28	7	3	5	23	25	1	5	7	12	25	32	-15
Boston Utd	27	6	5	2	23	12	2	2	10	7	23	31	-5
Rochdale	29	4	4	6	17	19	4	3	8	15	20	31	-7
Macclesfield	29	5	6	3	20	14	2	4	9	18	33	31	-9
Kidderminster	28	4	3	6	14	19	4	4	7	12	18	31	-11
Southend	28	3	2	9	11	18	4	3	7	12	23	26	-18
Darlington	29	6	3	6	16	16	0	4	10	11	26	25	-15
Carlisle	28	4	2	8	13	19	1	1	12	10	26	18	-22

January matches table

	P	W	D	L	F	A	P
Hull	4	4	0	0	9	2	1[illegible]
Huddersfield	4	4	0	0	9	2	1[illegible]
Torquay	**4**	**3**	**0**	**1**	**10**	**4**	[illegible]
Doncaster	5	3	0	2	9	5	[illegible]
Leyton Orient	5	3	0	2	6	8	[illegible]
Lincoln City	5	2	2	1	5	4	[illegible]
Bristol Rovers	4	2	1	1	5	4	[illegible]
Mansfield	4	2	1	1	3	3	[illegible]
Carlisle	4	2	0	2	4	4	[illegible]
Cheltenham	5	1	3	1	2	3	[illegible]
Oxford Utd	4	1	2	1	4	5	[illegible]
Bury	4	1	2	1	3	2	[illegible]
Rochdale	5	1	2	2	3	4	[illegible]
Macclesfield	5	1	1	3	6	11	[illegible]
Yeovil	4	1	1	2	4	6	[illegible]
York	4	1	1	2	3	4	[illegible]
Darlington	4	1	1	2	2	3	[illegible]
Cambridge Utd	4	1	1	2	2	4	[illegible]
Boston Utd	3	1	0	2	4	5	[illegible]
Northampton	3	1	0	2	3	5	[illegible]
Kidderminster	4	0	2	2	2	4	[illegible]
Southend	4	0	2	2	1	4	[illegible]
Scunthorpe	3	0	2	1	0	1	[illegible]
Swansea	3	0	2	1	0	2	[illegible]

January team stats details

Club Name	Ply	Shots On	Shots Off	Corners	Hit W'work	Caught Offside	Offside Trap	Fouls	Yellow Cards	Red Cards	Pens Awarded	Pe C[illegible]
Boston Utd	3	19	17	14	3	7	9	34	7	0	- (-)	-
Bristol Rovers	4	23	15	14	2	5	21	77	4	0	2 (2)	-
Bury	4	17	14	20	1	15	8	57	5	0	- (-)	-
Cambridge Utd	4	15	15	20	2	5	11	69	6	0	1 (-)	-
Carlisle	4	29	15	21	1	14	16	47	6	0	- (-)	1
Cheltenham	5	21	38	26	1	30	12	47	5	1	- (-)	-
Darlington	4	15	21	37	0	13	8	56	7	0	- (-)	-
Doncaster	5	30	22	29	2	25	24	52	6	0	- (-)	-
Huddersfield	4	35	24	29	1	13	7	71	4	0	1 (1)	1
Hull	4	36	20	24	2	6	10	30	3	0	- (-)	-
Kidderminster	4	28	19	23	2	6	11	43	3	0	1 (-)	1
Leyton Orient	5	17	14	22	1	18	27	64	9	0	- (-)	-
Lincoln City	5	22	22	32	0	13	16	52	4	0	- (-)	-
Macclesfield	5	30	20	24	0	19	17	45	6	2	1 (1)	1
Mansfield	4	16	17	19	1	14	12	42	6	0	1 (1)	-
Northampton	3	17	12	14	0	16	19	42	4	0	- (-)	-
Oxford Utd	4	24	10	27	2	14	8	52	8	0	- (-)	-
Rochdale	5	20	9	25	1	20	10	63	6	0	1 (1)	1
Scunthorpe	3	24	19	33	3	12	14	27	5	0	- (-)	1
Southend	4	25	16	28	2	14	16	48	4	0	- (-)	1
Swansea	3	16	10	18	0	3	20	37	1	1	- (-)	-
Torquay	**4**	**37**	**14**	**22**	**0**	**14**	**16**	**48**	**5**	**0**	**- (-)**	1
Yeovil	4	27	15	21	1	24	10	55	2	0	- (-)	-
York	4	17	22	19	1	11	9	47	4	0	- (-)	-

 Monthly Match Details: Games 49 **Home Wins** 27 **Away Wins** 9 **Draws** 13

...January Player Stats..... Player Stats...... Player Stats......Pla

Monthly Top scorers

Leo Fortune-West (Doncaster)	4
Colin Little (Macclesfield)	3
Gary Alexander (Leyton Orient)	3
Stuart Elliott (Hull)	3
Danny Allsopp (Hull)	3
Jonathan Stead (Huddersfield)	2
Kevin Hill (Torquay)	2
Gary Fletcher (Lincoln City)	2
Craig Taylor (Torquay)	2
Steve Basham (Oxford Utd)	2

Penalties scored

2 W Carlisle (Bristol Rovers),
1 M Tipton (Macclesfield), J Stead (Huddersfield), K Townson (Rochdale)

Assists

Gregg Blundell (Doncaster)	3
Alex Russell (Torquay)	3
Jamie Forrester (Hull)	2
Dean Whitehead (Oxford Utd)	2
Nat Brown (Huddersfield)	2
Stuart Elliott (Hull)	2
John Melligan (Doncaster)	2

Quickest goals

3:01 mins - Leo Fortune-West (Southend vs Doncaster)

3:50 mins - Gary Fletcher (Lincoln City vs Bury)

5:14 mins - Gary Alexander (Leyton Orient vs Mansfield)

6:13 mins - Steve Basham (Oxford Utd vs Kidderminster)

6:30 mins - Adam Murray (Kidderminster vs Darlington)

Top Keeper

	Mins	Gls
Tom Evans (Scunthorpe)	287	1
Phillip Senior (Huddersfield)	386	2
Boaz Myhill (Hull)	381	2
Glyn Garner (Bury)	377	2
Shane Higgs (Cheltenham)	474	3
Roger Freestone (Swansea)	283	2
K Pilkington (Mansfield)	382	3
Michael Price (Darlington)	378	3

Shots on target

Ben Burgess (Hull)	12
Jonathan Stead (Huddersfield)	10
Paul Simpson (Carlisle)	10
Colin Little (Macclesfield)	9
Adam Murray (Kidderminster)	9
Danny Allsopp (Hull)	8
Kevin Hill (Torquay)	8
Gavin Williams (Yeovil)	7
Alex Russell (Torquay)	7
Andy Robinson (Swansea)	7

Shots off target

Leo Fortune-West (Doncaster)	9
Grant McCann (Cheltenham)	9
Jonathan Stead (Huddersfield)	8
Neil Redfearn (Boston Utd)	8
Paul Simpson (Carlisle)	6
Ben Burgess (Hull)	6
Neil Wainwright (Darlington)	6
Martin Devaney (Cheltenham)	6
Paul Hayes (Scunthorpe)	6
John Miles (Macclesfield)	5

Caught offside

Kevin Gall (Yeovil)	12
Jon Daly (Bury)	11
Gregg Blundell (Doncaster)	10
Paul Brayson (Cheltenham)	10
Barry Conlon (Darlington)	9
Steve Basham (Oxford Utd)	9
Damian Spencer (Cheltenham)	9
Gary Alexander (Leyton Orient)	8
Derek Asamoah (Northampton)	8

Free-kicks won

Nat Brown (Huddersfield)	16
Ben Sedgemore (Lincoln City)	13
Paul Arnison (Carlisle)	11
Andy Preece (Carlisle)	11
Ashley Nicholls (Darlington)	10
Adam Murray (Kidderminster)	10
Lewis Haldane (Bristol Rovers)	10
Jonathan Stead (Huddersfield)	10
Simon Weaver (Lincoln City)	9

Gritton & Canoville share their delight

Fouls conceded

Daryl Burgess (Rochdale)	13
Nat Brown (Huddersfield)	13
Daniel Webb (Cambridge Utd)	13
Glenn Whelan (Bury)	13
Kevin Gray (Carlisle)	13
J Worthington (Huddersfield)	13
Paul Ellender (Boston Utd)	11
Lee Matthews (Darlington)	11
Barry Conlon (Darlington)	11

Fouls without a card

Nat Brown (Huddersfield)	13
Lee Matthews (Darlington)	11
Barry Conlon (Darlington)	11
Graham Hyde (Bristol Rovers)	10
Jake Edwards (Yeovil)	10
Martin Carruthers (Macclesfield)	9
Wayne Carlisle (Bristol Rovers)	8
Jefferson Louis (Oxford Utd)	8
Kevin Austin (Bristol Rovers)	8

Brian McGlinchey gets in a pin point second half cross despite the attentions of a Macclesfield defender.
Torquay v Macclesfield
HPL01313_TNA_054

GOAL GOAL GOAL. . . Kevin Hill scores Torquay's first with a spectacular overhead kick.
Torquay v Macclesfield
HPL01313_TNA_047

Swansea [0] 1 TORQUAY [1] 2

7th February

Two top quality finishes by leading scorer David Graham and substitute Jo Kuffour topped off yet another terrific performance by Torquay United against Swansea City.

It was United's fourth successive victory and the way in which they reacted when City equalised in the 82nd minute spoke volumes for the mood of Rosenior's squad right now.

Instead of settling for a barely adequate point, they roared back, completely took the wind out of Swansea's sails and settled all arguments with Kuffour's show-stopping winner.

The first goal came in the 18th minute. Michael Howard headed weakly towards O'Leary, Graham was onto it, went into the box, checked back onto his right foot past Shaun Byrne and beat Roger Freestone from ten yards for his 14th goal of the season.

And on the stroke of half-time Fowler, drifting inside cleverly, helped to set up a good opening for Matt Hockley, who pulled his angled shot just wide across the face of goal.

But Swansea, with Robinson always lively, did have their moments. It took the save of the match by Dearden, in the 64th minute, to tip a Thomas volley over his bar before they equalized in the 82nd minute.

Most teams would have settled for a point at that stage, but United responded as if Swansea had just questioned their mother's morals.

Within a minute, they nearly regained the lead when a nervous backpass by Howard beat Freestone and bobbled only a foot wide. Taylor's header from the corner was on its way in when it was blocked.

Then, in the 85th minute, Kuffour crowned his livewire display with the winner. One on one in the box against Howard, he dropped his left shoulder, jinked past his man on the right and then unleashed a shot which no keeper would have stopped.

Result.......Result.......Result.

SWANSEA ....(0) **1** **TORQUAY** ......(1) **2**
Nugent 81 | Graham 18, Kuffour 85

Att 7,323
Referee: S Mathieson

Stats......Stats.......Stats......Stats

SWANSEA				TORQUAY		
1st	2nd	Total		Total	2nd	1st
6	4	10	**Corners**	7	6	1
4	6	10	**Fouls**	6	3	3
0	1	1	**Yellow cards**	2	0	2
0	0	0	**Red cards**	0	0	0
0	2	2	**Caught Offside**	6	2	4
3	6	9	**Shots on target**	4	2	2
0	5	5	**Shots off target**	4	2	2
0	0	0	**Hit woodwork**	0	0	0
53	44	48%	**Possession**	52%	56	47

> **TORQUAY** are a good side and we were second-best. They are in form, we aren't and it showed as we were very predictable, particularly in the first half.
>
> **Brian Flynn**

> **HE** didn't train until Thursday, but I knew if Jo Kuffour had hold of the ball he would cause Swansea problems and that is exactly what happened.
>
> **Leroy Rosenior**

Other Div 3 Results

Carlisle 2 Bury 1, Huddersfield 0 Darlington 2, Hull 2 York 1, Kidderminster 0 Yeovil 1, Leyton Orient 1 Oxford Utd 0, Macclesfield 1 Cheltenham 2, Northampton 2 Bristol Rovers 0, Rochdale 3 Mansfield 0, Scunthorpe 2 Doncaster 2, Southend 1 Cambridge Utd 0

Swansea [0] 1 TORQUAY [1] 2

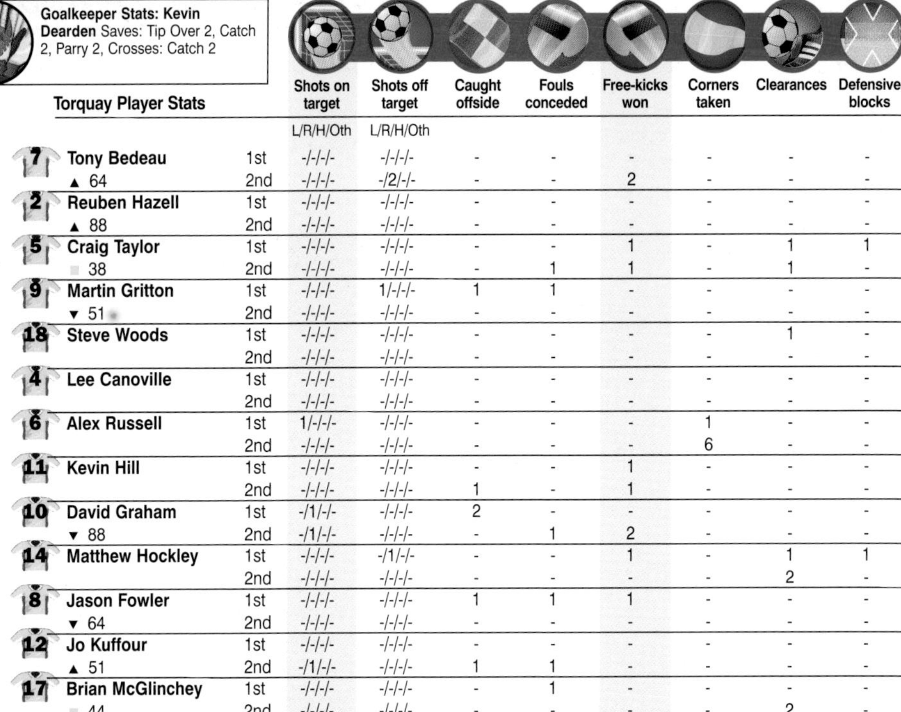

Goalkeeper Stats: Kevin Dearden Saves: Tip Over 2, Catch 2, Parry 2, Crosses: Catch 2

Torquay Player Stats		Shots on target L/R/H/Oth	Shots off target L/R/H/Oth	Caught offside	Fouls conceded	Free-kicks won	Corners taken	Clearances	Defensive blocks
7 Tony Bedeau	1st	-/-/-/-	-/-/-/-	-	-	-	-	-	-
▲ 64	2nd	-/-/-/-	-/2/-/-	-	-	2	-	-	-
2 Reuben Hazell	1st	-/-/-/-	-/-/-/-	-	-	-	-	-	-
▲ 88	2nd	-/-/-/-	-/-/-/-	-	-	-	-	-	-
5 Craig Taylor	1st	-/-/-/-	-/-/-/-	-	-	1	-	1	1
■ 38	2nd	-/-/-/-	-/-/-/-	-	1	1	-	1	-
9 Martin Gritton	1st	-/-/-/-	1/-/-/-	1	1	-	-	-	-
▼ 51	2nd	-/-/-/-	-/-/-/-	-	-	-	-	-	-
18 Steve Woods	1st	-/-/-/-	-/-/-/-	-	-	-	-	1	-
	2nd	-/-/-/-	-/-/-/-	-	-	-	-	-	-
4 Lee Canoville	1st	-/-/-/-	-/-/-/-	-	-	-	-	-	-
	2nd	-/-/-/-	-/-/-/-	-	-	-	-	-	-
6 Alex Russell	1st	1/-/-/-	-/-/-/-	-	-	-	1	-	-
	2nd	-/-/-/-	-/-/-/-	-	-	-	6	-	-
11 Kevin Hill	1st	-/-/-/-	-/-/-/-	-	-	1	-	-	-
	2nd	-/-/-/-	-/-/-/-	1	-	1	-	-	-
10 David Graham	1st	-/1/-/-	-/-/-/-	2	-	-	-	-	-
▼ 88	2nd	-/1/-/-	-/-/-/-	-	1	2	-	-	-
14 Matthew Hockley	1st	-/-/-/-	-/1/-/-	-	-	1	-	1	1
	2nd	-/-/-/-	-/-/-/-	-	-	-	-	2	-
8 Jason Fowler	1st	-/-/-/-	-/-/-/-	1	1	1	-	-	-
▼ 64	2nd	-/-/-/-	-/-/-/-	-	-	-	-	-	-
12 Jo Kuffour	1st	-/-/-/-	-/-/-/-	-	-	-	-	-	-
▲ 51	2nd	-/1/-/-	-/-/-/-	1	1	-	-	-	-
17 Brian McGlinchey	1st	-/-/-/-	-/-/-/-	-	1	-	-	-	-
■ 44	2nd	-/-/-/-	-/-/-/-	-	-	-	-	2	-

Subs not used: Van Heusden, Woozley. - **Formation: 4-4-2**

Goalkeeper Stats: Roger Freestone Saves: Catch 4, Parry 2, Crosses: Catch 6, Parry 2

Player Stats	Shots on target	Shots off target	Caught offside	Fouls conceded	Free-kicks won	Corners taken	Clearances	Defensive blocks
15 Jonathon Coates ▲ 55	-/-/-/-	1/-/-/-	-	-	-	-	-	-
14 Bradley Maylett	-/1/-/-	-/1/-/-	1	-	1	-	-	-
18 Andy Robinson	2/1/-/-	1/1/-/-	-	3	-	7	-	-
6 Roberto Martinez	-/1/-/-	-/-/-/-	-	1	1	1	-	-
4 Kristian O'Leary	-/-/-/-	-/-/-/-	-	-	-	-	1	-
16 Karl Connolly ▼ 55	-/-/-/-	-/-/-/-	-	-	-	1	-	-
3 Michael Howard	1/-/-/-	-/-/-/-	-	1	-	1	-	-
5 Alan Tate ▲ 78	-/-/-/-	-/-/-/-	-	-	-	-	-	-
9 James Thomas ▼ 72	1/-/-/-	1/-/-/-	1	-	-	-	1	-
26 Mark Pritchard ▲ 72	-/-/-/-	-/-/-/-	-	-	-	-	-	-
22 Izzy Iriekpen ▼ 78 ■ 55	-/-/-/-	-/-/-/-	-	2	3	-	2	-
8 Kevin Nugent	1/1/-/-	-/-/-/-	-	3	1	-	2	-
2 Shaun Byrne	-/-/-/-	-/-/-/-	-	-	-	-	-	-

Subs not used: Hylton, Murphy. - **Formation: 4-4-2**

Torquay Played: 29 **Won** 14 **Drawn** 7 **Lost** 8 **For** 40 **Against** 30 **Pos** 6

Torquay [0] 0 HUDDERSFIELD [0] 1 — 14th February

Play-Off rivals Huddersfield Town took all three points from a shell-shocked Torquay at Plainmoor.

Referee Iain Williamson failed to protect Gulls strikers David Graham and Jo Kuffour from some blatant strong-arm tactics early on, which was the green light for Huddersfield's defenders to turn in one of the most physical displays seen at Plainmoor this season.

In fairness the visitors, who packed their midfield and defence to combat United's in-form attack, certainly battled, riding their luck until snatching what turned out to be the winner through young centre-back Nathan Clarke in the 71st minute.

By that stage, United had already hit the woodwork twice and had one goal disallowed. And when, just after Huddersfield winger Tony Carss was sent off for a second yellow card, skipper Craig Taylor thumped home an equalising header in the 86th minute, United seemed to have earned a point they more than deserved.

But Mr. Williamson wasn't finished yet. He disallowed the goal, claiming that Taylor had fouled Steve Yates to get in the header.

Early on, it looked like Torquay would walk this game and should have scored twice in the first dozen minutes. Kuffour, released by Alex Russell down the left, beat Yates but failed to roll a simple, goal-scoring pass into the path of Matt Hockley, who missed.

Then, on a Russell free-kick from the left, Kuffour escaped Huddersfield's goalmouth marking and, when he looked certain to score from close-range, headed against the far-post.

A brilliant lob by Jason Fowler, from 20 yards on the right with the outside of his right boot, forced the back-pedalling Phil Senior to tip the ball on to his post and away in the 49th minute, sparking United's renewed superiority in the second half.

But Huddersfield managed to hang on to their lead. When Carss received his marching orders in the 84th minute, after scything down Bedeau, he became the ninth player to be sent off for Huddersfield this season.

But it was little consolation to United, and Mr. Williamson's decision to disallow Taylor's header was just about the last straw.

Result.......Result.......Result.

TORQUAY ....(0) **0** **H'DERSFIELD** (0) **1**
Clarke 71

Att 3,821
Referee: I Williamson

Stats......Stats.......Stats......Stats

TORQUAY				HUDDERSFIELD		
1st	2nd	Total		Total	2nd	1st
4	3	7	**Corners**	6	1	5
9	10	19	**Fouls**	14	7	7
1	2	3	**Yellow cards**	2	0	2
0	0	0	**Red cards**	1	1	0
1	2	3	**Caught Offside**	2	0	2
2	4	6	**Shots on target**	4	2	2
4	3	7	**Shots off target**	3	1	2
1	0	1	**Hit woodwork**	0	0	0
52	55	53%	**Possession**	47%	45	48

"I thought it was an exciting game and a good advert for the Third Division and I'm just disappointed that we didn't get the result we deserved.

Leroy Rosenior"

"IT was an excellent result, Torquay are not in this position for nothing - they are a very good team indeed - but we defended very well.

Peter Jackson"

Other Div 3 Results

Bristol Rovers 0 Darlington 3, Bury 1 Cambridge Utd 0, Carlisle 1 Hull 1, Cheltenham 1 Boston Utd 0, Doncaster 1 Macclesfield 0, Northampton 3 Rochdale 1, Southend 3 Kidderminster 0, Yeovil 1 Oxford Utd 0, York 1 Mansfield 2

TORQUAY [0] 0 Huddersfield [0] 1

Goalkeeper Stats: Kevin Dearden Saves: Round Post 2, Crosses: Catch 2

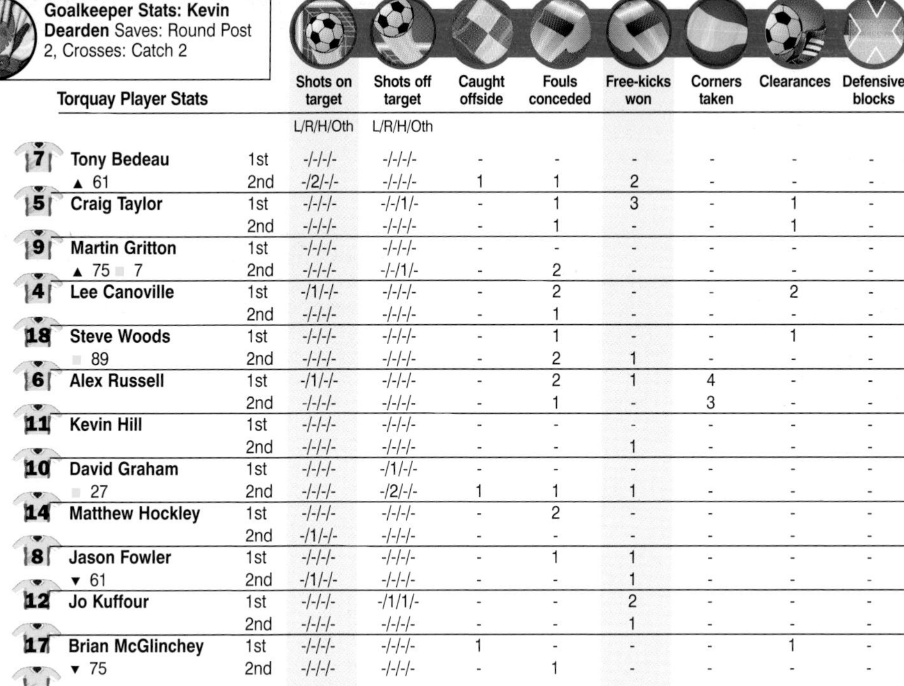

Torquay Player Stats		Shots on target L/R/H/Oth	Shots off target L/R/H/Oth	Caught offside	Fouls conceded	Free-kicks won	Corners taken	Clearances	Defensive blocks
7 Tony Bedeau	1st	-/-/-/-	-/-/-/-	-	-	-	-	-	-
▲ 61	2nd	-/2/-/-	-/-/-/-	1	1	2	-	-	-
5 Craig Taylor	1st	-/-/-/-	-/-/1/-	-	1	3	-	1	-
	2nd	-/-/-/-	-/-/-/-	-	1	-	-	1	-
9 Martin Gritton	1st	-/-/-/-	-/-/-/-	-	-	-	-	-	-
▲ 75 □ 7	2nd	-/-/-/-	-/-/1/-	-	2	-	-	-	-
4 Lee Canoville	1st	-/1/-/-	-/-/-/-	-	2	-	-	2	-
	2nd	-/-/-/-	-/-/-/-	-	1	-	-	-	-
18 Steve Woods	1st	-/-/-/-	-/-/-/-	-	1	-	-	1	-
□ 89	2nd	-/-/-/-	-/-/-/-	-	2	1	-	-	-
6 Alex Russell	1st	-/1/-/-	-/-/-/-	-	2	1	4	-	-
	2nd	-/-/-/-	-/-/-/-	-	1	-	3	-	-
11 Kevin Hill	1st	-/-/-/-	-/-/-/-	-	-	-	-	-	-
	2nd	-/-/-/-	-/-/-/-	-	-	1	-	-	-
10 David Graham	1st	-/-/-/-	-/1/-/-	-	-	-	-	-	-
□ 27	2nd	-/-/-/-	-/2/-/-	1	1	1	-	-	-
14 Matthew Hockley	1st	-/-/-/-	-/-/-/-	-	2	-	-	-	-
	2nd	-/1/-/-	-/-/-/-	-	-	-	-	-	-
8 Jason Fowler	1st	-/-/-/-	-/-/-/-	-	1	1	-	-	-
▼ 61	2nd	-/1/-/-	-/-/-/-	-	-	1	-	-	-
12 Jo Kuffour	1st	-/-/-/-	-/1/1/-	-	-	2	-	-	-
	2nd	-/-/-/-	-/-/-/-	-	-	1	-	-	-
17 Brian McGlinchey	1st	-/-/-/-	-/-/-/-	1	-	-	-	1	-
▼ 75	2nd	-/-/-/-	-/-/-/-	-	1	-	-	-	-

Subs not used: Van Heusden, Hazell, Woozley. - **Formation: 4-4-2**

Goalkeeper Stats: Phillip Senior Saves: Catch 4, Parry 4, Round Post 2, Crosses: Catch 6

	Player Stats	Shots on target	Shots off target	Caught offside	Fouls conceded	Free-kicks won	Corners taken	Clearances	Defensive blocks
16	Efetobore Sodje	-/-/-/-	-/-/1/-	1	-	1	-	1	-
23	Andy Booth ▼ 77	-/-/-/-	-/1/-/-	-	5	1	-	4	-
21	Andy Holdsworth	-/-/1/-	-/1/-/-	-	-	1	-	4	-
11	Danny Schofield	-/1/-/-	-/-/-/-	1	1	1	1	-	-
20	Nat Brown ▲ 77	-/-/-/-	-/-/-/-	-	2	1	-	-	-
15	Nathan Clarke	-/-/1/-	-/-/-/-	-	1	5	-	4	-
24	Anthony Lloyd	-/-/-/-	-/-/-/-	-	-	1	-	3	1
5	Steve Yates	-/1/-/-	-/-/-/-	-	2	2	-	1	-
27	David Mirfin ▲ 90	-/-/-/-	-/-/-/-	-	-	-	-	-	-
4	Lee Fowler ▼ 90 □ 25	-/-/-/-	-/-/-/-	-	2	2	-	1	-
8	Anthony Carss □ 8 ■ 85	-/-/-/-	-/-/-/-	-	1	3	5	1	-

Subs not used: Giles, Newby, Edwards. - **Formation: 5-4-1**

Torquay Played: 30 **Won** 14 **Drawn** 7 **Lost** 9 **For** 40 **Against** 31 **Pos** 7

Hull [0] 0 TORQUAY [1] 1

21st February

If doubts surfaced after the disheartening loss to Huddersfield the week before, Torquay did not show them in this great victory against the league leaders Hull City.

Substitute Martin Gritton's goal on the stroke of half-time earned United's first win on Humberside for 43 years. But it was the way in which this victory was achieved that was truly impressive.

Hull went into Saturday's game on a run of seven wins and a draw and showed good form. After soaking up a fair bit of early pressure, United strikers Jo Kuffour and David Graham started to stretch Hull's defence and it was only the brilliance of City goalkeeper Boaz Myhill that stopped United from scoring four times in the first 25 minutes.

Yet, whenever the Gulls made a mistake, Hull were ready to pounce. Kevin Dearden had to make a smart low save from Jon Walters' near-post header in the 34th minute and Walters hit the side-netting.

Then, in first-half stoppage time, Graham flicked on Russell's ball forward, Gritton dashed on to it, beat the advancing Myhill and tucked a cool shot home from six yards.

After the break, the home fans expected their side to press. Crosses poured in from all ranges and all angles. Time and again United's defenders repelled them. Centre-backs Steve Woods and Craig Taylor would not give an inch.

Even with their backs to the wall, United showed enough quality and ambition to hit Hull on the break. Taylor had a header cleared off the line and Graham hooked an overhead volley wide.

But it was backs-to-the-wall stuff for United. Elliott headed inches wide from a Ryan France cross. Taylor and Woods kept booming headers away.

The Gulls nearly got a second goal to ease their nerves. Gritton looked certain to score, but held his head in anguish after missing the target. It didn't matter, for not even four minutes of stoppage-time was enough for Hull to save themselves.

Result.......Result.......Result.

HULL ....(0) **0** **TORQUAY** ......(1) **1**
Gritton 45

Att 15,222
Referee: M Ryan

Stats......Stats.......Stats......Stats

HULL 1st	2nd	Total		Total	2nd	TORQUAY 1st
4	2	6	**Corners**	6	3	3
7	8	15	**Fouls**	15	9	6
0	3	3	**Yellow cards**	2	2	0
0	0	0	**Red cards**	0	0	0
0	0	0	**Caught Offside**	5	2	3
4	5	9	**Shots on target**	12	4	8
3	6	9	**Shots off target**	8	3	5
0	0	0	**Hit woodwork**	1	1	0
43	44	43%	**Possession**	57%	56	57

I thought Torquay shaded it. We came back at them in the second half but I was disappointed with some of our defending because it was indecisive.

Peter Taylor

OUR first-half performance won us the match. I am delighted with the way that we played and it is great to come here and win.

Leroy Rosenior

Other Div 3 Results

Boston Utd 2 York 0, Cambridge Utd 3 Bristol Rovers 1, Darlington 3 Yeovil 2, Kidderminster 2 Swansea 0, Leyton Orient 2 Southend 1, Macclesfield 1 Carlisle 1, Mansfield 1 Doncaster 2, Oxford Utd 1 Bury 1, Rochdale 0 Cheltenham 0, Scunthorpe 1 Northampton 0

Hull [0] 0 TORQUAY [1] 1

Goalkeeper Stats: Kevin Dearden Crosses: Catch 16

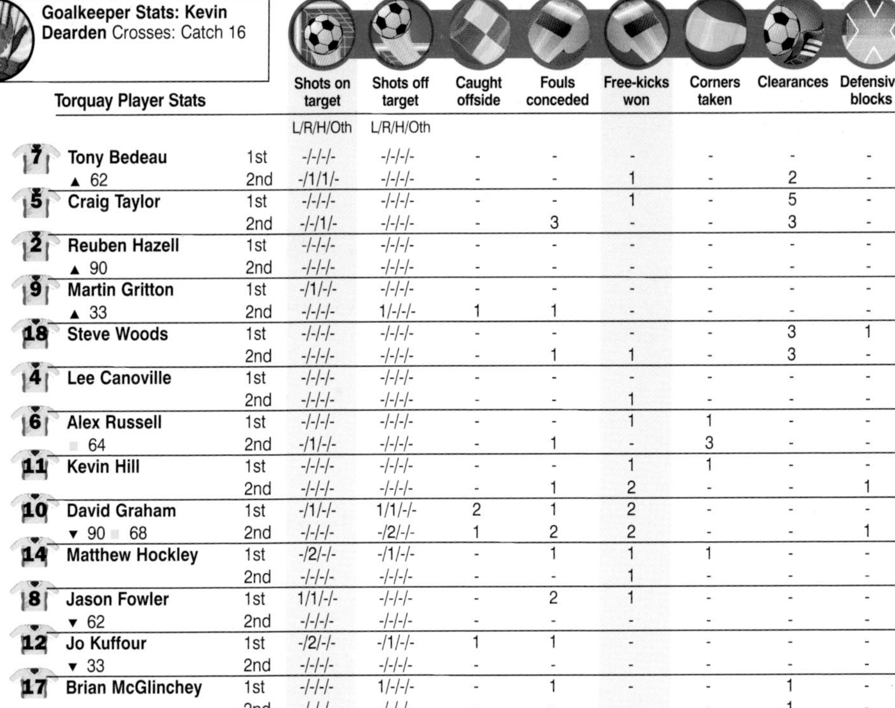

	#	Torquay Player Stats	Half	Shots on target L/R/H/Oth	Shots off target L/R/H/Oth	Caught offside	Fouls conceded	Free-kicks won	Corners taken	Clearances	Defensive blocks
7		Tony Bedeau	1st	-/-/-/-	-/-/-/-	-	-	-	-	-	-
		▲ 62	2nd	-/1/1/-	-/-/-/-	-	-	1	-	2	-
5		Craig Taylor	1st	-/-/-/-	-/-/-/-	-	-	1	-	5	-
			2nd	-/-/1/-	-/-/-/-	-	3	-	-	3	-
2		Reuben Hazell	1st	-/-/-/-	-/-/-/-	-	-	-	-	-	-
		▲ 90	2nd	-/-/-/-	-/-/-/-	-	-	-	-	-	-
9		Martin Gritton	1st	-/1/-/-	-/-/-/-	-	-	-	-	-	-
		▲ 33	2nd	-/-/-/-	1/-/-/-	1	1	-	-	-	-
18		Steve Woods	1st	-/-/-/-	-/-/-/-	-	-	-	-	3	1
			2nd	-/-/-/-	-/-/-/-	-	1	1	-	3	-
4		Lee Canoville	1st	-/-/-/-	-/-/-/-	-	-	-	-	-	-
			2nd	-/-/-/-	-/-/-/-	-	-	1	-	-	-
6		Alex Russell	1st	-/-/-/-	-/-/-/-	-	-	1	1	-	-
		■ 64	2nd	-/1/-/-	-/-/-/-	-	1	-	3	-	-
11		Kevin Hill	1st	-/-/-/-	-/-/-/-	-	-	1	1	-	-
			2nd	-/-/-/-	-/-/-/-	-	1	2	-	-	1
10		David Graham	1st	-/1/-/-	1/1/-/-	2	1	2	-	-	-
		▼ 90 ■ 68	2nd	-/-/-/-	-/2/-/-	1	2	2	-	-	1
14		Matthew Hockley	1st	-/2/-/-	-/1/-/-	-	1	1	1	-	-
			2nd	-/-/-/-	-/-/-/-	-	-	1	-	-	-
8		Jason Fowler	1st	1/1/-/-	-/-/-/-	-	2	1	-	-	-
		▼ 62	2nd	-/-/-/-	-/-/-/-	-	-	-	-	-	-
12		Jo Kuffour	1st	-/2/-/-	-/1/-/-	1	1	-	-	-	-
		▼ 33	2nd	-/-/-/-	-/-/-/-	-	-	-	-	-	-
17		Brian McGlinchey	1st	-/-/-/-	1/-/-/-	-	1	-	-	1	-
			2nd	-/-/-/-	-/-/-/-	-	-	-	-	1	-

Subs not used: Van Heusden, Woozley. - **Formation: 4-4-2**

Goalkeeper Stats: Boaz Myhill Saves: Tip Over 4, Parry 4, Crosses: Catch 8

#	Player Stats	Shots on target	Shots off target	Caught offside	Fouls conceded	Free-kicks won	Corners taken	Clearances	Defensive blocks
7	Stuart Elliott	-/1/2/-	1/1/2/-	-	1	1	-	1	-
16	Damien Delaney ■ 75	-/-/1/-	-/-/-/-	-	1	-	-	-	1
9	Ben Burgess ▼ 71	-/-/-/-	1/1/1/-	-	3	5	-	-	-
8	Jamie Forrester ▲ 71	-/-/-/-	-/-/-/-	-	-	-	-	-	-
28	Richard Hinds ▼ 66	-/1/-/-	-/-/-/-	-	1	-	-	2	-
14	Stuart Green	-/2/-/-	-/-/-/-	-	-	-	6	1	-
21	Nathan Peat ▲ 66	-/-/-/-	-/-/-/-	-	-	-	-	-	-
11	Jonathan Walters	-/-/1/-	-/1/-/-	-	1	3	-	2	-
24	Andrew Holt ▼ 66 ■ 48	-/-/-/-	-/-/-/-	-	2	2	-	-	1
29	Ryan France ▲ 66	-/-/1/-	-/-/-/-	-	2	1	-	-	-
20	Lee Marshall ■ 86	-/-/-/-	-/-/-/-	-	1	-	-	3	1
6	Marc Joseph	-/-/-/-	-/-/1/-	-	-	1	-	1	1
2	Alton Thelwell	-/-/-/-	-/-/-/-	-	3	2	-	2	-

Subs not used: Musselwhite, Melton. - **Formation: 4-4-2**

Torquay Played: 31 **Won** 15 **Drawn** 7 **Lost** 9 **For** 41 **Against** 31 **Pos** 7

Torquay [1] 1 SCUNTHORPE [0] 0

24th February

Digging deep into their reserves of resilience, discipline and sheer bloody-mindedness, Torquay United gradually squeezed the life out of bogey team Scunthorpe United to clinch their sixth win in seven games.

Midfielder Matt Hockley's first-half header, finishing a six-man move, was enough to earn three more precious points. But just as important in pushing United ever higher in the promotion race was another no-quarter-given display by their defence.

Overall, the display might not always have been pretty but it was mighty effective.

After soaking up some early pressure, United hit Scunthorpe on the break. Woods, Martin Gritton, Jason Fowler and Taylor were all involved down the right, finally releasing Canoville for a cross to the near-post.

Hockley gambled, threw himself at the ball and looped a header over the stranded Tommy Evans and under the bar from ten yards. Then on the half-hour Graham produced a lovely turn to beat his man 35 yards out and let fly with a crisp volley which was held well by Evans.

There had been many times in the past when United were unable to hold on to slender leads, but they were in no mood to give this one up in the second half.

On the hour Gritton put Bedeau away on the right, he pulled back a low near-post cross and Graham nipped in to hit the post from a tight angle. Five minutes later Alex Russell pulled a top-class save from Evans with a 25-yard volley which was destined for the bottom left-hand corner.

But the decisive stuff was happening in United's half of the pitch, where the defence would let nothing pass. Scunthorpe were unable to test Dearden until the 92nd minute, and even that was a speculative effort, Dearden arching back to tip Taylor's cross-shot for a corner.

Result.......Result.......Result.

TORQUAY ....(1) **1** **SCUNTHORPE**(0) **0**
Hockley 13

Att 2,561
Referee: S Tomlin

Stats......Stats.......Stats......Stats

TORQUAY				SCUNTHORPE		
1st	**2nd**	**Total**		**Total**	**2nd**	**1st**
2	2	4	**Corners**	7	2	5
8	8	16	**Fouls**	18	11	7
0	0	0	**Yellow cards**	2	2	0
0	0	0	**Red cards**	0	0	0
1	3	4	**Caught Offside**	3	1	2
2	3	5	**Shots on target**	1	0	1
1	2	3	**Shots off target**	3	1	2
0	1	1	**Hit woodwork**	0	0	0
46	51	49%	**Possession**	51%	49	54

I know we can play and so does everybody else, but we've come off with cuts and bruises and we had to go right to the edge.

Leroy Rosenior

IN the second half our midfield was very, very poor and I thought that Torquay were better than us all the way across the park.

Brian Laws

Other Div 3 Results

Bury 1 Southend 1, Swansea 2 Leyton Orient 1

TORQUAY [1] 1 Scunthorpe [0] 0

Goalkeeper Stats: Kevin Dearden Crosses: Catch 2, Parry 1

Torquay Player Stats

No.	Player	Half	Shots on target L/R/H/Oth	Shots off target L/R/H/Oth	Caught offside	Fouls conceded	Free-kicks won	Corners taken	Clearances	Defensive blocks
7	Tony Bedeau	1st	-/-/-/-	-/-/-/-	-	-	1	-	1	-
	▲ 42	2nd	-/-/-/-	-/-/-/-	1	1	1	-	-	-
5	Craig Taylor	1st	-/-/-/-	-/-/-/-	-	-	2	-	3	1
		2nd	-/-/-/-	-/-/-/-	-	1	-	-	-	-
3	David Woozley	1st	-/-/-/-	-/-/-/-	-	-	-	-	-	-
	▲ 87	2nd	-/-/-/-	-/-/-/-	1	-	-	-	-	-
9	Martin Gritton	1st	-/-/-/-	-/-/-/-	-	1	-	-	-	-
	▼ 73	2nd	-/-/-/-	-/-/-/-	-	-	-	-	-	-
18	Steve Woods	1st	-/-/-/-	-/-/-/-	-	2	-	-	-	-
		2nd	-/-/-/-	-/-/-/-	-	-	1	-	2	-
4	Lee Canoville	1st	-/-/-/-	-/-/-/-	-	1	-	-	1	-
		2nd	-/-/-/-	-/-/-/-	-	-	1	-	1	-
6	Alex Russell	1st	-/-/-/-	-/-/-/-	-	-	1	2	1	-
		2nd	-/1/-/-	-/-/-/-	-	-	3	2	1	-
11	Kevin Hill	1st	-/-/-/-	-/-/-/-	-	-	-	-	1	-
		2nd	-/-/-/-	-/-/-/-	-	-	1	-	-	-
15	Kevin Wills	1st	-/-/-/-	-/-/-/-	-	-	-	-	-	-
	▲ 73	2nd	-/-/-/-	-/-/-/-	-	3	2	-	-	-
10	David Graham	1st	-/1/-/-	1/-/-/-	1	2	-	-	-	-
	▼ 87	2nd	-/1/-/-	-/2/-/-	1	2	1	-	-	-
14	Matthew Hockley	1st	-/-/1/-	-/-/-/-	-	1	1	-	-	-
		2nd	-/1/-/-	-/-/-/-	-	1	1	-	-	-
8	Jason Fowler	1st	-/-/-/-	-/-/-/-	-	1	1	-	1	-
	▼ 42	2nd	-/-/-/-	-/-/-/-	-	-	-	-	-	-
17	Brian McGlinchey	1st	-/-/-/-	-/-/-/-	-	-	-	-	-	-
		2nd	-/-/-/-	-/-/-/-	-	-	-	-	-	-

Subs not used: Van Heusden, Hazell. - **Formation: 4-4-2**

Goalkeeper Stats: Tom Evans Saves: Catch 1, Round Post 1, Parry 1, Crosses: Catch 3

No.	Player Stats	Shots on target	Shots off target	Caught offside	Fouls conceded	Free-kicks won	Corners taken	Clearances	Defensive blocks
17	Andy Parton ▲ 68	-/-/-/-	-/-/-/-	-	1	-	-	-	-
2	Nathan Stanton ▲ 68	-/-/-/-	-/-/-/-	-	-	1	-	-	-
6	Cliff Byrne	-/-/-/-	-/-/-/-	-	1	1	-	4	-
22	Steven MacLean	-/1/-/-	-/1/-/-	-	5	1	4	-	-
7	Matthew Sparrow	-/-/-/-	-/-/-/-	-	1	1	-	-	-
27	Cleveland Taylor	-/-/-/-	-/1/-/-	1	-	-	-	-	-
16	Terry Barwick ▼ 81 ■ 77	-/-/-/-	-/-/-/-	1	4	-	-	1	-
10	Steve Torpey	-/-/-/-	-/-/-/-	1	1	2	-	-	-
18	Andy Butler	-/-/-/-	-/-/-/-	-	2	4	-	-	-
3	Kevin Sharp ▼ 68	-/-/-/-	-/-/-/-	-	-	3	2	-	-
8	Wayne Graves ▼ 68	-/-/-/-	-/1/-/-	-	-	1	-	2	-
4	Jamie McCombe ▲ 81	-/-/-/-	-/-/-/-	-	1	-	-	-	-
12	Lee Ridley ■ 80	-/-/-/-	-/-/-/-	-	2	1	1	-	-

Subs not used: Hayes, Capp. - **Formation: 4-4-2**

Torquay Played: 32 **Won** 16 **Drawn** 7 **Lost** 9 **For** 42 **Against** 31 **Pos** 6

Torquay [1] 2 BOSTON UTD [0] 0

28th February

Torquay United completed a smashing seven-week spell by disposing of lowly Boston United at Plainmoor. It meant that since their 0-2 defeat at Rochdale on January 3, United had won seven out of eight games.

The breakthrough came in the 27th minute. Hockley produced a great covering-back tackle to deny Jermaine Brown just outside his own area, and within a split-second Russell was on the ball and spotted Graham on a run.

There is nobody in the division better at finding the target from long-range, and one sumptuous 40-yard pass later Graham was clear for a steadying touch and an angled right-foot volley from 12 yards which was too sweet and too strong for Paul Bastock to save. It was a top-class strike for Graham's 15th goal of the season.

Boston had scored only eight goals in 17 away games this season, and it wasn't hard to see why. They played with just one man, veteran targetman Graeme Jones, up front and seldom troubled a solid United defence .

And as United went hunting for the second goal, the Pilgrims found themselves hanging on ever more desperately. Kuffour and Russell combined to rob Bennett in possession in the 51st minute, setting up Graham for a shot which shaved the outside of the right-hand post.

The clincher came in the 57th minute. From a free-kick nearly 30 yards out, Taylor had a low shot parried by Bastock. Bedeau was on to the rebound quickly, placing himself between the ball and defender Ben Chapman, Chapman scythed him down and referee Richard Beeby's decision was hardly a difficult one.

Up stepped Woods to sidefoot a firm shot to Bastock's left. The keeper got his fingtertips to the ball, but could not keep it out.

Near the end Woods and Kuffour were both unlucky not to score a third goal as the Gulls concentrated on giving little away at the back and catching Boston on the break.

Result.......Result.......Result.

TORQUAY ....(1) **2** **BOSTON UTD** (0) **0**
Graham 27
Woods 57(p)

Att 3,000
Referee: R Beeby

Stats......Stats.......Stats......Stats

TORQUAY				BOSTON UTD		
1st	**2nd**	**Total**		**Total**	**2nd**	**1st**
3	2	5	**Corners**	5	4	1
6	11	17	**Fouls**	12	7	5
0	0	0	**Yellow cards**	0	0	0
0	0	0	**Red cards**	0	0	0
0	0	0	**Caught Offside**	4	0	4
5	4	9	**Shots on target**	3	2	1
4	5	9	**Shots off target**	8	5	3
0	0	0	**Hit woodwork**	0	0	0
48	51	49%	**Possession**	51%	49	52

THE performance was solid and we showed bits of quality when we needed to. I don't think Boston had many shots and we should have scored more.

Leroy Rosenior

TORQUAY were far better than us. We weren't pulling up any trees before I took over and we aren't pulling up trees at the moment.

Jim Rodwell

Other Div 3 Results

Bristol Rovers 1 Oxford Utd 1, Bury 1 Darlington 1, Carlisle P Huddersfield P, Cheltenham 4 Mansfield 2, Northampton 1 Leyton Orient 0, Southend 1 Macclesfield 0, Swansea P Rochdale P, Yeovil 4 Cambridge Utd 1, York P Scunthorpe P

TORQUAY [1] 2 Boston Utd [0] 0

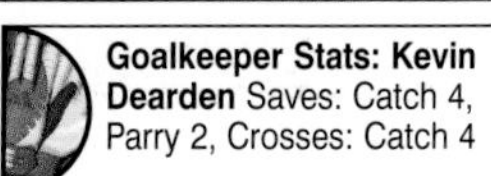

Goalkeeper Stats: Kevin Dearden Saves: Catch 4, Parry 2, Crosses: Catch 4

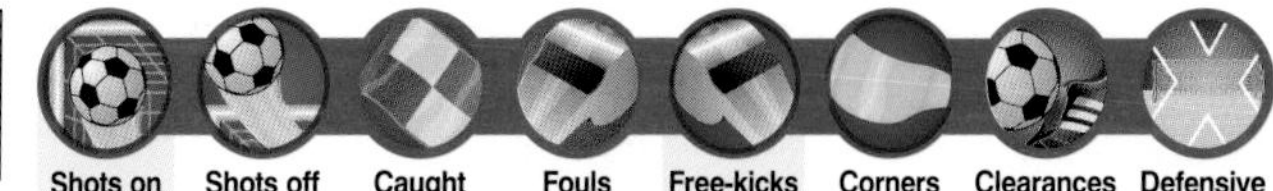

#	Torquay Player Stats		Half	Shots on target L/R/H/Oth	Shots off target L/R/H/Oth	Caught offside	Fouls conceded	Free-kicks won	Corners taken	Clearances	Defensive blocks
7	Tony Bedeau		1st	2/-/-/-	-/1/-/-	-	-	2	-	-	-
			2nd	-/-/-/-	-/-/-/-	-	-	3	-	2	-
5	Craig Taylor		1st	-/-/-/-	-/-/-/-	-	1	-	-	-	-
			2nd	-/-/-/-	-/-/-/-	-	3	-	-	-	-
2	Reuben Hazell		1st	-/-/-/-	-/-/-/-	-	-	-	-	-	-
		▲ 76	2nd	-/-/-/-	-/-/-/-	-	-	-	-	-	-
9	Martin Gritton		1st	-/-/-/-	-/-/-/-	-	-	-	-	-	-
		▲ 79	2nd	-/-/-/-	-/-/-/-	-	-	1	-	1	-
4	Lee Canoville		1st	-/-/-/-	-/-/-/-	-	1	-	-	2	-
		▼ 76	2nd	-/-/-/-	-/-/-/-	-	1	-	-	-	-
18	Steve Woods		1st	-/-/-/-	-/-/-/-	-	1	1	-	-	-
			2nd	-/-/-/-	-/-/1/-	-	2	1	-	-	-
6	Alex Russell		1st	-/-/-/-	-/1/-/-	-	-	1	3	-	-
		▼ 90	2nd	-/-/-/-	-/-/-/-	-	1	-	2	-	-
11	Kevin Hill		1st	1/1/-/-	-/-/-/-	-	2	-	-	-	-
			2nd	-/-/-/-	-/-/-/-	-	-	1	-	1	-
29	Joe Broad		1st	-/-/-/-	-/-/-/-	-	-	-	-	-	-
		▲ 90	2nd	-/-/-/-	-/-/-/-	-	-	-	-	-	-
10	David Graham		1st	-/1/-/-	-/1/1/-	-	1	-	-	-	-
		▼ 79	2nd	2/1/-/-	-/2/-/-	-	-	-	-	-	-
14	Matthew Hockley		1st	-/-/-/-	-/-/-/-	-	-	-	-	-	-
			2nd	-/-/-/-	-/-/-/-	-	2	-	-	-	-
12	Jo Kuffour		1st	-/-/-/-	-/-/-/-	-	-	1	-	-	-
			2nd	-/-/-/-	-/2/-/-	-	-	1	-	-	-
17	Brian McGlinchey		1st	-/-/-/-	-/-/-/-	-	-	-	-	-	-
			2nd	-/-/-/-	-/-/-/-	-	2	-	-	-	-

Subs not used: Van Heusden, Woozley. - **Formation: 4-4-2**

Goalkeeper Stats: Paul Bastock Saves: Catch 6, Parry 2, Crosses: Catch 8

#	Player Stats	Shots on target	Shots off target	Caught offside	Fouls conceded	Free-kicks won	Corners taken	Clearances	Defensive blocks
7	Tom Bennett	-/-/-/-	-/-/-/-	-	-	-	1	3	-
8	Graeme Jones ▼ 58	-/-/-/-	-/-/1/-	2	2	1	-	-	-
20	Lee Beevers	-/-/-/-	-/-/-/-	-	1	-	-	3	-
17	Stuart Douglas ▲ 58	-/-/-/-	-/1/-/-	-	1	5	-	-	-
11	Mark Angel ▲ 45	1/1/-/-	-/-/1/-	-	2	3	4	-	-
9	Peter Duffield	-/1/-/-	-/-/-/-	1	-	1	-	-	-
23	Jermaine Brown	-/-/-/-	1/-/-/-	1	1	1	-	-	-
5	Stuart Balmer	-/-/-/-	-/-/-/-	-	-	-	-	3	1
27	David Noble	-/-/-/-	-/3/-/-	-	1	3	-	-	-
3	Ben Chapman	-/-/-/-	-/-/-/-	-	2	1	-	-	-
4	Paul Ellender ▼ 45	-/-/-/-	-/-/-/-	-	1	-	-	1	1
18	Lee Thompson	-/-/-/-	-/1/-/-	-	1	1	-	-	-

Subs not used: Croudson, Rodwell, Clarke. - **Formation: 4-3-3**

Torquay Played: 33 **Won** 17 **Drawn** 7 **Lost** 9 **For** 44 **Against** 31 **Pos** 4

...February Team Stats.....Team Stats......Team Stats......Team S

League table at the end of February

	HOME						AWAY					
	P	W	D	L	F	A	W	D	L	F	A	Pts	Df
Doncaster	33	13	2	2	36	9	8	3	5	27	20	68	34
Hull	33	12	3	2	39	17	6	6	4	21	14	63	29
Oxford Utd	33	12	4	0	29	10	4	9	4	18	17	61	20
Torquay	**33**	**11**	**4**	**2**	**30**	**14**	**6**	**3**	**7**	**14**	**17**	**58**	**13**
Mansfield	32	10	2	3	33	16	7	3	7	25	26	56	16
Yeovil	33	12	1	4	32	14	6	1	9	18	24	56	12
Huddersfield	32	11	3	2	26	11	5	5	6	21	29	56	7
Lincoln City	33	7	8	2	24	14	7	4	5	21	17	54	14
Northampton	33	10	2	5	20	16	4	4	8	14	22	48	-4
Swansea	31	8	5	3	27	15	4	4	7	14	23	45	3
Leyton Orient	33	8	5	3	23	17	4	3	10	16	28	44	-6
Cheltenham	33	9	3	5	28	27	2	7	7	14	26	43	-11
Bury	34	7	5	5	20	21	4	2	11	18	28	40	-11
York	33	7	4	5	18	17	3	6	8	11	25	40	-13
Scunthorpe	32	5	8	3	27	18	3	6	7	20	26	38	3
Bristol Rovers	33	6	5	6	17	19	4	3	9	18	25	38	-9
Cambridge U	33	3	6	7	19	26	6	5	6	21	24	38	-10
Boston Utd	32	7	6	2	26	13	2	3	12	8	27	36	-6
Southend	33	6	2	9	16	18	4	4	8	14	26	36	-14
Rochdale	32	5	5	6	20	19	4	3	9	16	23	35	-6
Darlington	34	7	3	7	20	20	2	5	10	17	27	35	-10
Kidderminster	33	5	4	7	16	20	4	4	9	12	26	35	-18
Macclesfield	33	5	7	4	22	17	2	4	11	18	35	32	-12
Carlisle	32	5	3	8	16	21	1	3	12	13	29	24	-21

February matches table

	P	W	D	L	F	A	Pts
Northampton	6	5	0	1	10	3	15
Torquay	**5**	**4**	**0**	**1**	**6**	**2**	**12**
Cheltenham	5	3	2	0	7	3	11
Doncaster	4	3	1	0	10	3	10
Darlington	5	3	1	1	10	5	10
Southend	5	3	1	1	7	3	10
Yeovil	5	3	0	2	8	6	9
Lincoln City	5	2	2	1	9	5	8
Huddersfield	4	2	1	1	4	4	7
Carlisle	4	1	3	0	6	5	6
Bury	5	1	3	1	5	5	6
Leyton Orient	4	2	0	2	4	4	6
Scunthorpe	5	1	2	2	6	7	5
Oxford Utd	5	1	2	2	5	6	5
Boston Utd	5	1	2	2	4	5	5
Cambridge Utd	5	1	1	3	6	9	4
Rochdale	3	1	1	1	4	3	4
Swansea	4	1	1	2	4	6	4
Hull	4	1	1	2	3	5	4
Kidderminster	5	1	1	3	2	9	4
Mansfield	4	1	0	3	5	10	3
Bristol Rovers	5	0	2	3	3	10	2
Macclesfield	4	0	1	3	2	5	1
York	4	0	0	4	3	10	0

February team stats details

Club Name	Ply	Shots On	Shots Off	Corners	Hit W'work	Caught Offside	Offside Trap	Fouls	Yellow Cards	Red Cards	Pens Awarded	Pens Con
Boston Utd	5	20	31	26	0	21	10	70	12	0	- (-)	1
Bristol Rovers	5	26	26	31	1	20	20	67	5	0	- (-)	-
Bury	5	29	15	20	0	14	13	55	5	1	1 (-)	-
Cambridge U	5	41	20	37	2	15	17	70	4	0	- (-)	1
Carlisle	4	38	21	28	2	13	13	46	6	0	- (-)	-
Cheltenham	5	34	23	21	0	12	22	64	3	0	- (-)	-
Darlington	5	26	26	30	1	29	9	67	6	2	1 (1)	1
Doncaster	4	38	26	33	2	12	23	46	6	1	2 (1)	2
Huddersfield	4	19	20	19	1	14	10	45	5	1	- (-)	-
Hull	4	31	22	17	3	4	18	52	8	0	- (-)	-
Kidderminster	5	23	27	28	0	14	15	67	9	1	1 (-)	2
Leyton Orient	4	13	27	21	4	17	18	62	10	0	1 (-)	-
Lincoln City	5	36	18	42	1	14	23	70	7	0	1 (1)	1
Macclesfield	4	21	18	19	0	11	7	29	4	0	- (-)	1
Mansfield	4	26	15	31	0	18	13	49	9	0	1 (1)	1
Northampton	6	44	34	43	2	14	43	90	5	1	1 (1)	1
Oxford Utd	5	16	22	27	0	15	12	60	3	0	- (-)	-
Rochdale	3	21	11	21	0	18	8	34	6	1	1 (1)	-
Scunthorpe	5	22	22	33	1	22	18	78	10	0	- (-)	-
Southend	5	32	41	23	1	24	11	52	6	0	2 (2)	2
Swansea	4	23	25	33	0	11	20	27	2	0	- (-)	-
Torquay	**5**	**36**	**31**	**29**	**3**	**18**	**11**	**73**	**7**	**0**	**1 (1)**	**-**
Yeovil	5	33	31	32	2	18	15	67	4	1	1 (1)	1
York	4	15	17	12	0	12	11	42	2	1	- (-)	-

 Monthly Match Details: Games 55 **Home Wins** 30 **Away Wins** 11 **Draws** 14

FEBRUARY STATS

...February Player Stats..... Player Stats...... Player Stats......Pla

Monthly Top scorers

Gregg Blundell (Doncaster)	5
Barry Conlon (Darlington)	4
Lawrie Dudfield (Southend)	3
Paul Simpson (Carlisle)	3
Peter Gain (Lincoln City)	3
Steve Torpey (Scunthorpe)	3
Gareth Seddon (Bury)	3
David Bridges (Cambridge Utd)	2
David Graham (Torquay)	2
Neil Wainwright (Darlington)	2

Penalties scored

2 L Constantine (Southend), **1** Ian Clark (Darlington), G Williams (Yeovil), M McIndoe (Doncaster)

Assists

Martin Devaney (Cheltenham)	3
Fred Murray (Cambridge Utd)	2
Lee Johnson (Yeovil)	2
Simon Bryant (Bristol Rovers)	2
Michael McIndoe (Doncaster)	2
Andy Booth (Huddersfield)	2
Liam Lawrence (Mansfield)	2

Quickest goals

1:01 mins - Gareth Seddon (Bury vs Cambridge Utd)

4:25 mins - Mark Albrighton (Doncaster vs Kidderminster)

5:05 mins - Neil Redfearn (Lincoln City vs Boston Utd)

6:24 mins - Paul Simpson (Cambridge Utd vs Carlisle)

9:22 mins - Steve Torpey (Scunthorpe vs Doncaster)

Top Keeper

	Mins	Gls
Kevin Dearden (Torquay)	476	2
Lee Harper (Northampton)	567	3
Darryl Flahavan (Southend)	486	3
Shane Higgs (Cheltenham)	473	3
A Warrington (Doncaster)	384	3
Alan Marriott (Lincoln City)	483	5
Glenn Morris (Leyton O)	385	4
Ryan Clarke (Bristol R)	96	1

Shots on target

Martin Smith (Northampton)	11
Paul Simpson (Carlisle)	11
Luke Guttridge (Cambridge Utd)	9
Stuart Elliott (Hull)	9
Lawrie Dudfield (Southend)	9
David Graham (Torquay)	9
Gregg Blundell (Doncaster)	8
Barry Conlon (Darlington)	8
Leon Constantine (Southend)	8
Simon Yeo (Lincoln City)	7

Shots off target

David Graham (Torquay)	14
Neil Redfearn (Boston Utd)	9
Adam Murray (Kidderminster)	9
Leon Constantine (Southend)	8
Lawrie Dudfield (Southend)	8
Marc Richards (Northampton)	8
Stuart Elliott (Hull)	8
Kevin Gall (Yeovil)	8
Martin Smith (Northampton)	7
Gavin Williams (Yeovil)	7

Caught offside

Barry Conlon (Darlington)	15
Lawrie Dudfield (Southend)	12
Junior Agogo (Bristol Rovers)	11
Neil Teggart (Darlington)	11
Matt Fryatt (Carlisle)	10
Graeme Jones (Boston Utd)	9
Iyseden Christie (Mansfield)	9
Kevin Townson (Rochdale)	9
David Graham (Torquay)	8

Free-kicks won

Junior Agogo (Bristol Rovers)	16
Steve Torpey (Scunthorpe)	15
Gavin Williams (Yeovil)	12
Tony Bedeau (Torquay)	12
Ashley Nicholls (Darlington)	12
Martin Smith (Northampton)	12
Paul Reid (Northampton)	11
Chris Brass (York)	11
Andy Butler (Scunthorpe)	11

David Graham (v Boston)

Fouls conceded

Marc Richards (Northampton)	23
Daniel Webb (Cambridge Utd)	17
Barry Conlon (Darlington)	16
Ian Sampson (Northampton)	14
Paul Ellender (Boston Utd)	13
Ben Burgess (Hull)	13
Graeme Jones (Boston Utd)	12
Marcus Richardson (Lincoln City)	11
Mark Greaves (Boston Utd)	11

Fouls without a card

Daniel Webb (Cambridge Utd)	17
Barry Conlon (Darlington)	16
Paul Ellender (Boston Utd)	13
Ben Burgess (Hull)	13
Adam Lockwood (Yeovil)	11
Andy Booth (Huddersfield)	10
Andy Butler (Scunthorpe)	10
Chris Willmott (Northampton)	10
Mark Bailey (Lincoln City)	9

Lee Canoville takes the ball past two Huddersfield defenders.
Torquay v Huddersfield
HPL01359_TNA_005

Steve Woods celebrates his penalty goal with David Graham, Jo Kuffour and Kevin Hill.
Torquay v Boston
HPL01397_TNA_071

Brian McGlinchey gets in a saving tackle in the first half.
Torquay v Huddersfield
HPL01360_TNA_066

Jo Kuffour takes it on the chest.
Torquay v Boston
HPL01397_TNA_021

Torquay [2] 4 CARLISLE [0] 1

6th March

Carlisle, who had given themselves a sniff of safety with only two defeats in 12 games, did precious little wrong for the first 20 minutes in this game, but still found themselves 2-0 down.

Veteran striker Andy Preece is a great pro, but there's a saying about forwards' marking in their own penalty-areas, and so it proved after only four minutes.

Preece was supposed to pick up Hill on Alex Russell's left-wing corner, but he only half did the job, Hill soared above him and nodded Russell's flag-kick down and inside the near-post.

Carlisle must still have fancied themselves when, following a Russell free-kick in the 20th minute, Lee Andrews half-cleared the ball. It broke out to Hill, who unleashed a dipping 22-yard volley which beat keeper Matt Glennon all ends up.

Without showing anywhere near the mental alertness and physical bite of their recent run, United did start to pick up towards half-time, Jo Kuffour going close with a lovely bit of skill.

Then Graham produced a show-stopper in the 52nd minute. Cutting in from the right on Hockley's through ball and under pressure from a recovering defender, he suddenly unleashed an angled right-foot shot from 15 yards which Glennon never even sniffed.

Eleven minutes later, Graham got goalside of Carlisle defender Kevin Gray, who fouled him from behind. Referee Paul Taylor pointed straight to the spot. Up stepped Steve Woods but he blasted the penalty onto the post and out.

After that, Carlisle began to fight their way back into the game and Dearden had to make several saves, highlighted by an acrobatic tip-over from a Craig Farrell header.

Carlisle deserved something out of the match and the Cumbrians duly grabbed a consolation goal in the 73rd minute. Preece hooked the ball into the goalmouth from the left and it eventually reached McGill to volley home from eight yards at the far post.

Result.......Result.......Result.

TORQUAY ....(2) **4** **CARLISLE** ......(0) **1**
Hill 4, 21 McGill 73
Graham 52
Woods 63(p)

Att 3,366
Referee: P Taylor

Stats......Stats.......Stats......Stats

TORQUAY						CARLISLE
1st	2nd	Total		Total	2nd	1st
2	1	3	Corners	3	1	2
6	2	8	Fouls	8	2	6
0	2	2	Yellow cards	3	2	1
0	0	0	Red cards	0	0	0
3	0	3	Caught Offside	2	0	2
6	4	10	Shots on target	9	2	7
1	1	2	Shots off target	2	0	2
0	0	0	Hit woodwork	0	0	0
43	49	44%	Possession	56%	51	57

"I thought Carlisle played really well and did not deserve the difference in the scoreline between the sides, but our finishing was outstanding."

Leroy Rosenior

"**WE** were poor and we have let ourselves, the club and the supporters down. At one stage it looked as if we might lose by five or six."

Paul Simpson

Other Div 3 Results

Boston Utd 2 Rochdale 0, Bristol Rovers 1 Southend 1, Bury 1 Leyton Orient 1, Cambridge Utd 0 Northampton 1, Kidderminster 4 York 1, Macclesfield 0 Darlington 1, Mansfield 1 Hull 0, Oxford Utd 0 Huddersfield 1, Scunthorpe 3 Yeovil 0

6th March

TORQUAY [2] 4 Carlisle [0] 1

Goalkeeper Stats: Kevin Dearden Saves: Catch 8, Parry 2, Crosses: Catch 4

Torquay Player Stats

No.	Player	Half	Shots on target L/R/H/Oth	Shots off target L/R/H/Oth	Caught offside	Fouls conceded	Free-kicks won	Corners taken	Clearances	Defensive blocks
7	**Tony Bedeau**	1st	-/-/-/-	-/-/-/-	-	2	-	-	-	-
		2nd	-/-/1/-	-/-/-/-	-	-	1	-	1	-
3	**David Woozley**	1st	-/-/-/-	-/-/-/-	-	-	-	-	-	-
	▲ 89	2nd	-/-/-/-	-/-/-/-	-	-	-	-	-	-
5	**Craig Taylor**	1st	-/-/-/-	1/-/-/-	-	1	-	-	2	-
	▼ 89 ■ 73	2nd	-/-/-/-	-/-/-/-	-	-	-	-	-	-
9	**Martin Gritton**	1st	-/-/-/-	-/-/-/-	-	-	-	-	-	-
	▲ 64	2nd	-/-/-/-	-/-/-/-	-	-	-	-	-	-
4	**Lee Canoville**	1st	-/-/-/-	-/-/-/-	-	-	-	-	-	-
	■ 90	2nd	-/-/-/-	-/-/-/-	-	-	-	-	-	-
18	**Steve Woods**	1st	-/-/-/-	-/-/-/-	-	3	-	-	-	1
		2nd	-/-/-/-	-/-/-/-	-	-	-	-	1	-
6	**Alex Russell**	1st	-/-/-/-	-/-/-/-	-	-	2	2	-	-
		2nd	-/-/-/-	-/-/-/-	-	1	-	4	1	-
29	**Joe Broad**	1st	-/-/-/-	-/-/-/-	-	-	-	-	-	-
	▲ 83	2nd	-/-/-/-	-/-/-/-	-	-	-	-	-	-
11	**Kevin Hill**	1st	1/-/1/-	-/-/-/-	-	-	-	-	1	-
	▼ 83	2nd	-/-/-/-	-/-/-/-	-	-	-	-	-	-
10	**David Graham**	1st	-/1/1/-	-/-/-/-	1	-	1	-	-	-
		2nd	-/1/-/-	-/-/-/-	-	1	1	-	-	-
14	**Matthew Hockley**	1st	-/-/-/-	-/-/-/-	-	-	-	-	1	-
		2nd	-/1/-/-	-/1/-/-	-	-	-	-	-	-
12	**Jo Kuffour**	1st	-/1/1/-	-/-/-/-	2	-	3	-	-	-
	▼ 64	2nd	-/-/-/-	-/-/-/-	-	-	-	-	-	-
17	**Brian McGlinchey**	1st	-/-/-/-	-/-/-/-	-	-	-	-	1	-
		2nd	-/-/-/-	-/-/-/-	-	-	-	-	-	-

Subs not used: Van Heusden, Hazell. - **Formation: 4-4-2**

Goalkeeper Stats: Matthew Glennon Saves: Catch 2, Parry 2, Crosses: Catch 6

No.	Player Stats	Shots on target	Shots off target	Caught offside	Fouls conceded	Free-kicks won	Corners taken	Clearances	Defensive blocks
14	**Kevin Gray**	-/-/-/-	-/-/1/-	-	2	-	-	-	-
31	**Andy Preece** ▼ 80 ■ 28	1/-/-/-	-/-/-/-	2	-	2	-	-	-
5	**Brian Shelley**	-/-/-/-	-/-/-/-	-	-	-	-	2	-
20	**Brendan McGill** ■ 73	1/2/-/-	-/-/-/-	-	-	-	1	-	-
18	**Kelvin Langmead** ▲ 54	-/-/-/-	-/-/-/-	-	-	-	-	-	-
7	**Peter Murphy**	-/-/1/-	-/-/-/-	-	1	1	-	1	-
8	**Chris Billy** ▼ 54	-/-/-/-	-/-/-/-	-	2	-	-	1	-
3	**Tom Cowan** ■ 90	1/-/-/-	-/-/-/-	-	1	2	-	1	-
12	**Lee Andrews**	-/-/-/-	-/-/-/-	-	1	-	-	-	-
26	**Paul Simpson**	3/-/-/-	-/1/-/-	-	-	1	5	-	-
11	**Adam Rundle** ▲ 80	-/-/-/-	-/-/-/-	-	-	-	-	-	-
19	**Craig Farrell**	-/-/-/-	-/-/-/-	-	1	2	-	-	-

Subs not used: McDonagh, Keen, Jack. - **Formation: 4-4-2**

Torquay Played: 34 **Won** 18 **Drawn** 7 **Lost** 9 **For** 48 **Against** 32 **Pos** 5

York [0] 0 TORQUAY [0] 0

13th March

Torquay United's increasingly miserly defence ensured that they emerged with a point from this tough game against York City at Bootham Crescent.

Captain Craig Taylor, central defensive partner Steve Woods and goalkeeper Kevin Dearden were all outstanding as York eventually ran out of steam and ideas.

And counter-attacking United, cheered on by hundreds of traveling fans, went agonisingly close to a late winner when lively substitute Martin Gritton hit the post four minutes from time.

After a bright start by the Gulls, York started testing out the middle of United's defence with a series of corners and free-kicks of their own.

One breakaway goal by the Gulls would surely have been enough to win it, and one of the best chances came soon after half-time.

Picking up the ball just inside York's half, Graham set off on a thrilling run to the left and then picked out the supporting Broad on the edge of the area but his finish was weak and easily saved.

Nullified in midfield, City found little space, but from a rare cross by Nogan in the 52nd minute Andy Bell must have thought he had scored with a header, until Dearden got the faintest but most important of touches to deflect it onto his bar and away.

But United repeatedly hit York on the counter during the second half and Grahamclearly fancied himself to earn all three points. Twice he went close, with a shot deflected wide and then a first-time volley just over the bar after a McGlinchey throw from the left had been helped on.

The best chances continued to fall United's way in the closing stages. Hill should have hit the target and then came that so-near finish four minutes from time, Gritton first feeding Graham down the left and then going for the return pass into the goalmouth. He just about got there, but at full stretch he could only direct the ball on to the far post instead of just inside it.

Result.......Result.......Result.

YORK....................(0) **0** **TORQUAY** ......(0) **0**
Att 3,150
Referee: M Warren

Stats......Stats.......Stats......Stats

YORK				TORQUAY		
1st	2nd	Total		Total	2nd	1st
3	2	5	**Corners**	2	1	1
11	8	19	**Fouls**	15	9	6
0	0	0	**Yellow cards**	1	1	0
0	0	0	**Red cards**	0	0	0
2	2	4	**Caught Offside**	3	2	1
3	2	5	**Shots on target**	4	2	2
2	2	4	**Shots off target**	8	5	3
0	1	1	**Hit woodwork**	1	1	0
46	51	49%	**Possession**	51%	49	54

I'VE wanted to try the 3-4-3 all season - it's just getting the personnel in. Now we've got Richard Offiong he gives us a bit of pace.

Chris Brass

I was pleased given the changes we had to make, with Alex Russell going down late and Jason Fowler too. We were solid and organised.

Leroy Rosenior

Other Div 3 Results

Carlisle 2 Oxford Utd 0, Darlington 3 Cambridge Utd 4, Doncaster 1 Cheltenham 1, Huddersfield 4 Macclesfield 0, Hull 2 Scunthorpe 1, Leyton Orient 1 Kidderminster 1, Northampton 2 Boston Utd 0, Rochdale 0 Bury 0, Southend 1 Swansea 1, Yeovil 4 Bristol Rovers 0

York [0] 0 TORQUAY [0] 0

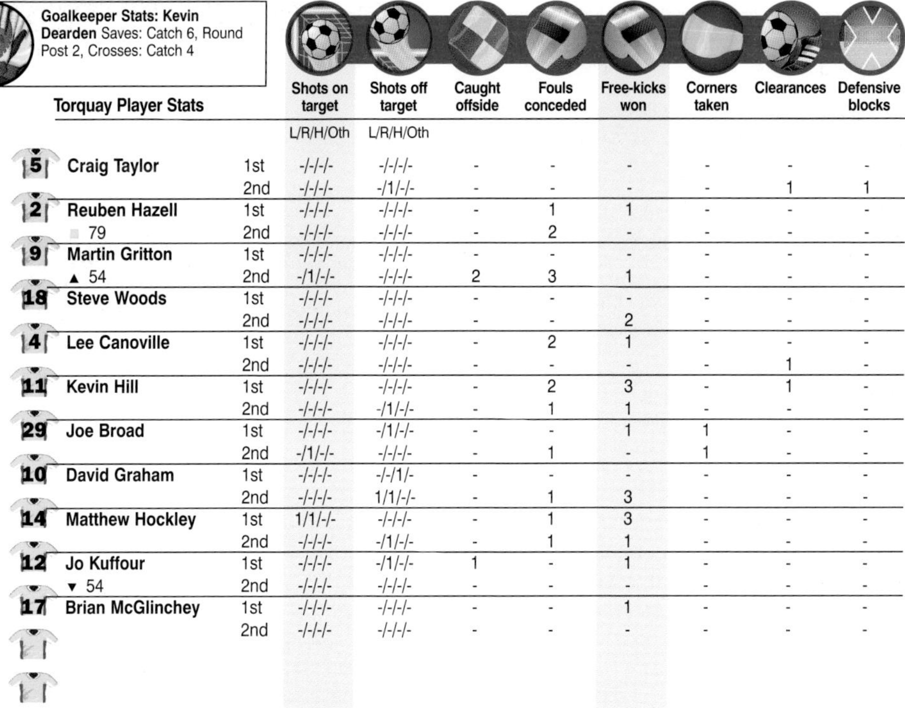

Goalkeeper Stats: Kevin Dearden Saves: Catch 6, Round Post 2, Crosses: Catch 4

No.	Torquay Player Stats		Shots on target L/R/H/Oth	Shots off target L/R/H/Oth	Caught offside	Fouls conceded	Free-kicks won	Corners taken	Clearances	Defensive blocks
5	Craig Taylor	1st	-/-/-/-	-/-/-/-	-	-	-	-	-	-
		2nd	-/-/-/-	-/1/-/-	-	-	-	-	1	1
2	Reuben Hazell	1st	-/-/-/-	-/-/-/-	-	1	1	-	-	-
	■ 79	2nd	-/-/-/-	-/-/-/-	-	2	-	-	-	-
9	Martin Gritton	1st	-/-/-/-	-/-/-/-	-	-	-	-	-	-
	▲ 54	2nd	-/1/-/-	-/-/-/-	2	3	1	-	-	-
18	Steve Woods	1st	-/-/-/-	-/-/-/-	-	-	-	-	-	-
		2nd	-/-/-/-	-/-/-/-	-	-	2	-	-	-
4	Lee Canoville	1st	-/-/-/-	-/-/-/-	-	2	1	-	-	-
		2nd	-/-/-/-	-/-/-/-	-	-	-	-	1	-
11	Kevin Hill	1st	-/-/-/-	-/-/-/-	-	2	3	-	1	-
		2nd	-/-/-/-	-/1/-/-	-	1	1	-	-	-
29	Joe Broad	1st	-/-/-/-	-/1/-/-	-	-	1	1	-	-
		2nd	-/1/-/-	-/-/-/-	-	1	-	1	-	-
10	David Graham	1st	-/-/-/-	-/-/1/-	-	-	-	-	-	-
		2nd	-/-/-/-	1/1/-/-	-	1	3	-	-	-
14	Matthew Hockley	1st	1/1/-/-	-/-/-/-	-	1	3	-	-	-
		2nd	-/-/-/-	-/1/-/-	-	1	1	-	-	-
12	Jo Kuffour	1st	-/-/-/-	-/1/-/-	1	-	1	-	-	-
	▼ 54	2nd	-/-/-/-	-/-/-/-	-	-	-	-	-	-
17	Brian McGlinchey	1st	-/-/-/-	-/-/-/-	-	-	1	-	-	-
		2nd	-/-/-/-	-/-/-/-	-	-	-	-	-	-

Subs not used: Van Heusden, Woozley, Wills, Benefield. - **Formation: 4-4-2**

Goalkeeper Stats: Chris Porter Saves: Catch 6, Crosses: Catch 2

No.	Player Stats	Shots on target	Shots off target	Caught offside	Fouls conceded	Free-kicks won	Corners taken	Clearances	Defensive blocks
24	Dave Merris	-/-/-/-	-/2/-/-	-	1	3	-	-	-
4	Richard Cooper	-/-/-/-	-/-/-/-	-	2	3	-	-	-
29	Richard Offiong ▼ 66	-/-/-/-	-/-/-/-	1	5	1	-	-	-
23	Richard Hope	-/-/1/-	-/-/-/-	1	2	-	-	-	-
9	Lee Nogan	-/2/-/-	-/1/-/-	2	2	1	-	-	-
5	Andy Bell	1/-/1/-	-/1/-/-	-	2	4	-	-	-
12	Stuart Wise	-/-/-/-	-/-/-/-	-	3	2	-	-	-
6	Chris Smith	-/-/-/-	-/-/-/-	-	1	-	-	-	-
18	Levent Yalcin ▲ 66	-/-/-/-	-/-/-/-	-	1	-	-	-	-
22	Darren Dunning	-/-/-/-	-/-/-/-	-	-	1	5	-	-
15	Leigh Wood	-/-/-/-	-/-/-/-	-	-	-	-	-	-

Subs not used: Ovendale, Ward, Davies, Donovan. - **Formation: 3-5-2**

Torquay Played: 35 **Won** 18 **Drawn** 8 **Lost** 9 **For** 48 **Against** 32 **Pos** 5

Bristol Rovers [1] 2 TORQUAY [2] 2

16th March

Two up in only 16 minutes, Torquay United were forced to hang on grimly for a point as Bristol Rovers rediscovered their pride In the Westcountry derby at the Memorial Ground.

More than a thousand Gulls fans rejoiced as Jo Kuffour, switched from a striker role to the left wing, struck twice early on, taking his tally to nine goals this season.

After only four minutes. Reuben Hazell and Lee Canoville had one attack blocked on the right, but when the ball broke out to Hazell for a second time, he curled a cross to the far post where Kuffour swept home a right-foot volley from five yards.

United nearly scored again in the 15th minute and then did so a minute later.

Gritton nodded down goalkeeper Kevin Dearden's long kick, Kuffour beat Sonny Parker and headed for the penalty-area.

With defenders retreating before him, he tried a shot across the goalmouth, but the ball hit Christian Edwards and screwed just inside the near-post with Kevin Miller hopelessly wrong-footed.

It was a dream start for United, but there was a long way to go and Rovers were not about to accept defeat. United needed to keep their two-goal cushion until half-time, but in the 28th minute Rovers pulled a goal back.

Suddenly it was all Rovers. Tait headed just over from a Hyde free-kick on the half-hour and on the stroke of half-time Dearden had to come up with a brave near-post smother from a cross by the lively Matthews.

Rovers, now in full cry, equalized in the 52nd minute. Gary Twigg crossed from the left and Parker, unmarked beyond the far-post, looped a 12-yard header over Dearden and into the left-hand corner of the net.

Hill did pull one shot just wide across the face of goal and Kuffour tested Miller with a 25-yard half-volley. But for the last half-hour it was one-way traffic and agony for Gulls fans.

Result.......Result.......Result.

BRISTOL ROV......(1) **2** **TORQUAY** ......(2) **2**
Tait 28 Kuffour 5, 17
Parker 52

Att 6,461
Referee: E Evans

Stats......Stats.......Stats......Stats

BRISTOL ROVERS **TORQUAY**

1st	2nd	Total		Total	2nd	1st
3	5	8	**Corners**	5	2	3
7	2	9	**Fouls**	7	5	2
2	3	5	**Yellow cards**	2	2	0
0	0	0	**Red cards**	0	0	0
0	1	1	**Caught Offside**	2	0	2
3	1	4	**Shots on target**	4	1	3
3	0	3	**Shots off target**	1	1	0
0	0	0	**Hit woodwork**	0	0	0
36	41	38%	**Possession**	62%	59	64

“**ALL** I can say is that my record hasn't been good enough as caretaker manager and I understand that the directors must look at changing things.

Phil Bater

“**ONCE** we failed to kill the game off and allowed Rovers to equalise I was delighted with the way the players dug in and
battled for the result.

Leroy Rosenior

Other Div 3 Results

Bury 3 Mansfield 0, Cambridge Utd 0 Boston Utd 1, Carlisle 1 Northampton 1, Huddersfield 1 Rochdale 1, Hull 3 Leyton Orient 0, Macclesfield 2 Swansea 1, Scunthorpe 0 Kidderminster 2, Yeovil 0 Doncaster 1

Bristol Rovers [1] 2 TORQUAY [2] 2

Goalkeeper Stats: Kevin Dearden Saves: Catch 3, Crosses: Fumble 1, Punch 1

Torquay Player Stats

No.	Player	Half	Shots on target L/R/H/Oth	Shots off target L/R/H/Oth	Caught offside	Fouls conceded	Free-kicks won	Corners taken	Clearances	Defensive blocks
21	Kevin Dearden	1st	-/-/-/-	-/-/-/-	-	-	-	-	-	-
		2nd	-/-/-/-	-/-/-/-	-	-	-	-	-	-
5	Craig Taylor	1st	-/-/-/-	-/-/-/-	-	-	1	-	4	-
		2nd	-/-/-/-	-/-/-/-	-	-	-	-	1	-
3	David Woozley	1st	-/-/-/-	-/-/-/-	-	-	-	-	-	-
	▲ 82 ■ 83	2nd	-/-/-/-	-/-/-/-	-	1	-	-	-	-
2	Reuben Hazell	1st	-/-/-/-	-/-/-/-	-	1	-	-	-	-
	■ 67	2nd	-/-/-/-	-/-/-/-	-	1	-	-	2	-
9	Martin Gritton	1st	-/-/-/-	-/-/-/-	1	-	1	-	-	-
	▼ 82	2nd	-/-/-/-	-/-/-/-	-	-	-	-	-	-
18	Steve Woods	1st	-/-/-/-	-/-/-/-	-	-	1	-	2	-
		2nd	-/-/-/-	-/-/-/-	-	2	-	-	2	-
4	Lee Canoville	1st	-/1/-/-	-/-/-/-	1	-	1	-	-	1
	▼ 72	2nd	-/-/-/-	-/-/-/-	-	-	-	-	-	-
11	Kevin Hill	1st	-/-/-/-	-/-/-/-	-	-	1	-	2	1
		2nd	-/-/-/-	1/-/-/-	-	1	-	-	3	-
10	David Graham	1st	-/-/-/-	-/-/-/-	-	-	1	-	-	-
		2nd	-/-/-/-	-/-/-/-	-	-	-	-	-	-
15	Kevin Wills	1st	-/-/-/-	-/-/-/-	-	-	-	-	-	-
	▲ 72	2nd	-/-/-/-	-/-/-/-	-	-	1	-	-	-
14	Matthew Hockley	1st	-/-/-/-	-/-/-/-	-	-	-	3	-	-
		2nd	-/1/-/-	-/-/-/-	-	-	-	2	1	-
12	Jo Kuffour	1st	1/1/-/-	-/-/-/-	-	1	1	-	-	-
		2nd	-/-/-/-	-/-/-/-	-	-	1	-	-	-
17	Brian McGlinchey	1st	-/-/-/-	-/-/-/-	-	-	-	-	-	1
		2nd	-/-/-/-	-/-/-/-	-	-	-	-	-	-

Subs not used: Van Heusden, Benefield, Broad. - **Formation: 4-3-3**

Goalkeeper Stats: Kevin Miller Saves: Parry 1, Crosses: Catch 1, Punch 1

No.	Player Stats	Shots on target	Shots off target	Caught offside	Fouls conceded	Free-kicks won	Corners taken	Clearances	Defensive blocks
6	Kevin Austin	-/-/-/-	-/-/-/-	-	-	-	-	1	-
32	Lee Matthews	-/1/-/-	-/-/-/-	-	1	3	-	-	-
10	Junior Agogo ▲ 85	-/-/-/-	-/-/-/-	1	-	1	-	-	-
9	Paul Tait	-/2/-/-	-/1/-/-	-	1	-	-	-	-
33	Gary Twigg ▼ 86 ■ 61	-/-/-/-	-/-/-/-	-	1	-	2	1	-
5	Adam Barrett	-/-/-/-	-/-/-/-	-	1	-	-	3	-
8	Robert Quinn ■ 85	-/1/-/-	-/1/-/-	-	-	-	-	-	-
14	Graham Hyde ▼ 85 ■ 45	-/-/-/-	-/-/-/-	-	1	1	1	-	1
18	Sonny Parker ▼ 77 ■ 9	-/-/-/-	-/-/-/-	-	2	-	-	1	-
30	Ryan Williams ▲ 86	-/-/-/-	-/-/-/-	-	-	-	-	-	-
20	Christian Edwards	-/-/-/-	-/-/-/-	-	2	1	-	1	1
7	David Savage ■ 51	-/-/-/-	-/1/-/-	-	-	-	5	3	-
24	Neil Arndale ▲ 77	-/-/-/-	-/-/-/-	-	-	-	-	-	-

Subs not used: Bryant, Hodges. - **Formation: 5-3-2**

Torquay Played: 36 **Won** 18 **Drawn** 9 **Lost** 9 **For** 50 **Against** 34 **Pos** 4

Torquay [2] 3 CAMBRIDGE UTD [0] 0 — 20th March

It was a family affair when Torquay met Cambridge. In just over an hour's non-stop debut action Liam Rosenior grabbed a place in the affections of Torquay United fans.

And it was only fitting that it was his run and cross, with his weaker left foot, which laid on United's clinching third and David Graham's second goal just after half-time.

After midfielder Matt Hockley's deflected opener, two more top-quality finishes by leading scorer Graham took the Scot's tally for the season to 18 goals.

But it was the visitors who had the best of the early stages, Webb going close with his eleventh minute header and John Turner outpacing Steve Woods in another dangerous break.

In the 22nd minute Torquay took the lead. Lee Canoville took a throw on the right, Graham put Jo Kuffour away down the same flank, he pulled back a low cross, Hockley met it with a first-time shot from 20 yards and the ball deflected past Marshall off lunging defender Steve Angus.

The goal settled any nerves that United might have had. Hockley and Graham both went close, and Graham apologised to the lively Rosenior for shooting weakly instead of passing to him, before the second goal came in the 39th minute.

Martin Gritton's shot was parried by Marshall, but Graham had followed up and he buried an angled shot past Marshall from eight yards.

The wind dropped a little at Plainmoor for a spell in the second half, but United were in no mood to slacken off. Four minutes after the interval, they made the points certain.

Brian McGlinchey fed Rosenior on the left, he swept past Ashley Nicholls in a determined run, his near-post cross caught the boot of poor Angus again and Graham was there to flick the ball over Marshall from close-range.

Result.......Result.......Result.

TORQUAY ....(2) **3** **C'BRIDGE U** ..(0) **0**
Hockley 22
Graham 39, 50

Att 2,975
Referee: T Parkes

Stats......Stats.......Stats......Stats

TORQUAY				CAMBRIDGE UTD		
1st	**2nd**	**Total**		**Total**	**2nd**	**1st**
4	5	9	**Corners**	5	1	4
4	6	10	**Fouls**	14	4	10
1	1	2	**Yellow cards**	2	1	1
0	0	0	**Red cards**	0	0	0
1	2	3	**Caught Offside**	6	5	1
6	3	9	**Shots on target**	3	1	2
2	3	5	**Shots off target**	5	3	2
0	0	0	**Hit woodwork**	0	0	0
48	54	51%	**Possession**	49%	46	52

"**IT** was scrappy and a bit horrible because of the wind, but I was delighted to come in 2-0 up at half-time. We defended tremendously in the second half.

Leroy Rosenior"

"**THIS** is going to be a dogfight until the end of the season.

Dale Brooks"

Other Div 3 Results

Boston Utd 1 Bristol Rovers 0, Cheltenham 1 Bury 2, Doncaster 1 Darlington 1, Kidderminster 1 Macclesfield 4, Mansfield A Oxford Utd A, Northampton A Huddersfield A, Rochdale 2 Carlisle 0, Southend P Hull P, Swansea 4 Scunthorpe 2, York P Yeovil P

TORQUAY [2] 3 Cambridge Utd [0] 0

Goalkeeper Stats: Kevin Dearden Crosses: Tip Over 2, Catch 2

Torquay Player Stats		Shots on target L/R/H/Oth	Shots off target L/R/H/Oth	Caught offside	Fouls conceded	Free-kicks won	Corners taken	Clearances	Defensive blocks
5 Craig Taylor	1st	1/-/-/-	1/-/-/-	-	-	-	-	1	-
	2nd	-/-/-/-	-/-/1/-	-	-	-	-	2	-
2 Reuben Hazell	1st	-/-/-/-	-/-/-/-	-	-	-	-	-	-
▲ 84	2nd	-/-/-/-	-/-/-/-	-	-	-	-	-	-
9 Martin Gritton	1st	1/-/-/-	-/-/-/-	-	-	3	-	1	-
	2nd	-/-/-/-	-/-/-/-	2	1	-	-	-	-
18 Steve Woods	1st	-/-/-/-	-/-/-/-	-	1	1	-	-	-
	2nd	-/-/-/-	-/-/1/-	-	1	1	-	1	-
4 Lee Canoville	1st	-/-/-/-	-/-/-/-	-	-	-	-	-	-
■ 82	2nd	-/-/-/-	1/-/-/-	-	2	1	-	-	-
20 Liam Rosenior	1st	-/-/-/-	-/-/-/-	-	2	1	-	-	-
▼ 61	2nd	-/-/-/-	-/-/-/-	-	-	1	3	-	-
11 Kevin Hill	1st	-/-/-/-	-/-/-/-	-	-	2	-	1	-
▼ 84	2nd	1/-/-/-	-/-/-/-	-	-	-	-	1	-
10 David Graham	1st	-/2/-/-	-/1/-/-	1	1	-	-	-	-
▼ 76 ■ 24	2nd	-/1/-/-	-/-/-/-	-	1	1	-	-	-
15 Kevin Wills	1st	-/-/-/-	-/-/-/-	-	-	-	-	-	-
▲ 76	2nd	-/-/-/-	-/-/-/-	-	-	-	-	-	-
14 Matthew Hockley	1st	-/2/-/-	-/-/-/-	-	-	-	4	-	-
	2nd	-/-/-/-	-/-/-/-	-	-	-	-	-	-
8 Jason Fowler	1st	-/-/-/-	-/-/-/-	-	-	-	-	-	-
▲ 61	2nd	-/-/-/-	-/-/-/-	-	1	-	2	-	-
12 Jo Kuffour	1st	-/-/-/-	-/-/-/-	-	-	3	-	-	-
	2nd	1/-/-/-	-/-/-/-	-	-	-	-	-	-
17 Brian McGlinchey	1st	-/-/-/-	-/-/-/-	-	-	-	-	-	-
	2nd	-/-/-/-	-/-/-/-	-	-	-	-	1	-

Subs not used: Van Heusden, Woozley. - **Formation: 4-4-2**

Goalkeeper Stats: Shaun Marshall Saves: Catch 6, Parry 4, Crosses: Catch 4

	Player Stats	Shots on target	Shots off target	Caught offside	Fouls conceded	Free-kicks won	Corners taken	Clearances	Defensive blocks
14	Luke Guttridge ▼ 67	-/1/-/-	-/-/-/-	-	1	1	3	-	-
3	Fred Murray	-/-/-/-	1/-/-/-	-	1	1	-	-	-
16	Alex Revell ▲ 79	-/-/-/-	-/-/-/-	1	-	-	-	-	-
5	Adam Tann ■ 41	-/-/-/-	-/-/-/-	-	1	2	-	-	-
18	David Bridges ▲ 67	-/-/-/-	-/1/-/-	-	-	-	-	-	-
22	Stuart Bimson ▲ 72	-/-/-/-	-/-/-/-	-	-	-	-	-	-
2	Warren Goodhind	-/-/-/-	-/-/1/-	-	2	-	-	1	-
7	Daniel Webb	-/-/2/-	-/-/-/-	2	3	2	-	2	-
10	Shane Tudor ▼ 72	-/-/-/-	-/1/-/-	1	2	2	2	1	-
6	Stevland Angus	-/-/-/-	-/-/-/-	-	2	1	-	2	-
15	John Turner ■ 49	-/-/-/-	-/-/-/-	-	-	1	-	1	-
9	Jermaine Easter ▼ 79	-/-/-/-	-/1/-/-	2	2	-	-	-	-

Subs not used: Brennan, Gleeson. - **Formation: 4-4-2**

Torquay Played: 37 **Won** 19 **Drawn** 9 **Lost** 9 **For** 53 **Against** 34 **Pos** 3

Darlington [1] 1 TORQUAY [0] 1 — 27th March

Torquay United supporters must have breathed a sigh of relief when Deadline Day without anybody coming up with the sort of offer which would have bought David Graham.

Less than 48 hours later, at Darlington's new 30,000-capacity Reynolds Arena, Graham showed just how valuable he is to the Gulls with the brilliant second-half equaliser which earned another precious point.

With Darlington desperate for points to pull away from relegation trouble, this was always going to be one of the most difficult away games of United's run-in and they hardly helped themselves by starting slowly and giving the Quakers a goal after only two minutes.

Chris Hughes had time and space to pick out his cross from Darlington's right, and when Canoville did go to whack the ball clear, he drove it against the broad, bald head of home centre-forward Barry Conlon.

United made and missed a good early chance to equalise, defender Steve Woods volleying over at the far-post when he should have hit the target after headers by Graham and Craig Taylor following an Alex Russell cross.

True to their principles, Russell & Co kept passing the ball on a stodgy pitch, but finding any space through Darlington's packed midfield and defence was like trying to pick a lock with a hair-grip.

Canoville tested Darlington keeper Michael Price and McGlinchey fired just wide, both from long range, and just before half-time Rosenior was narrowly off-target with a clever chip from 20 yards.

With substitute Neil Wainwright starting to test Hill and McGlinchey, United had their work cut out to make sure they didn't slip further behind. Dearden had to make a goalline save when Conlon's head met a Wainwright cross at the far-post.

But then United equalized. In the 66th minute Woods' diagonal pass was nodded down by Gritton on the edge of the Darlington box. A burst of pace and a deft touch took Graham past defender Joey Hutchison and he scored with an angled volley past Price from eight yards.

Result.......Result.......Result.

DARLINGTON ......(1) **1** **TORQUAY** ......(0) **1**
Conlon 2 — Graham 66

Att 4,317
Referee: E Ilderton

Stats......Stats.......Stats......Stats

DARLINGTON 1st	2nd	Total		TORQUAY Total	2nd	1st
0	7	7	**Corners**	4	2	2
4	4	8	**Fouls**	10	5	5
0	0	0	**Yellow cards**	3	2	1
0	0	0	**Red cards**	0	0	0
4	1	5	**Caught Offside**	2	0	2
3	5	8	**Shots on target**	4	1	3
1	2	3	**Shots off target**	7	1	6
0	0	0	**Hit woodwork**	0	0	0
45	48	47%	**Possession**	53%	52	55

AFTER the start that we had in the game we should have gone on and really punished them, but we sat back and let them dictate the play.

Dave Hodgson

DARLINGTON have an excellent defence and they defended well. But once we got the equaliser we bossed the game and only allowed them a couple of chances.

Leroy Rosenior

Other Div 3 Results

Bristol Rovers 3 York 0, Bury 1 Boston Utd 3, Cambridge Utd 2 Cheltenham 1, Carlisle 1 Southend 2, Huddersfield 3 Swansea 0, Hull 1 Rochdale 0, Macclesfield 0 Northampton 4, Oxford Utd 0 Doncaster 0, Scunthorpe 1 Leyton Orient 1, Yeovil 1 Mansfield 1

27th March

Darlington [1] 1 TORQUAY [0] 1

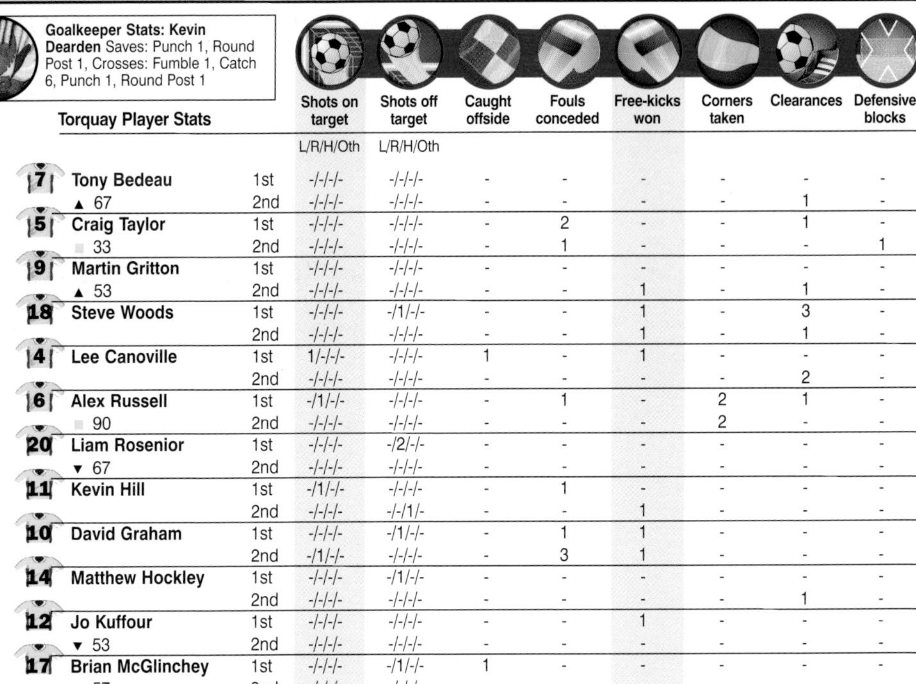

Goalkeeper Stats: Kevin Dearden Saves: Punch 1, Round Post 1, Crosses: Fumble 1, Catch 6, Punch 1, Round Post 1

Torquay Player Stats		Shots on target L/R/H/Oth	Shots off target L/R/H/Oth	Caught offside	Fouls conceded	Free-kicks won	Corners taken	Clearances	Defensive blocks
7 Tony Bedeau	1st	-/-/-/-	-/-/-/-	-	-	-	-	-	-
▲ 67	2nd	-/-/-/-	-/-/-/-	-	-	-	-	1	-
5 Craig Taylor	1st	-/-/-/-	-/-/-/-	-	2	-	-	1	-
■ 33	2nd	-/-/-/-	-/-/-/-	-	1	-	-	-	1
9 Martin Gritton	1st	-/-/-/-	-/-/-/-	-	-	-	-	-	-
▲ 53	2nd	-/-/-/-	-/-/-/-	-	-	1	-	1	-
18 Steve Woods	1st	-/-/-/-	-/1/-/-	-	-	1	-	3	-
	2nd	-/-/-/-	-/-/-/-	-	-	1	-	1	-
4 Lee Canoville	1st	1/-/-/-	-/-/-/-	1	-	1	-	-	-
	2nd	-/-/-/-	-/-/-/-	-	-	-	-	2	-
6 Alex Russell	1st	-/1/-/-	-/-/-/-	-	1	-	2	1	-
■ 90	2nd	-/-/-/-	-/-/-/-	-	-	-	2	-	-
20 Liam Rosenior	1st	-/-/-/-	-/2/-/-	-	-	-	-	-	-
▼ 67	2nd	-/-/-/-	-/-/-/-	-	-	-	-	-	-
11 Kevin Hill	1st	-/1/-/-	-/-/-/-	-	1	-	-	-	-
	2nd	-/-/-/-	-/-/1/-	-	-	1	-	-	-
10 David Graham	1st	-/-/-/-	-/1/-/-	-	1	1	-	-	-
	2nd	-/1/-/-	-/-/-/-	-	3	1	-	-	-
14 Matthew Hockley	1st	-/-/-/-	-/1/-/-	-	-	-	-	-	-
	2nd	-/-/-/-	-/-/-/-	-	-	-	-	1	-
12 Jo Kuffour	1st	-/-/-/-	-/-/-/-	-	-	1	-	-	-
▼ 53	2nd	-/-/-/-	-/-/-/-	-	-	-	-	-	-
17 Brian McGlinchey	1st	-/-/-/-	-/1/-/-	1	-	-	-	-	-
■ 57	2nd	-/-/-/-	-/-/-/-	-	-	-	-	-	-

Subs not used: Van Heusden, Fowler, Hazell. - **Formation: 4-4-2**

Goalkeeper Stats: Michael Price Saves: Punch 1, Crosses: Catch 4

	Player Stats	Shots on target	Shots off target	Caught offside	Fouls conceded	Free-kicks won	Corners taken	Clearances	Defensive blocks
2	Ryan Valentine	-/-/-/-	1/-/-/-	-	-	-	-	1	-
18	Craig Russell ▼ 60	1/-/-/-	-/-/-/-	-	-	-	1	-	-
16	Mark Convery ▼ 67	-/-/-/-	-/-/-/-	2	-	1	1	1	-
27	Brian Close ▲ 60	-/-/-/-	-/-/-/-	-	-	1	2	-	-
4	Craig Liddle	-/-/-/-	-/-/-/-	-	3	-	-	-	-
21	Jonathan Hutchinson	-/-/-/-	-/-/-/-	-	-	1	2	3	1
25	Neil Teggart	-/-/1/-	-/1/-/-	-	1	1	-	-	-
22	Neil Maddison	-/-/-/-	-/-/-/-	-	-	1	-	2	-
13	Barry Conlon	2/-/2/1	-/-/1/-	3	2	2	-	-	-
34	Danny Graham ▲ 67	-/-/1/-	-/-/-/-	-	-	-	-	-	-
5	Matthew Clarke	-/-/-/-	-/-/-/-	-	-	2	-	1	-
14	Neil Wainwright ▲ 59	-/-/-/-	-/-/-/-	-	1	-	1	1	-
17	Chris Hughes ▼ 59	-/-/-/-	-/-/-/-	-	-	1	-	-	1

Subs not used: Clark, Norton. - **Formation: 3-5-2**

Torquay Played: 38 **Won** 19 **Drawn** 10 **Lost** 9 **For** 54 **Against** 35 **Pos** 4

Mansfield [2] 2 TORQUAY [1] 1 — 30th March

Promotion rivals Mansfield Town caused Torquay United's first defeat in nine games in a thrilling match at Field Mill.

Apart from a slow start, which saw Colin Larkin and Junior Mendes both score for the Stags, United played their full part in a contest that was far above Third Division quality.

But United gave themselves the proverbial mountain to climb when they found themselves two down in ten minutes.

For the opener, Neil MacKenzie's shot was going well wide when Colin Larkin swung his boot at it from 12 yards and the ball spun into the net past a hopelessly wrong-footed Kevin Dearden.

United were still trying to pull themselves together when they let in another goal. Craig Taylor appeared to have controlled a long pass until he stumbled under pressure from Junior Mendes, who took the ball away from the Gulls' captain and volleyed over Dearden from just inside the box.

It was vital that United establish a foothold in a match that was threatening to run away from them, and they did so only six minutes later.

Gritton nodded down Brian McGlinchey's free-kick from the left, David Graham's first shot was parried by Kevin Pilkington, but Gritton side-footed the loose ball home.

From being in danger of losing before they had started, United were suddenly up and running. In the 55th minute, with United giving it everything, Rosenior hit the post from a slick Graham-Gritton build-up and in one desperate spell, United had three shots blocked in quick succession.

In the 63rd minute Graham had the retreating Mansfield defence in big trouble. He got into the box, turned cleverly, appeared to have his legs taken by Rhys Day and United fans behind the goal howled unsuccessfully for a penalty.

Gritton had a goal disallowed for offside, another tight decision but probably just right, as United drove forward in search of the equaliser.

Result.......Result.......Result.

MANSFIELD ....(2) **2** **TORQUAY** ......(1) **1**
Larkin 5 Gritton 17
Mendes 10

Att 4,552
Referee: A Leake

Stats......Stats.......Stats......Stats

MANSFIELD						TORQUAY
1st	**2nd**	**Total**		**Total**	**2nd**	**1st**
6	4	10	**Corners**	6	2	4
3	4	7	**Fouls**	9	4	5
0	1	1	**Yellow cards**	0	0	0
0	0	0	**Red cards**	0	0	0
1	1	2	**Caught Offside**	5	3	2
3	0	3	**Shots on target**	6	2	4
5	6	11	**Shots off target**	9	6	3
1	0	1	**Hit woodwork**	1	1	0
58	57	58%	**Possession**	42%	43	42

THAT was a cracking game between two teams trying to play football the right way. It was a massive game and winning has given us a massive boost.

Keith Curle

IT was a great game of football between two good sides and it was just a shame it was spoilt by the referee and two linesmen.

Leroy Rosenior

Other Div 3 Results

Rochdale 1 Doncaster 1

Mansfield [2] 2 TORQUAY [1] 1

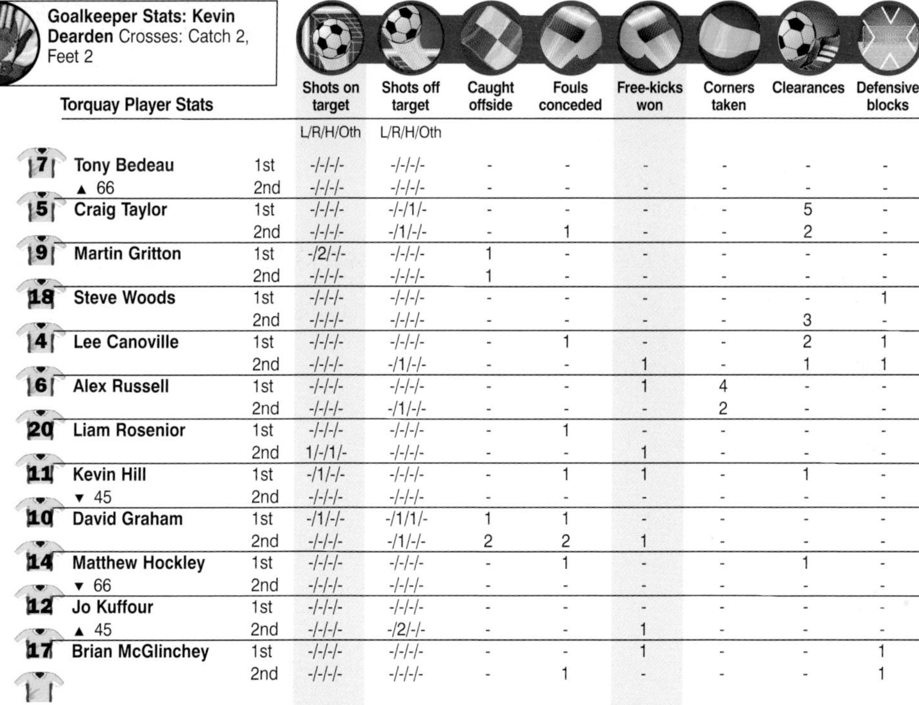

Goalkeeper Stats: Kevin Dearden Crosses: Catch 2, Feet 2

Torquay Player Stats		Shots on target L/R/H/Oth	Shots off target L/R/H/Oth	Caught offside	Fouls conceded	Free-kicks won	Corners taken	Clearances	Defensive blocks
7 Tony Bedeau	1st	-/-/-/-	-/-/-/-	-	-	-	-	-	-
▲ 66	2nd	-/-/-/-	-/-/-/-	-	-	-	-	-	-
5 Craig Taylor	1st	-/-/-/-	-/-/1/-	-	-	-	-	5	-
	2nd	-/-/-/-	-/1/-/-	-	1	-	-	2	-
9 Martin Gritton	1st	-/2/-/-	-/-/-/-	1	-	-	-	-	-
	2nd	-/-/-/-	-/-/-/-	1	-	-	-	-	-
18 Steve Woods	1st	-/-/-/-	-/-/-/-	-	-	-	-	-	1
	2nd	-/-/-/-	-/-/-/-	-	-	-	-	3	-
4 Lee Canoville	1st	-/-/-/-	-/-/-/-	-	1	-	-	2	1
	2nd	-/-/-/-	-/1/-/-	-	-	1	-	1	1
6 Alex Russell	1st	-/-/-/-	-/-/-/-	-	-	1	4	-	-
	2nd	-/-/-/-	-/1/-/-	-	-	-	2	-	-
20 Liam Rosenior	1st	-/-/-/-	-/-/-/-	-	1	-	-	-	-
	2nd	1/-/1/-	-/-/-/-	-	-	1	-	-	-
11 Kevin Hill	1st	-/1/-/-	-/-/-/-	-	1	1	-	1	-
▼ 45	2nd	-/-/-/-	-/-/-/-	-	-	-	-	-	-
10 David Graham	1st	-/1/-/-	-/1/1/-	1	1	-	-	-	-
	2nd	-/-/-/-	-/1/-/-	2	2	1	-	-	-
14 Matthew Hockley	1st	-/-/-/-	-/-/-/-	-	1	-	-	1	-
▼ 66	2nd	-/-/-/-	-/-/-/-	-	-	-	-	-	-
12 Jo Kuffour	1st	-/-/-/-	-/-/-/-	-	-	-	-	-	-
▲ 45	2nd	-/-/-/-	-/2/-/-	-	-	1	-	-	-
17 Brian McGlinchey	1st	-/-/-/-	-/-/-/-	-	-	1	-	-	1
	2nd	-/-/-/-	-/-/-/-	-	1	-	-	-	1

Subs not used: Van Heusden, Woozley, Hazell. - **Formation: 4-4-2**

Goalkeeper Stats: Kevin Pilkington Crosses: Catch 4, Parry 2

	Player Stats	Shots on target	Shots off target	Caught offside	Fouls conceded	Free-kicks won	Corners taken	Clearances	Defensive blocks
8	Craig Disley ▲ 83	-/-/-/-	-/-/-/-	-	-	-	-	1	-
20	Junior Mendes	-/2/-/-	1/1/1/-	1	-	1	-	-	-
6	Tony Vaughan	-/-/-/-	-/-/-/-	-	-	-	-	-	-
5	Rhys Day	-/-/-/-	-/-/-/-	-	-	1	-	4	1
7	Liam Lawrence	-/-/-/-	-/2/-/-	-	2	2	5	2	1
24	Lee Williamson ▲ 80	-/-/-/-	-/-/-/-	-	-	-	-	-	-
15	Alex Baptiste	-/-/-/-	-/-/-/-	-	-	2	-	-	1
9	Colin Larkin ▼ 70	-/1/-/-	-/-/-/-	1	-	-	-	-	1
4	Tom Curtis	-/-/-/-	-/-/-/-	-	3	-	-	3	2
12	Bobby Hassell	-/-/-/-	-/-/-/-	-	1	-	-	1	3
19	Andy White ▲ 70 ■ 73	-/-/-/-	-/1/-/-	-	1	-	-	-	-
11	Wayne Corden ▼ 80	-/-/-/-	1/-/-/-	-	-	1	5	1	-
14	Neil MacKenzie ▼ 83	-/-/-/-	1/3/-/-	-	-	2	-	-	-

Subs not used: Artell, Beardsley. - **Formation: 4-4-2**

Torquay Played: 39 **Won** 19 **Drawn** 10 **Lost** 10 **For** 55 **Against** 37 **Pos** 4

...March Team Stats.....Team Stats......Team Stats......Team S

League table at the end of March

	HOME						AWAY						
	P	W	D	L	F	A	W	D	L	F	A	Pts	Df
Doncaster	39	13	4	2	38	11	9	6	5	30	22	76	35
Hull	38	15	3	2	45	18	7	6	5	23	16	75	34
Huddersfield	38	14	4	2	37	13	6	5	7	22	30	69	16
Torquay	**39**	**13**	**4**	**2**	**37**	**15**	**6**	**6**	**8**	**18**	**22**	**67**	**18**
Oxford Utd	38	13	6	1	30	11	4	9	5	18	19	66	18
Mansfield	38	12	3	3	37	18	7	4	9	27	34	64	12
Lincoln City	39	8	10	2	31	18	8	5	6	25	20	63	18
Yeovil	38	13	2	5	37	16	6	1	11	19	30	60	10
Northampton	38	11	2	5	22	16	6	5	9	21	25	58	2
Swansea	39	9	7	3	33	19	5	6	9	18	30	55	2
Boston Utd	39	9	6	4	30	17	4	3	13	12	30	48	-5
Bury	39	8	6	6	25	25	5	3	11	20	29	48	-9
Leyton Orient	39	8	7	4	25	21	4	5	11	18	33	48	-11
Cheltenham	39	10	3	6	32	31	2	8	10	17	32	47	-14
Kidderminster	39	7	4	8	23	26	5	6	9	16	28	46	-15
Scunthorpe	39	6	9	5	33	24	4	6	9	26	33	45	2
Southend	38	6	3	9	17	19	6	6	8	21	30	45	-11
Bristol Rovers	39	7	7	6	23	22	4	4	11	19	31	44	-11
Cambridge Utd	39	4	6	10	21	30	7	5	7	25	30	44	-14
Darlington	39	8	4	8	26	26	3	6	10	19	28	43	-9
Rochdale	39	6	7	6	23	20	4	5	11	18	28	42	-7
York	38	7	5	6	19	20	3	7	10	12	32	42	-21
Macclesfield	39	6	8	6	24	23	3	4	12	22	40	39	-17
Carlisle	39	7	4	9	21	24	2	3	14	17	37	34	-23

March matches table

	P	W	D	L	F	A	Pts
Huddersfield	6	4	1	1	12	3	13
Hull	5	4	0	1	8	3	12
Boston Utd	7	4	0	3	8	7	12
Kidderminster	6	3	2	1	11	8	11
Swansea	8	2	4	2	10	11	10
Northampton	5	3	1	1	9	3	10
Carlisle	7	3	1	3	9	11	10
Torquay	**6**	**2**	**3**	**1**	**11**	**6**	**9**
Lincoln City	6	2	3	1	11	7	9
Southend	5	2	3	0	8	5	9
Darlington	5	2	2	1	8	7	8
Bury	5	2	2	1	7	5	8
Mansfield	6	2	2	2	6	10	8
Doncaster	6	1	5	0	5	4	8
Scunthorpe	7	2	1	4	12	13	7
Macclesfield	6	2	1	3	6	11	7
Rochdale	7	1	4	2	5	6	7
Bristol Rovers	6	1	3	2	7	9	6
Cambridge Utd	6	2	0	4	6	10	6
Oxford Utd	5	1	2	2	1	3	5
Cheltenham	6	1	1	4	7	10	4
Yeovil	5	1	1	3	6	8	4
Leyton Orient	6	0	4	2	4	9	4
York	5	0	2	3	2	10	2

March team stats details

Club Name	Ply	Shots On	Shots Off	Corners	Hit W'work	Caught Offside	Offside Trap	Fouls	Yellow Cards	Red Cards	Pens Awarded	Pens Con
Boston Utd	7	39	32	35	1	31	21	104	16	1	1 (1)	1
Bristol Rovers	6	31	21	35	0	21	19	91	16	2	- (-)	-
Bury	5	30	20	26	2	27	10	79	6	0	2 (2)	1
Cambridge U	6	41	27	33	2	30	19	76	8	0	1 (1)	-
Carlisle	7	45	31	33	0	22	19	84	12	1	- (-)	3
Cheltenham	6	18	30	30	0	12	30	59	3	0	- (-)	2
Darlington	5	29	23	41	0	22	10	43	1	0	- (-)	-
Doncaster	6	34	40	53	1	25	26	64	15	0	- (-)	-
Huddersfield	6	40	27	36	0	18	10	71	7	0	- (-)	-
Hull	5	32	26	23	2	26	14	50	4	0	- (-)	-
Kidderminster	6	33	25	40	1	22	7	86	13	1	2 (2)	1
Leyton Orient	6	33	31	31	4	16	39	82	15	1	- (-)	-
Lincoln City	6	39	11	41	2	19	30	73	7	1	1 (1)	1
Macclesfield	6	22	34	29	2	20	12	71	6	1	1 (1)	1
Mansfield	6	25	16	25	2	11	30	71	11	1	2 (2)	2
Northampton	5	29	23	18	1	17	26	63	5	0	- (-)	-
Oxford Utd	5	26	20	25	3	20	23	64	6	0	1 (1)	-
Rochdale	7	37	26	31	0	26	16	94	15	0	2 (1)	1
Scunthorpe	7	38	34	31	2	19	32	98	12	2	2 (2)	2
Southend	5	44	32	33	0	15	21	67	6	0	1 (1)	1
Swansea	8	45	28	37	1	20	27	89	13	2	1 (1)	1
Torquay	**6**	**37**	**32**	**29**	**2**	**18**	**20**	**59**	**10**	**0**	**1 (1)**	**-**
Yeovil	5	27	22	26	2	21	10	63	11	0	- (-)	-
York	5	16	12	16	2	13	20	60	9	0	1 (-)	2

 Monthly Match Details: Games 71 **Home Wins** 29 **Away Wins** 18 **Draws** 24

...March Player Stats..... Player Stats...... Player Stats......Pla

Monthly Top scorers

Marc Richards (Northampton)	5
Danny Schofield (Huddersfield)	4
Steven MacLean (Scunthorpe)	4
David Graham (Torquay)	4
Gary Fletcher (Lincoln City)	4
Craig Farrell (Carlisle)	3
Ben Burgess (Hull)	3
Paul Tait (Bristol Rovers)	3
Gareth Seddon (Bury)	3
Leon Constantine (Southend)	3

Penalties scored

2 Steven MacLean (Scunthorpe), Danny Swailes (Bury), Liam Lawrence (Mansfield)

Assists

Danny Schofield (Huddersfield)	3
Anthony Carss (Huddersfield)	2
Lee Matthews (Bristol Rovers)	2
Marcus Richardson (Lincoln City)	2
Paul Groves (Grimsby)	2
Gary Twigg (Bristol Rovers)	2
Ian Foster (Chester)	2

Quickest goals

1:59 mins - Barry Conlon (Darlington vs Torquay)

2:19 mins - Marcus Richardson (Cheltenham vs Lincoln City)

2:37 mins - Gary Fletcher (Leyton Orient vs Lincoln City)

3:26 mins - Kevin Hill (Torquay vs Carlisle)

4:27 mins - John Turner (Cambridge Utd vs Cheltenham)

Top Keeper

	Mins	Gls
P Rachubka (Huddersfield)	474	2
Boaz Myhill (Hull)	478	3
Lee Harper (Northampton)	472	3
A Warrington (Doncaster)	581	4
Steven Collis (Yeovil)	289	2
Andy Woodman (Oxford U)	386	3
Neil Edwards (Rochdale)	677	6
Paul Bastock (Boston Utd)	675	7

Shots on target

Andy Robinson (Swansea)	14
Craig Farrell (Carlisle)	14
Barry Conlon (Darlington)	11
Peter Duffield (Boston Utd)	10
Chris Brown (Doncaster)	10
Leon Constantine (Southend)	10
Ben Burgess (Hull)	9
Lawrie Dudfield (Southend)	9
Jermaine Easter (Cambridge Utd)	9
Gary Fletcher (Lincoln City)	9

Shots off target

Craig Farrell (Carlisle)	10
Matthew Tipton (Macclesfield)	10
John Doolan (Doncaster)	9
Grant McCann (Cheltenham)	9
Jermaine Easter (Cambridge Utd)	8
Steve Torpey (Scunthorpe)	8
Gary Alexander (Leyton Orient)	8
David Graham (Torquay)	8
Kevin Maher (Southend)	8
Roberto Martinez (Swansea)	8

Caught offside

Gareth Seddon (Bury)	14
Jermaine Easter (Cambridge Ut)	14
Grant Holt (Rochdale)	12
Leo Fortune-West (Doncaster)	11
Martin Carruthers (Macclesfield)	11
Steven MacLean (Scunthorpe)	11
Jonathan Walters (Hull)	10
David Nugent (Bury)	9
Barry Conlon (Darlington)	9

Free-kicks won

Grant Holt (Rochdale)	26
Leon Britton (Swansea)	21
Eric Sabin (Northampton)	18
Craig Farrell (Carlisle)	17
Anthony Carss (Huddersfield)	16
Andy Booth (Huddersfield)	16
Andy Preece (Carlisle)	15
Adam Murray (Kidderminster)	15
Steve Torpey (Scunthorpe)	15

David Graham scores (v Carlisle)

Fouls conceded

Paul Ellender (Boston Utd)	25
Steve Torpey (Scunthorpe)	21
John Mackie (Leyton Orient)	18
Grant Holt (Rochdale)	17
Efetobore Sodje (Huddersfield)	17
Kevin Gray (Carlisle)	16
Jamie McCombe (Lincoln City)	16
Ben Burgess (Hull)	15
David Flitcroft (Bury)	15

Fouls without a card

Ben Burgess (Hull)	15
Andy Booth (Huddersfield)	15
Paul Groves (Grimsby)	13
Gareth Seddon (Bury)	12
Stuart Wise (York)	10
Kevin Nugent (Swansea)	10
Craig Liddle (Darlington)	10
Adam Barrett (Bristol Rovers)	10
Andy Robinson (Swansea)	10

Goal, goal, goal!...David Graham scores.
Torquay v Carlisle
HPL01415_TNA_005

Jo Kuffour.
Torquay v Carlisle
HPL01415_TNA_038

Grenada international Tony Bedeau gets into the Caribbean spirit.
Torquay v Carlisle
HPL01415_TNA_003

Goal heroes Kevin Hill and David Graham in first half action.
Torquay v Carlisle
HPL01415_TNA_022

Torquay [1] 2 YEOVIL [2] 2

3rd April

A bold tactical decision sparked a tingling fightback against Yeovil Town in a sold-out Westcountry derby at Plainmoor.

When the Glovers took a 2-0 lead after only 26 minutes, Rosenior knew that his response would be vital. The Gulls boss' reaction was swift, taking off Bedeau and Kevin Hill, and sending on his young son Liam Rosenior and Jo Kuffour.

The effect was immediate. Rosenior and Kuffour breathed pace and urgency into United's attitude as they stormed back to draw a match they had nearly thrown away.

At the start of the game, United had the edge, with Gritton nearly scoring twice from a close-range shot and a glancing header. But Yeovil faught back and took the lead in the 16th minute. El Kholti's shot from outside the area hit the left-hand post. Darren Way was quickest to the rebound and scored on the volley.

And United had only themselves to blame for the second. Trying to find Lee Canoville, Bedeau's touch let him down and a terrible pass found Gavin Williams instead. All Williams had to do was deliver a short, low cross and Jake Edwards could hardly miss an open goal from point-blank range.

Rosenior had seen enough. Off came Bedeau and Hill and on went Rosenior Jr and Kuffour. They may have been 0-2 down, but United were at least up and running.

They needed to cut the deficit before half-time to give themselves a real chance , and did just that in the 43rd minute. Gritton was fouled by Colin Pluck outside the box, Russell rolled a short free-kick to Taylor and his 22-yard left-foot shot beat Yeovil's 'wall' and keeper Collis all ends up.

Torquay, with the wind behind them, were gradually getting on top and two minutes after the Skiverton header, they equalized through a Steve Woods penalty.

United were favourites to win now but they couldn't quite press home the advantage that their equaliser should have given them.

Result.......Result.......Result.

TORQUAY ....(1) **2** **YEOVIL** ....(2) **2**
Taylor 44 — Way 17
Woods 59 — Edwards 27

Att 6,156
Referee: R Styles

Stats......Stats.......Stats......Stats

TORQUAY				YEOVIL		
1st	**2nd**	**Total**		**Total**	**2nd**	**1st**
3	5	8	**Corners**	11	4	7
3	5	8	**Fouls**	15	7	8
0	4	4	**Yellow cards**	2	2	0
0	0	0	**Red cards**	1	1	0
2	2	4	**Caught Offside**	1	0	1
5	2	7	**Shots on target**	8	3	5
5	3	8	**Shots off target**	5	3	2
1	0	1	**Hit woodwork**	1	1	0
48	48	48%	**Possession**	52%	52	52

IT was a great advert for football in the west country. After our equaliser, it could've gone either way, so a draw was a fair result.

Leroy Rosenior

WE had a super first 25 minutes, got the goals we were looking to get with the wind behind us and we used the wind to good effect.

Gary Johnson

Other Div 3 Results

Boston Utd 1 Darlington 0, Cheltenham 1 Bristol Rovers 2, Doncaster 3 Bury 1, Kidderminster 1 Hull 1, Leyton Orient 1 Huddersfield 1, Mansfield 1 Cambridge Utd 1, Northampton 2 Oxford Utd 1, Swansea 1 Carlisle 2

3rd April

TORQUAY [1] 2 Yeovil [2] 2

Goalkeeper Stats: Kevin Dearden Saves: Catch 4, Crosses: Catch 6

No.	Torquay Player Stats		Shots on target L/R/H/Oth	Shots off target L/R/H/Oth	Caught offside	Fouls conceded	Free-kicks won	Corners taken	Clearances	Defensive blocks
7	Tony Bedeau	1st	-/-/-/-	-/-/-/-	-	-	1	-	-	-
	▼ 29	2nd	-/-/-/-	-/-/-/-	-	-	-	-	-	-
5	Craig Taylor	1st	1/-/-/-	-/-/1/-	-	-	1	-	4	-
		2nd	-/-/-/-	-/-/-/-	-	-	-	-	-	1
9	Martin Gritton	1st	-/1/-/-	-/1/1/-	2	1	2	-	-	-
	▼ 78 □ 61	2nd	1/-/-/-	-/-/-/-	-	-	1	-	-	-
4	Lee Canoville	1st	-/1/-/-	-/-/-/-	-	-	1	-	-	-
		2nd	-/-/-/-	-/-/-/-	-	2	-	-	-	-
18	Steve Woods	1st	-/-/-/-	-/-/-/-	-	-	-	-	-	-
	□ 80	2nd	1/-/-/-	-/-/-/-	-	2	-	-	-	-
6	Alex Russell	1st	-/-/-/-	-/-/1/-	-	-	-	3	1	-
		2nd	-/-/-/-	-/-/-/-	-	-	1	4	-	-
20	Liam Rosenior	1st	-/-/-/-	-/-/1/-	-	-	-	-	-	-
	▲ 29	2nd	-/-/-/-	-/-/-/-	-	-	1	-	1	-
11	Kevin Hill	1st	-/-/-/-	-/-/-/-	-	-	1	-	-	-
	▼ 29	2nd	-/-/-/-	-/-/-/-	-	-	-	-	-	-
10	David Graham	1st	-/1/-/-	-/-/-/-	-	1	2	-	-	-
	□ 8	2nd	-/-/-/-	-/2/-/-	1	-	2	-	-	-
14	Matthew Hockley	1st	-/-/1/-	-/-/-/-	-	1	-	-	-	-
	□ 71	2nd	-/-/-/-	-/1/-/-	-	1	-	1	1	-
12	Jo Kuffour	1st	-/-/-/-	-/-/-/-	-	-	-	-	-	-
	▲ 29	2nd	-/-/-/-	-/-/-/-	1	-	1	-	-	-
17	Brian McGlinchey	1st	-/-/-/-	-/-/-/-	-	-	-	-	-	-
		2nd	-/-/-/-	-/-/-/-	-	-	-	-	-	-
25	Daryl McMahon	1st	-/-/-/-	-/-/-/-	-	-	-	-	-	-
	▲ 78	2nd	-/-/-/-	-/-/-/-	-	-	-	-	-	-

Subs not used: Van Heusden, Hazell. - **Formation: 4-4-2**

Goalkeeper Stats: Steven Collis Saves: Catch 2, Feet 2, Penalty 2, Parry 2, Crosses: Catch 4

No.	Player Stats	Shots on target	Shots off target	Caught offside	Fouls conceded	Free-kicks won	Corners taken	Clearances	Defensive blocks
7	Adam Stansfield ▲ 78	-/-/-/-	-/-/-/-	-	-	-	-	-	-
11	Lee Matthews	-/1/-/-	-/-/-/-	1	-	2	-	-	-
5	Colin Pluck	-/-/-/-	1/-/-/-	-	4	-	-	2	1
8	Lee Johnson	-/1/-/-	-/-/-/-	-	1	1	7	1	-
10	Nick Crittenden ▼ 68	-/-/-/-	-/-/-/-	-	1	-	-	-	-
17	Jake Edwards ▼ 78	-/1/-/-	-/1/1/-	-	1	3	-	-	-
20	Gavin Williams □ 53 ■ 88	-/1/-/-	-/-/-/-	-	4	2	4	-	-
24	Paul Terry □ 61	-/-/-/-	-/-/-/-	-	1	-	-	3	-
4	Terry Skiverton	-/-/-/-	-/-/1/-	-	1	-	-	1	-
6	Darren Way	-/2/-/-	-/1/-/-	-	-	-	-	1	-
9	Kevin Gall ▲ 68	-/-/-/-	-/-/-/-	-	-	-	-	-	-
3	Abdelhalim El Kholti	-/1/-/-	-/-/-/-	-	2	-	-	-	-

Subs not used: Talbott, Weatherstone, Northmore. - **Formation: 4-4-2**

Torquay Played: 40 **Won** 19 **Drawn** 11 **Lost** 10 **For** 57 **Against** 39 **Pos** 4

Bury [1] 2 TORQUAY [1] 1

9th April

Torquay United lost not just three vital points at Bury, but goalkeeper Kevin Dearden may have been knocked out of the Third Division promotion race.

Dearden limped through the closing stages of the 1-2 defeat at Gigg Lane after pulling a hamstring, and Arjan Van Heusden looked certain to take over for Monday's key six-pointer against Oxford United at Plainmoor.

Bury came from behind to cancel out David Graham's 20th goal of the season, winning with goals by Gareth Seddon and David Nugent.

The result left United struggling to overtake Huddersfield for the third automatic promotion spot.

But head coach Leroy Rosenior refused to be downhearted. He said that United had got five games left, and he believed that they were capable of winning all five. This was despite them stuttering in a spell of only one win in seven matches however.

They were very disappointed to lose, but Rosenior was delighted with his players. He believed that the performance was outstanding at times, especially in the first half, and in difficult conditions.

Unfortunately the rub of the green was just not going for the Gulls. The players gave everything against a battling Bury side. Their attitude was spot-on and the football was good.

David Graham scored a great goal, although he should have hit the target a few more times later in the game. Bury were strong and the refereeing was poor. David Flitcroft must have committed 12 fouls without getting booked.

Torquay were not getting the rub of the green. Earlier in the season, they would have taken all three points from a performance like that. Instead Bury stole all the points after they came behind to score an unlikely victory, with the winning goal being scored by David Nugent.

Rosenior was not worried about what the other teams were doing. He believed that the Gulls had keep going and keep playing good football.

Result.......Result.......Result.

BURY ....(1) **2** **TORQUAY** ......(1) **1**
Seddon 35 Graham 30
Nugent 67

Att 2,770
Referee: A Penn

Stats......Stats.......Stats......Stats

BURY 1st	2nd	Total		TORQUAY Total	2nd	1st
0	2	2	**Corners**	10	7	3
9	11	20	**Fouls**	8	4	4
0	3	3	**Yellow cards**	4	3	1
0	0	0	**Red cards**	0	0	0
1	1	2	**Caught Offside**	4	1	3
2	7	9	**Shots on target**	11	7	4
3	2	5	**Shots off target**	6	2	4
0	1	1	**Hit woodwork**	0	0	0
32	48	40%	**Possession**	60%	52	68

WE gave a good account of ourselves and now we've got to make sure no-one takes their foot off the pedal for the rest of the season.

Graham Barrow

I'M disappointed we didn't get anything from the game but I'm not disappointed by the performance. We've got to keep trying and driving forward.

Leroy Rosenior

Other Div 3 Results

Cambridge Utd 2 York 0, Oxford Utd 0 Boston Utd 0

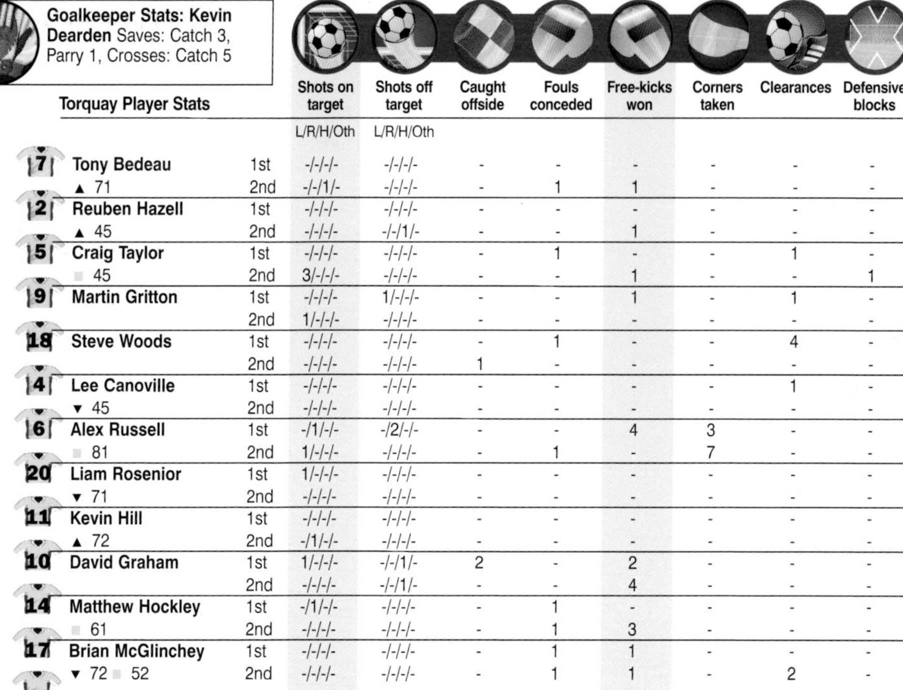

Goalkeeper Stats: Kevin Dearden Saves: Catch 3, Parry 1, Crosses: Catch 5

Torquay Player Stats		Shots on target	Shots off target	Caught offside	Fouls conceded	Free-kicks won	Corners taken	Clearances	Defensive blocks
		L/R/H/Oth	L/R/H/Oth						
7 Tony Bedeau	1st	-/-/-/-	-/-/-/-	-	-	-	-	-	-
▲ 71	2nd	-/-/1/-	-/-/-/-	-	1	1	-	-	-
2 Reuben Hazell	1st	-/-/-/-	-/-/-/-	-	-	-	-	-	-
▲ 45	2nd	-/-/-/-	-/-/1/-	-	-	1	-	-	-
5 Craig Taylor	1st	-/-/-/-	-/-/-/-	-	1	-	-	1	-
■ 45	2nd	3/-/-/-	-/-/-/-	-	-	1	-	-	1
9 Martin Gritton	1st	-/-/-/-	1/-/-/-	-	-	1	-	1	-
	2nd	1/-/-/-	-/-/-/-	-	-	-	-	-	-
18 Steve Woods	1st	-/-/-/-	-/-/-/-	-	1	-	-	4	-
	2nd	-/-/-/-	-/-/-/-	1	-	-	-	-	-
4 Lee Canoville	1st	-/-/-/-	-/-/-/-	-	-	-	-	1	-
▼ 45	2nd	-/-/-/-	-/-/-/-	-	-	-	-	-	-
6 Alex Russell	1st	-/1/-/-	-/2/-/-	-	-	4	3	-	-
■ 81	2nd	1/-/-/-	-/-/-/-	-	1	-	7	-	-
20 Liam Rosenior	1st	1/-/-/-	-/-/-/-	-	-	-	-	-	-
▼ 71	2nd	-/-/-/-	-/-/-/-	-	-	-	-	-	-
11 Kevin Hill	1st	-/-/-/-	-/-/-/-	-	-	-	-	-	-
▲ 72	2nd	-/1/-/-	-/-/-/-	-	-	-	-	-	-
10 David Graham	1st	1/-/-/-	-/-/1/-	2	-	2	-	-	-
	2nd	-/-/-/-	-/-/1/-	-	-	4	-	-	-
14 Matthew Hockley	1st	-/1/-/-	-/-/-/-	-	1	-	-	-	-
■ 61	2nd	-/-/-/-	-/-/-/-	-	1	3	-	-	-
17 Brian McGlinchey	1st	-/-/-/-	-/-/-/-	-	1	1	-	-	-
▼ 72 ■ 52	2nd	-/-/-/-	-/-/-/-	-	1	1	-	2	-

Subs not used: Van Heusden, Woozley. - **Formation: 4-4-2**

Goalkeeper Stats: Glyn Garner Crosses: Catch 1

	Player Stats	Shots on target	Shots off target	Caught offside	Fouls conceded	Free-kicks won	Corners taken	Clearances	Defensive blocks
3	Colin Woodthorpe ■ 90	-/-/-/-	-/-/-/-	-	2	-	-	2	1
17	Terry Dunfield	-/-/-/-	-/-/-/-	-	2	1	-	1	-
22	Harpal Singh	-/-/-/-	-/1/-/-	-	1	1	1	-	-
4	Danny Swailes	-/-/-/-	-/-/-/-	-	1	-	-	-	3
30	David Challinor	-/-/-/-	-/-/-/-	-	-	-	-	3	-
11	David Flitcroft	-/1/-/-	-/-/-/-	-	5	1	-	2	-
12	Chris Porter ▲ 90	-/-/-/-	-/-/-/-	-	-	-	-	-	-
19	Gareth Seddon ▼ 77 ■ 76	1/3/2/-	-/2/-/-	2	1	-	-	2	-
2	Matthew Barrass	-/1/-/-	-/-/-/-	-	-	-	-	2	3
9	David Nugent ▼ 90	1/-/-/-	1/-/-/-	-	3	2	-	-	-
18	Thomas Kennedy ■ 58	-/-/-/-	-/-/-/-	-	3	-	1	-	-
14	Paul O'Shaughnessy ▲ 77	-/-/-/-	-/1/-/-	-	1	1	-	-	-

Subs not used: Whaley, Cartledge, Solly. - **Formation: 3-4-3**

Torquay Played: 41 **Won** 19 **Drawn** 11 **Lost** 11 **For** 58 **Against** 41 **Pos** 4

Torquay [1] 3 OXFORD UTD [0] 0

12th April

Torquay United silenced the doubters when they destroyed Oxford United in front of a bumper holiday crowd at Plainmoor.

A run of one win in seven previous games had piled on the pressure forTorquay, but they didn't show it.

Nobody played better than a man apparently out of position in Reuben Hazell. His second-half goal was just reward for a performance full of character and intent.

Rosenior restored the striking partnership of Jo Kuffour and David Graham up front, and their combination of pace and trickery was too much for Oxford's overworked defence.

When the breakthrough came in the 32nd minute, it was with an own-goal. Liam Rosenior left Danny Brown for dead on United's right and, when Graham's headed lunge just missed the cross from close-range, Paul Wanless could only turn it into his own net.

In the space of 60 seconds around the 37th minute, one brilliant solo run by Graham set up Kuffour for a left-foot miss, and then Graham had two shots blocked after a sparkling Rosenior-Hazell build-up.

Oxford started brightly in the second-half, but Van Heusden's handling was still sure, and the U's ended up with only three scoring attempts to United's 15.

In the 63rd minute Fowler combined with Kuffour on the right, Kuffour's pass inside Matt Bound beat the offside trap and found Hazell on the overlap, and he steadied himself before slipping the ball past Woodman on an angle from ten yards.

Eleven minutes later Fowler was involved in the build-up to a goal which saw United at their best.

Fowler started it, setting Russell away down the left. Just when Oxford were expecting Russell to cut back on his favoured right foot, he delivered a terrific cross with his left, Craig Taylor nodded the ball back from beyond the far-post and Graham was there to head into the roof of the net from four yards.

Result.......Result.......Result.

TORQUAY ....(1) **3** **OXFORD UTD** (0) **0**
Wanless 33 (og)
Hazell 63
Graham 75

Att 5,114
Referee: R Beeby

Stats......Stats.......Stats......Stats

TORQUAY				OXFORD UTD		
1st	**2nd**	**Total**		**Total**	**2nd**	**1st**
5	2	7	**Corners**	5	4	1
6	6	12	**Fouls**	12	5	7
0	0	0	**Yellow cards**	1	1	0
0	0	0	**Red cards**	1	0	1
5	2	7	**Caught Offside**	0	0	0
2	3	5	**Shots on target**	2	1	1
6	3	9	**Shots off target**	2	1	1
0	0	0	**Hit woodwork**	0	0	0
45	54	49%	**Possession**	51%	46	55

THAT performance put the doubters in their place. We did it with pace and skill, playing the football we like to play.

Leroy Rosenior

TO an extent I feel a bit let down. We ran about and tried our best but were naive, and there are many other things I could say.

Graham Rix

Other Div 3 Results

Boston Utd 3 Yeovil 2, Cheltenham 2 Scunthorpe 1, Doncaster 2 Cambridge Utd 0, Kidderminster 2 Huddersfield 1, Leyton Orient 1 Carlisle 1, Mansfield 0 Bristol Rovers 0, Rochdale 1 Macclesfield 2, Southend 3 Darlington 2, Swansea 2 Hull 3

TORQUAY [1] 3 Oxford Utd [0] 0

Goalkeeper Stats: Arjan Van Heusden Saves: Catch 6, Crosses: Catch 6

	Torquay Player Stats		Shots on target	Shots off target	Caught offside	Fouls conceded	Free-kicks won	Corners taken	Clearances	Defensive blocks
			L/R/H/Oth	L/R/H/Oth						
5	Craig Taylor	1st	-/-/-/-	-/-/-/-	-	3	2	-	1	-
		2nd	-/-/-/-	-/-/-/-	-	-	-	-	3	-
3	David Woozley	1st	-/-/-/-	-/-/-/-	-	-	-	-	-	-
	▲ 77	2nd	-/-/-/-	-/-/-/-	-	-	-	-	-	-
2	Reuben Hazell	1st	-/-/-/-	-/-/-/-	-	1	-	-	-	-
		2nd	-/1/-/-	-/-/-/-	-	1	-	-	2	-
9	Martin Gritton	1st	-/-/-/-	-/-/-/-	-	-	-	-	-	-
	▲ 85	2nd	-/-/-/-	-/-/-/-	-	-	-	-	-	-
18	Steve Woods	1st	-/-/1/-	1/-/-/-	-	1	-	-	1	-
		2nd	-/-/-/-	-/-/-/-	-	1	-	-	-	-
6	Alex Russell	1st	-/-/-/-	-/-/-/-	-	-	1	5	-	-
		2nd	-/-/-/-	-/1/-/-	-	1	1	2	-	-
20	Liam Rosenior	1st	-/-/-/-	-/1/-/-	-	-	-	-	2	-
	▼ 62	2nd	-/-/-/-	-/-/-/-	-	-	-	-	-	-
11	Kevin Hill	1st	-/-/-/-	-/-/-/-	1	-	1	-	-	-
		2nd	-/-/-/-	-/1/-/-	1	1	1	-	-	-
10	David Graham	1st	-/1/-/-	1/1/-/-	3	1	-	-	-	-
	▼ 85	2nd	-/-/-/-	1/-/-/-	1	2	2	-	-	-
14	Matthew Hockley	1st	-/-/-/-	-/-/-/-	-	-	-	-	1	-
		2nd	-/-/-/-	-/-/-/-	-	-	1	-	-	-
8	Jason Fowler	1st	-/-/-/-	-/-/-/-	-	-	-	-	-	-
	▲ 62	2nd	-/-/-/-	-/-/-/-	-	-	-	-	-	-
12	Jo Kuffour	1st	-/-/-/-	1/-/-/-	1	-	2	-	-	1
		2nd	-/2/-/-	-/-/-/-	-	-	-	-	-	-
17	Brian McGlinchey	1st	-/-/-/-	1/-/-/-	-	-	1	-	1	-
	▼ 77	2nd	-/-/-/-	-/-/-/-	-	-	-	-	-	-

Subs not used: Wills, Bedeau. - **Formation: 4-4-2**

OXFORD UNITED F.C.

Goalkeeper Stats: Andy Woodman Saves: Catch 4, Crosses: Catch 4, Parry 2

	Player Stats	Shots on target	Shots off target	Caught offside	Fouls conceded	Free-kicks won	Corners taken	Clearances	Defensive blocks
18	Matthew Bound	-/-/-/-	-/-/-/-	-	-	2	-	4	-
23	Steve Basham ▼ 45	-/1/-/-	-/-/-/-	-	1	3	-	-	-
29	Jon Ashton	-/-/-/-	-/-/-/-	-	1	2	-	2	1
19	Daniel Brown	-/-/-/-	-/-/-/-	-	-	-	1	1	-
11	Mark Rawle	-/-/-/-	1/-/-/-	-	1	2	-	2	-
6	David Waterman	-/-/-/-	'-/-/-	-	2	-	-	2	-
10	Courtney Pitt ▲ 45	-/-/-/-	-/-/-/-	-	-	1	-	-	-
12	Dean Whitehead	-/1/-/-	-/1/-/-	-	3	-	4	-	-
7	Chris Hackett ▲ 45	-/-/-/-	-/-/-/-	-	-	1	-	-	-
5	Andy Crosby ■ 41	-/-/-/-	-/-/-/-	-	2	-	-	1	-
27	Paul Wanless ▼ 45	-/-/-/-	-/-/-/-	-	-	1	-	1	-
8	James Hunt ■ 83	-/-/-/-	-/-/-/-	-	2	-	-	-	-

Subs not used: Cox, McNiven, Walker. - **Formation: 3-5-2**

Torquay Played: 42 **Won** 20 **Drawn** 11 **Lost** 11 **For** 61 **Against** 41 **Pos** 4

Torquay [1] 1 DONCASTER [0] 0

17th April

After being totally outplayed for more than an hour, ten-man Doncaster Rovers put another bumper crowd through the emotional mincer.

Conceding territory and possession despite their extra man, United were backed up against the Babbacombe Away End in a torrid examination of their resolve.

When Fortune-West headed an 'equaliser', United's automatic promotion hopes seemed to have gone with it. But referee David Crick had spotted a push by Fortune-West on United goalscorer Kevin Hill.

United were forced to hang on desperately in the second half on Saturday but nobody can accuse Leroy Rosenior's side of caving in. In that tense finale, they threw heads, legs and bodies in the way of a barrage of shots, crosses and set-piece moves. It may not have been pretty but in the end it was just enough.

David Graham nearly scored after only eight seconds, shooting just wide after playing two one-twos with Alex Russell from the kick-off. Then Graham dashed clear on a Brian McGlinchey through-ball and his angled left-foot shot hit the inside of the post, stayed out and rebounded on to the knee of defender Dave Morley.

With Steve Woods and McGlinchey immaculate on the ball, the Gulls were able to build from the back. And in midfield and attack, they made Doncaster look anything but champions-elect.

The breakthrough came in the 37th minute. Liam Rosenior, lively on the right wing, swept past Richard McGrath on the outside, crossed to the far-post and Hill finished with a measured header back across goal from eight yards. It was his fifth goal of the season.

United needed a second goal to end Doncaster's resistance and, with Martin Gritton replacing the injured Jo Kuffour at the interval, they should have had it.

In the second-half United started conceding ground and the fans became tense.

Rovers poured long balls, from deep and wide into United's goalmouth and let Fortune-West fight for them.

Result.......Result.......Result.

TORQUAY ....(1) **1** **DONCASTER** (0) **0**
Hill 38

Att 5,808
Referee: D Crick

Stats......Stats.......Stats......Stats

TORQUAY				DONCASTER		
1st	**2nd**	**Total**		**Total**	**2nd**	**1st**
4	1	5	**Corners**	13	11	2
2	9	11	**Fouls**	13	7	6
1	2	3	**Yellow cards**	1	0	1
0	0	0	**Red cards**	1	0	1
2	3	5	**Caught Offside**	2	1	1
9	3	12	**Shots on target**	4	3	1
3	1	4	**Shots off target**	5	2	3
1	0	1	**Hit woodwork**	0	0	0
62	67	64%	**Possession**	36%	33	38

WE were absolutely scintillating. In the second half we got a bit nervous and it wasn't about tactics, it was about sheer guts and determination.

Leroy Rosenior

TORQUAY played well and were the better team in the first half but I thought we were better in the second half.

Dave Penney

Other Div 3 Results

Boston Utd 1 Mansfield 2, Bristol Rovers 2 Swansea 1, Cambridge Utd 0 Kidderminster 0, Darlington 2 Oxford Utd 0, Huddersfield 3 Scunthorpe 2, Macclesfield 1 Hull 1, Northampton 2 Southend 2, Rochdale 3 Leyton Orient 0, Yeovil 2 Bury 1, York 0 Cheltenham 2

TORQUAY [1] 1 Doncaster [0] 0

Goalkeeper Stats: Arjan Van Heusden Saves: Catch 2, Crosses: Catch 10, Feet 2

Torquay Player Stats		Shots on target L/R/H/Oth	Shots off target L/R/H/Oth	Caught offside	Fouls conceded	Free-kicks won	Corners taken	Clearances	Defensive blocks
2 Reuben Hazell	1st	-/-/-/-	-/-/-/-	-	-	-	-	-	-
	2nd	-/-/-/-	-/-/-/-	-	1	1	-	3	-
5 Craig Taylor	1st	-/-/-/-	-/-/-/-	-	-	-	-	1	-
	2nd	-/-/-/-	-/-/-/-	-	-	-	-	2	-
3 David Woozley	1st	-/-/-/-	-/-/-/-	-	-	-	-	-	-
▲ 89	2nd	-/-/-/-	-/-/-/-	-	-	-	-	-	-
9 Martin Gritton	1st	-/-/-/-	-/-/-/-	-	-	-	-	-	-
▲ 45	2nd	-/-/1/-	-/-/-/-	1	1	-	-	2	-
18 Steve Woods	1st	-/1/-/-	-/-/-/-	-	-	2	-	1	-
	2nd	-/-/-/-	-/-/-/-	-	-	-	-	4	-
20 Liam Rosenior	1st	-/-/-/-	-/-/-/-	-	-	-	-	-	-
▼ 71	2nd	-/-/-/-	-/-/-/-	-	-	2	-	-	-
6 Alex Russell	1st	1/-/-/-	-/-/-/-	-	1	-	4	-	-
■ 51	2nd	-/-/-/-	-/-/-/-	-	1	-	1	-	-
11 Kevin Hill	1st	-/-/1/-	-/-/1/-	-	-	1	-	-	-
	2nd	-/-/-/-	-/1/-/-	1	-	1	-	-	-
10 David Graham	1st	1/2/-/-	2/-/-/-	1	-	3	-	-	-
▼ 89	2nd	2/-/-/-	-/-/-/-	1	2	2	-	-	-
14 Matthew Hockley	1st	-/2/-/-	-/-/-/-	-	1	-	-	-	-
■ 90	2nd	-/-/-/-	-/-/-/-	-	3	1	-	-	-
8 Jason Fowler	1st	-/-/-/-	-/-/-/-	-	-	-	-	-	-
▲ 71	2nd	-/-/-/-	-/-/-/-	-	1	-	-	-	-
12 Jo Kuffour	1st	-/1/-/-	-/-/-/-	1	-	-	-	-	-
▼ 45	2nd	-/-/-/-	-/-/-/-	-	-	-	-	-	-
17 Brian McGlinchey	1st	-/-/-/-	-/-/-/-	-	-	-	-	2	-
■ 29	2nd	-/-/-/-	-/-/-/-	-	-	-	-	1	-

Subs not used: Wills, Bedeau. - **Formation: 4-4-2**

Goalkeeper Stats: Andy Warrington Saves: Catch 8, Feet 2, Parry 2, Crosses: Catch 4, Block 2, Parry 2

	Player Stats	Shots on target	Shots off target	Caught offside	Fouls conceded	Free-kicks won	Corners taken	Clearances	Defensive blocks
4	David Morley	-/-/-/-	-/-/1/-	-	1	1	-	2	-
20	Paul Green ▲ 63	-/-/-/-	-/-/1/-	-	-	1	7	-	-
14	Leo Fortune-West ▲ 63	-/1/1/-	-/-/-/-	-	1	-	-	-	-
3	Tim Ryan	-/-/-/-	-/-/-/-	-	-	2	-	1	-
12	John McGrath	-/-/-/-	-/-/-/-	-	2	-	6	-	-
19	Ricky Ravenhill	-/-/-/-	-/1/-/-	-	4	2	-	1	-
16	John Melligan ▼ 18	-/1/-/-	-/-/-/-	-	-	-	-	-	-
30	Dave Mulligan ■ 15	-/-/-/-	-/-/-/-	-	1	-	-	1	-
18	Jamie Price ▲ 18	-/-/-/-	-/-/-/-	-	-	1	-	-	-
9	Adebayo Akinfenwa ▼ 63	-/-/-/-	-/2/-/-	-	2	1	-	-	-
23	Stephen Foster ■ 34	-/-/-/-	-/-/-/-	-	2	2	-	5	3
5	John Doolan ▼ 63	-/-/-/-	-/-/-/-	-	-	1	-	-	-
8	Gregg Blundell	-/1/-/-	-/-/-/-	2	-	-	-	-	-

Subs not used: Brown, Collin. - **Formation: 4-4-2**

Torquay Played: 43 **Won** 21 **Drawn** 11 **Lost** 11 **For** 62 **Against** 41 **Pos** 4

Cheltenham [0] 1 TORQUAY [1] 3 — 24th April

Hull City and Huddersfield Town packed 23,500 fans into the KC Stadium hoping that they could both finally shake off Leroy Rosenior's men and celebrate promotion.

But two smashing goals by striker Jo Kuffour and a thunderous header from man-of-the-match Steve Woods beat outgunned Cheltenham at Whaddon Road as United refused to be shaken off the scent.

After a couple of early scares United ran the show. Graham had a 22-yard snapshot well saved before the breakthrough came in the 18th minute.

From a half-cleared free-kick, Russell's ball back into the area was flicked on by Craig Taylor's heel and Kuffour took a touch before punishing some slack marking with a firm right-foot shot from 12 yards.

With Graham and right-winger Liam Rosenior to the fore, United's quality on the ball started to open up the Cheltenham defence. And, after a brilliant solo run by Graham had forced a corner, Taylor headed inches over.

Cheltenham tried to gee up their outplayed midfield and for a worrying spell early in the second half United seemed to take their foot off the pedal. But they got themselves back into gear with a screaming 20-yard volley by Graham which keeper Shane Higgs just tipped over.

Then Woods scored the clinching second goal. Kuffour forced a corner on United's right, Russell's delivery was first-class and Woods powered an unstoppable header into the top right-hand corner from ten yards.

Cheltenham knew they were out of their depth and in the 78th minute Kuffour confirmed it. An inviting Russell lay-off in midfield gave Matt Hockley the chance to drive forward, his shot on the edge of the area was blocked, but the ball broke for Kuffour, who turned and thumped another right-foot shot low past Higgs' right hand from 16 yards.

That should have been it, but only three minutes later United squandered the chance of a third successive clean-sheet. A long ball down the middle by Higgs should not have been a problem yet Spencer managed to head the ball home.

Result.......Result.......Result.

CHELTENHAM ....(0) **1** **TORQUAY** ......(1) **3**
Spencer 81 — Kuffour 18, 78; Woods 65

Att 4,900
Referee: J Ross

Stats......Stats.......Stats......Stats

CHELTENHAM						TORQUAY
1st	**2nd**	**Total**		**Total**	**2nd**	**1st**
2	0	2	**Corners**	7	4	3
4	7	11	**Fouls**	8	3	5
0	2	2	**Yellow cards**	3	2	1
0	0	0	**Red cards**	0	0	0
1	2	3	**Caught Offside**	4	0	4
0	4	4	**Shots on target**	7	4	3
3	0	3	**Shots off target**	5	2	3
0	0	0	**Hit woodwork**	0	0	0
43	47	45%	**Possession**	55%	53	57

TORQUAY are an excellent side and I said that if we want to aspire to these things then we have got to be quicker and better in our play.

John Ward

I thought we were outstanding but there was no jumping up and down and celebrating - we have to keep on doing what we are doing.

Leroy Rosenior

Other Div 3 Results

Bury 0 Bristol Rovers 0, Doncaster 3 York 1, Hull 0 Huddersfield 0, Kidderminster 0 Rochdale 1, Leyton Orient 1 Boston Utd 3, Mansfield 2 Carlisle 3, Oxford Utd 2 Cambridge Utd 2, Scunthorpe 1 Macclesfield 0, Southend 0 Yeovil 2, Swansea 0 Northampton 2

Cheltenham [0] 1 TORQUAY [1] 3

Goalkeeper Stats: Arjan Van Heusden Saves: Catch 2, Crosses: Catch 1, Punch 1

Torquay Player Stats

No.	Player	Half	Shots on target L/R/H/Oth	Shots off target L/R/H/Oth	Caught offside	Fouls conceded	Free-kicks won	Corners taken	Clearances	Defensive blocks
7	Tony Bedeau	1st	-/-/-/-	-/-/-/-	-	-	-	-	-	-
	▲ 90	2nd	-/-/-/-	-/-/-/-	-	-	-	-	-	-
2	Reuben Hazell	1st	-/-/-/-	-/-/-/-	-	1	1	-	-	-
		2nd	-/-/-/-	-/-/-/-	-	-	1	-	2	-
5	Craig Taylor	1st	-/-/-/-	-/-/1/-	-	1	-	-	4	-
	■ 36	2nd	-/-/-/-	-/-/-/-	-	-	-	-	1	1
9	Martin Gritton	1st	-/-/-/-	-/-/-/-	-	-	-	-	-	-
	▲ 85	2nd	-/-/-/-	-/-/-/-	-	-	-	-	-	-
18	Steve Woods	1st	-/-/-/-	-/-/-/-	-	-	-	-	2	1
	■ 59	2nd	-/-/1/-	-/-/-/-	-	-	-	-	1	-
6	Alex Russell	1st	-/-/-/-	1/-/-/-	-	-	-	3	1	-
		2nd	-/-/-/-	-/-/-/-	-	-	1	4	-	-
20	Liam Rosenior	1st	1/-/-/-	-/-/-/-	-	1	2	-	-	-
	▼ 71	2nd	-/-/-/-	-/-/-/-	-	-	-	-	-	-
11	Kevin Hill	1st	-/-/-/-	1/-/-/-	-	1	1	-	1	-
	■ 67	2nd	-/-/-/-	-/-/-/-	-	2	1	-	-	-
10	David Graham	1st	1/-/-/-	-/-/-/-	3	1	-	-	-	-
	▼ 90	2nd	-/2/-/-	-/-/-/-	-	-	3	-	-	-
14	Matthew Hockley	1st	-/-/-/-	-/-/-/-	-	-	-	-	-	-
		2nd	-/-/-/-	-/1/-/-	-	1	-	-	-	-
8	Jason Fowler	1st	-/-/-/-	-/-/-/-	-	-	-	-	-	-
	▲ 71	2nd	-/-/-/-	-/-/1/-	-	-	-	-	-	-
12	Jo Kuffour	1st	-/1/-/-	-/-/-/-	1	-	-	-	-	-
	▼ 85	2nd	-/1/-/-	-/-/-/-	-	-	-	-	-	-
17	Brian McGlinchey	1st	-/-/-/-	-/-/-/-	-	-	-	-	-	-
		2nd	-/-/-/-	-/-/-/-	-	-	1	-	-	-

Subs not used: Woozley, Wills. - **Formation: 4-4-2**

Goalkeeper Stats: Shane Higgs Saves: Catch 3, Crosses: Catch 4, Punch 1

No.	Player Stats	Shots on target	Shots off target	Caught offside	Fouls conceded	Free-kicks won	Corners taken	Clearances	Defensive blocks
6	Michael Duff	-/-/-/-	-/-/-/-	-	-	1	-	-	1
9	Paul Brayson	-/-/-/-	-/1/-/-	3	1	1	-	-	-
29	Brian Wilson ■ 88	-/1/-/-	1/-/-/-	-	1	2	1	1	-
14	David Bird	-/1/-/-	-/-/-/-	-	-	-	-	2	-
28	John Finnigan ▼ 45	-/-/-/-	-/-/-/-	-	1	-	-	-	-
10	Damian Spencer	-/-/1/-	-/-/1/-	-	3	1	-	1	-
17	Kayode Odejayi ▲ 66	-/-/-/-	-/-/-/-	-	-	-	-	-	-
22	Graham Fyfe ▲ 45	-/-/-/-	-/-/-/-	-	-	-	-	-	-
18	Shane Duff	-/-/-/-	-/-/-/-	-	2	1	-	1	-
11	Grant McCann ■ 57	1/-/-/-	-/-/-/-	-	2	1	1	1	-
3	Jamie Victory	-/-/-/-	-/-/-/-	-	-	1	-	-	-
2	Antony Griffin ▼ 66	-/-/-/-	-/-/-/-	-	1	-	-	-	-

Subs not used: Book, Forsyth, Taylor. - **Formation: 3-5-2**

Torquay Played: 44 **Won** 22 **Drawn** 11 **Lost** 11 **For** 65 **Against** 42 **Pos** 4

...April Team Stats.....Team Stats......Team Stats......Team S

League table at the end of April

	HOME						AWAY						
	P	W	D	L	F	A	W	D	L	F	A	Pts	Df
Doncaster	44	16	4	2	46	13	10	6	6	32	24	88	41
Hull	44	15	4	3	47	21	8	9	5	30	22	82	34
Huddersfield	44	16	4	2	41	15	7	7	8	25	33	80	18
Torquay	**44**	**15**	**5**	**2**	**43**	**17**	**7**	**6**	**9**	**22**	**25**	**77**	**23**
Lincoln City	44	9	11	2	34	20	10	6	6	31	21	74	24
Mansfield	44	13	5	4	43	23	8	4	10	29	36	72	13
Yeovil	44	14	3	5	39	17	8	2	12	27	36	71	13
Northampton	44	12	4	6	27	21	8	5	9	26	27	69	5
Oxford Utd	44	13	8	1	32	13	4	9	9	20	29	68	10
Boston Utd	44	11	6	5	35	21	5	4	13	15	31	58	-2
Swansea	44	9	7	6	36	26	5	6	11	20	34	55	-4
Cheltenham	44	11	3	8	36	37	3	9	10	19	32	54	-14
Bury	44	9	7	6	27	26	5	4	13	23	35	53	-11
Southend	44	8	4	10	26	27	6	7	9	23	33	53	-11
Bristol Rovers	44	8	7	7	26	25	5	6	11	21	32	52	-10
Kidderminster	44	8	5	9	26	29	5	7	10	16	29	51	-16
Darlington	44	10	4	8	29	26	3	7	12	22	33	50	-8
Cambridge Utd	44	5	7	10	23	30	7	7	8	28	35	50	-14
Leyton Orient	44	8	9	5	28	26	4	5	13	18	37	50	-17
Scunthorpe	44	7	10	5	36	26	4	6	12	31	42	49	-1
Rochdale	44	7	7	8	27	25	5	6	11	21	30	49	-7
Macclesfield	44	7	9	6	26	24	5	4	13	26	42	49	-14
Carlisle	44	8	4	10	22	26	4	4	14	23	41	44	-22
York	44	7	6	9	21	27	3	7	12	13	37	43	-30

April matches table

	P	W	D	L	F	A	Pts
Doncaster	5	4	0	1	10	4	12
Northampton	6	3	2	1	10	7	11
Yeovil	6	3	2	1	10	7	11
Lincoln City	5	3	2	0	9	3	11
Huddersfield	6	3	2	1	7	5	11
Torquay	**5**	**3**	**1**	**1**	**10**	**5**	**10**
Boston Utd	5	3	1	1	8	5	10
Carlisle	5	3	1	1	7	6	10
Macclesfield	5	3	1	1	6	3	10
Southend	6	2	2	2	11	11	8
Mansfield	6	2	2	2	8	7	8
Bristol Rovers	5	2	2	1	5	4	8
Hull	6	1	4	1	9	9	7
Rochdale	5	2	1	2	7	7	7
Darlington	5	2	1	2	6	5	7
Cheltenham	5	2	1	2	6	6	7
Cambridge Utd	5	1	3	1	5	5	6
Bury	5	1	2	2	5	7	5
Kidderminster	5	1	2	2	3	4	5
Scunthorpe	5	1	1	3	8	11	4
Oxford Utd	6	0	2	4	4	12	2
Leyton Orient	5	0	2	3	3	9	2
York	6	0	1	5	3	12	1
Swansea	5	0	0	5	5	11	0

April team stats details

Club Name	Ply	Shots On	Shots Off	Corners	Hit W'work	Caught Offside	Offside Trap	Fouls	Yellow Cards	Red Cards	Pens Awarded	Per Co
Boston Utd	5	28	10	21	1	26	7	69	7	0	- (-)	-
Bristol Rovers	5	33	13	33	4	16	14	70	3	1	- (-)	-
Bury	5	33	22	27	3	13	13	56	7	0	- (-)	-
Cambridge Utd	5	20	21	20	1	9	16	87	15	0	- (-)	-
Carlisle	5	37	29	27	2	17	18	57	10	1	1 (1)	3
Cheltenham	5	33	29	24	1	13	23	58	5	0	1 (1)	1
Darlington	5	21	14	26	2	18	20	72	13	1	1 (1)	2
Doncaster	5	30	30	40	2	11	13	59	5	2	- (-)	-
Huddersfield	6	30	34	34	3	23	8	69	9	4	- (-)	-
Hull	6	43	34	32	2	12	21	67	7	0	- (-)	-
Kidderminster	5	23	18	27	1	10	3	76	9	2	- (-)	-
Leyton Orient	5	15	30	30	0	16	29	67	10	1	- (-)	-
Lincoln City	5	34	45	27	1	9	11	76	12	0	- (-)	-
Macclesfield	5	35	30	30	3	17	16	59	3	0	1 (1)	1
Mansfield	6	38	28	35	4	15	17	62	3	0	2 (1)	-
Northampton	6	38	25	35	1	16	24	71	7	0	2 (1)	1
Oxford Utd	6	26	27	46	0	11	20	76	6	1	- (-)	-
Rochdale	5	33	25	21	2	16	12	62	8	0	- (-)	-
Scunthorpe	5	28	17	33	0	23	18	83	12	0	1 (-)	1
Southend	6	42	37	41	1	24	30	85	9	0	2 (2)	2
Swansea	5	24	26	34	0	13	5	76	11	0	- (-)	-
Torquay	**5**	**42**	**32**	**37**	**2**	**24**	**8**	**47**	**14**	**0**	**1 (-)**	**-**
Yeovil	6	39	19	26	3	14	18	87	8	1	1 (-)	2
York	6	29	15	24	0	16	18	67	6	2	- (-)	-

Monthly Match Details: Games 64 **Home Wins** 26 **Away Wins** 19 **Draws** 19

..April Player Stats..... Player Stats...... Player Stats......Pla

Monthly Top scorers

aniel Rodrigues (Yeovil)	4
ric Sabin (Northampton)	4
imon Yeo (Lincoln City)	3
ınior Agogo (Bristol Rovers)	3
regg Blundell (Doncaster)	3
en Burgess (Hull)	3
debayo Akinfenwa (Doncaster)	3
teven MacLean (Scunthorpe)	2
ary Fletcher (Lincoln City)	2
eo Bertos (Rochdale)	2

Penalties scored

Leon Constantine (Southend), **1**
atthew Tipton (Macclesfield),
raig Farrell (Carlisle)

Assists

regg Blundell (Doncaster)	4
eil Redfearn (Rochdale)	3
en Burgess (Hull)	3
arc Richards (Northampton)	3
ichael McIndoe (Doncaster)	3
evin Ellison (Lincoln City)	2
oshua Low (Northampton)	2

Quickest goals

59 mins - Marc Richards (Hull vs orthampton)

27 mins - Leo Bertos cunthorpe vs Rochdale)

33 mins - Simon Weatherstone oston Utd vs Yeovil)

47 mins - Steven MacLean cunthorpe vs Rochdale)

47 mins - Gary Alexander (Leyton rient vs Huddersfield)

Top Keeper

	Mins	Gls
Van Heusden (Torquay)	287	1
an Marriott (Lincoln City)	481	3
eve Wilson (Macclesfield)	475	3
Warrington (Doncaster)	479	4
Danby (Kidderminster)	478	4
Rachubka (Huddersfield)	582	5
Marshall (Cambridge U)	485	5
chael Price (Darlington)	483	5

Shots on target

Junior Agogo (Bristol Rovers)	17
Matthew Tipton (Macclesfield)	12
Stuart Elliott (Hull)	11
David Graham (Torquay)	11
Paul Brayson (Cheltenham)	11
Marc Richards (Northampton)	10
Gareth Seddon (Bury)	9
Grant McCann (Cheltenham)	9
John McAliskey (Huddersfield)	9
Gregg Blundell (Doncaster)	9

Shots off target

Andy Booth (Huddersfield)	10
Neil Redfearn (Rochdale)	10
David Graham (Torquay)	9
Gary Fletcher (Lincoln City)	9
Ben Sedgemore (Lincoln City)	9
Mark Boyd (Carlisle)	8
Gary Alexander (Leyton Orient)	8
Francis Green (Lincoln City)	7
Adebayo Akinfenwa (Doncaster)	7
Steven MacLean (Scunthorpe)	7

Caught offside

Steve Torpey (Scunthorpe)	12
David Graham (Torquay)	12
Junior Agogo (Bristol Rovers)	11
Matthew Tipton (Macclesfield)	9
Andy Booth (Huddersfield)	9
Steven MacLean (Scunthorpe)	9
Leon Constantine (Southend)	8
Marc Richards (Northampton)	8
Andy Preece (Carlisle)	8

Free-kicks won

J Worthington (Huddersfield)	20
David Graham (Torquay)	20
Eric Sabin (Northampton)	19
Barry Conlon (Darlington)	16
John Taylor (Northampton)	16
Martin Smith (Northampton)	15
Liam Lawrence (Mansfield)	14
Steve Torpey (Scunthorpe)	13
Anthony Carss (Huddersfield)	13

Alex Russell celebrates (v Oxford)

Fouls conceded

Andy Crosby (Scunthorpe)	16
Mark Bentley (Southend)	16
Efetobore Sodje (Huddersfield)	15
Tom Curtis (Mansfield)	15
Paul Connor (Swansea)	15
Steven MacLean (Scunthorpe)	14
Andy Preece (Carlisle)	14
Damian Spencer (Cheltenham)	13
Graeme Jones (Boston Utd)	13

Fouls without a card

Paul Connor (Swansea)	15
Damian Spencer (Cheltenham)	13
Barry Conlon (Darlington)	12
Lee Thorpe (Bristol Rovers)	11
David Flitcroft (Bury)	10
Ben Burgess (Hull)	10
Hugo Rodrigues (Yeovil)	9
Jake Edwards (Yeovil)	9
Junior Agogo (Bristol Rovers)	9

Tony Bedeau goes after the ball.
Torquay v Carlisle
HPL01505_TNA_037

That's my boy. . . Liam Rosenior is the first to appeal for a penalty after David Graham is brought down in the box.
Torquay v Yeovil
HPL01456_TNA_027

Goal, goal, goal!... David Graham scores his 21st goal of the season to put Torquay 3-0 up.
Torquay v Oxford
HPL01492_TNA_037

Steve Wood goes close.
Torquay v Oxford
HPL01492_TNA_019

Torquay [1] 1 KIDDERMINSTER [0] 1 — 1st May

The nerves which have held up so well for so long, on the pitch and on the terraces, finally frayed in this tense game. From a position of complete command, before and just after half-time, United lost their way.

Kidderminster goalkeeper John Danby's brave save at the feet of David Graham in the 50th minute proved the turning point. A second goal for United's new Player Of The Year then and it would have been all over.

The miss gave Kidderminster new confidence and the crowd sensed it. Harriers began to create chances and the alarm-bells ringing all round Plainmoor when, in the 73rd minute, Burton's inswinging right-wing corner looped just over the head of Gulls skipper Craig Taylor and dropped for Harriers' captain Wayne Hatswell to score from six yards at the far post.

How different it had all been in the first half. United's passing game opened up the Harriers defence, with Alex Russell, Graham and Kufour all playing well.

Kuffour's pace was a threat, but it was Graham who stood out. In the space of four minutes around the half-hour, the Scot could have had a hat-trick. One brilliant control, turn and volley just over the bar, from a Steve Woods pass, was right out of the top drawer.

Then in the 41st minute Graham delivered. Hill's determination took him through two tackles in midfield, forced the ball loose and Graham seized the chance with a first-time right-foot shot from 22 yards which had Danby beaten from the moment it left Graham's boot for his 22nd goal of the season.

In the first few minutes of the second half a sumptuous touch and through-ball by Alex Russell saw Graham clear but just offside. Then came Danby's vital save at Graham's feet. The nerves started jangling and the doubts set in.

Result.......Result.......Result.

TORQUAY ....(1) **1** **KIDDERMINST**(0) **1**
Graham 42 Hatswell 73

Att 5,515
Referee: F Stretton

Stats......Stats.......Stats......Stats

TORQUAY				KIDDERMINSTER		
1st	2nd	Total		Total	2nd	1st
4	4	8	Corners	7	5	2
1	2	3	Fouls	17	7	10
0	1	1	Yellow cards	3	2	1
0	0	0	Red cards	0	0	0
1	2	3	Caught Offside	2	1	1
1	1	2	Shots on target	5	2	3
6	2	8	Shots off target	4	2	2
0	0	0	Hit woodwork	0	0	0
46	47	46%	Possession	54%	53	54

WE'RE disappointed to concede the goal we did from a set piece. But we will go to Southend, be positive, try and win the game and see what happens.

Leroy Rosenior

WE set out to try and frustrate them because Torquay are a good side and they move the ball around quickly. This is a difficult place to come to.

Jan Molby

Other Div 3 Results

Boston Utd 0 Doncaster 0, Cambridge Utd 3 Scunthorpe 2, Carlisle 1 Cheltenham 1, Darlington 1 Swansea 2, Huddersfield 1 Mansfield 3, Macclesfield 2 Oxford Utd 1, Northampton 3 Bury 2, Rochdale 1 Southend 1, Yeovil 1 Hull 2, York 1 Leyton Orient 2

TORQUAY [1] 1 Kidderminster [0] 1

Goalkeeper Stats: Arjan Van Heusden Saves: Fumble 2, Catch 4, Crosses: Catch 4, Parry 2

No.	Torquay Player Stats		Shots on target L/R/H/Oth	Shots off target L/R/H/Oth	Caught offside	Fouls conceded	Free-kicks won	Corners taken	Clearances	Defensive blocks
2	Reuben Hazell	1st	-/-/-/-	-/-/-/-	-	-	1	-	-	-
		2nd	-/-/-/-	-/-/-/-	-	-	-	-	2	-
5	Craig Taylor	1st	-/-/-/-	-/-/-/-	-	-	2	-	4	-
		2nd	-/-/-/-	-/-/-/-	-	-	-	-	-	-
9	Martin Gritton	1st	-/-/-/-	-/-/-/-	-	-	-	-	-	-
	▲ 81	2nd	-/-/-/-	-/-/-/-	-	-	1	-	-	-
18	Steve Woods	1st	-/-/-/-	-/-/-/-	-	-	1	-	1	-
		2nd	-/-/-/-	-/-/-/-	-	-	1	-	1	-
4	Lee Canoville	1st	-/-/-/-	-/-/-/-	-	-	-	-	-	-
	▲ 80	2nd	-/-/-/-	-/-/-/-	-	1	1	-	-	-
6	Alex Russell	1st	-/-/-/-	-/-/-/-	-	-	-	4	1	-
		2nd	-/-/-/-	-/-/-/-	-	-	-	3	1	-
20	Liam Rosenior	1st	-/-/-/-	-/1/-/-	-	-	-	-	-	-
	▼ 67	2nd	-/-/-/-	-/-/-/-	-	-	-	1	-	-
11	Kevin Hill	1st	-/-/-/-	-/-/-/-	1	-	1	-	-	-
		2nd	-/-/-/-	1/-/-/-	-	-	2	-	-	-
10	David Graham	1st	-/1/-/-	2/1/2/-	-	-	3	-	-	-
		2nd	1/-/-/-	-/1/-/-	2	-	2	-	-	-
14	Matthew Hockley	1st	-/-/-/-	-/-/-/-	-	-	-	-	-	-
	▼ 81	2nd	-/-/-/-	-/-/-/-	-	-	-	-	1	-
8	Jason Fowler	1st	-/-/-/-	-/-/-/-	-	-	-	-	-	-
	▲ 67 ■ 82	2nd	-/-/-/-	-/-/-/-	-	1	-	-	-	-
12	Jo Kuffour	1st	-/-/-/-	-/-/-/-	-	-	1	-	-	-
		2nd	-/-/-/-	-/-/-/-	-	-	-	-	-	-
17	Brian McGlinchey	1st	-/-/-/-	-/-/-/-	-	1	1	-	-	-
	▼ 80	2nd	-/-/-/-	-/-/-/-	-	-	-	-	-	-

Subs not used: Woozley, Bedeau. - **Formation: 4-4-2**

Goalkeeper Stats: John Danby Saves: Catch 4, Crosses: Catch 4

No.	Player Stats	Shots on target	Shots off target	Caught offside	Fouls conceded	Free-kicks won	Corners taken	Clearances	Defensive blocks
16	Scott Rickards ▲ 66	-/-/-/-	-/-/-/-	-	1	-	-	-	-
14	Sean Parrish ■ 54	-/-/-/-	-/-/-/-	-	-	-	-	2	-
23	Mark Yates	-/1/-/-	-/-/-/-	-	1	-	-	2	-
4	Steve Burton	1/-/-/-	-/-/-/-	-	-	1	6	-	-
9	John Williams ▼ 66	-/-/-/-	-/-/-/-	-	2	-	-	2	-
17	Adam Murray ▲ 62	-/1/-/-	-/1/-/-	-	-	-	1	-	-
10	Jesper Christiansen	-/-/-/-	-/-/-/-	1	5	1	-	-	-
6	Matthew Gadsby ▲ 89	-/-/-/-	-/-/-/-	-	-	-	-	-	-
5	Craig Hinton	-/-/-/-	-/-/-/-	-	2	-	-	2	-
22	Wayne Hatswell ■ 30	-/1/-/-	-/-/1/-	-	2	-	-	-	-
8	Lee Jenkins ■ 59	-/-/-/-	-/-/-/-	-	2	-	-	3	-
20	Graham Ward ▼ 62	1/-/-/-	-/-/-/-	-	1	-	-	-	-
24	Simon Brown ▼ 89	-/-/-/-	-/2/-/-	1	1	1	-	-	-

Subs not used: Stamps, McHale. - **Formation: 4-3-3**

Torquay Played: 45 **Won** 22 **Drawn** 12 **Lost** 11 **For** 66 **Against** 43 **Pos** 4

Southend [1] 1 TORQUAY [2] 2

8th May

When their final moment of triumph arrived, United had only beer and Coke to celebrate.

Typically modest and simply getting on with the job to the very end, Leroy Rosenior's Torquay United hadn't dared to take any of the real bubbly stuff along, for fear of tempting fate.

But when referee Tony Leake blew his whistle for the last time, he released an outpouring of joy which was as moving as it was deafening. Torquay United may not be a big city club, but their supporters are as passionate about them as any in the land.

The bond between Rosenior's team and its staunchest fans was so close you could almost touch it. And the greatest triumph of this wonderful 2003-2004 season was that United did it, unfancied and against all the odds, by playing football.

Under the greatest pressure of all, their pass-and-move style ripped Southend to shreds in an opening onslaught. They were 2-0 up before Southend had broken sweat.

First, defender Steve Woods volleyed in at the far-post when Southend failed to cut out Russell's left-wing corner.Then, left-back Brian McGlinchey fed Jo Kuffour down the left, he beat two defenders and hooked the ball into the goalmouth and David Graham stooped to head in from point-blank range for the second.

But Southend hit back only six minutes after Graham's 23rd goal of the season. Bramble cut in from his left past Woods, had a crack from 20 yards, Arjan Van Heusden fumbled and Lawrie Dudfield was there to score.

Graham nearly got Russell in, then Russell returned the compliment, Graham shooting only a foot wide. And then there was a goal at Cheltenham. United had to hang on and hope for the best.

And so the result came through from Whaddon Road. There were still a couple of stoppage-time minutes left at Roots Hall, but Southend had nothing more to give.

United had done it. Thirty-eight years after Frank O'Farrell's team had clinched automatic promotion at Darlington, Rosenior's men had followed suit in glorious style.

Result.......Result.......Result.

SOUTHEND..........(1) **1** **TORQUAY** ......(2) **2**
Dudfield 17 — Woods 3, Graham 11

Att 8,894
Referee: A Leake

Stats......Stats.......Stats......Stats

SOUTHEND				TORQUAY		
1st	2nd	Total		Total	2nd	1st
3	2	5	**Corners**	3	1	2
7	6	13	**Fouls**	7	2	5
0	1	1	**Yellow cards**	0	0	0
0	0	0	**Red cards**	0	0	0
1	2	3	**Caught Offside**	5	2	3
4	6	10	**Shots on target**	6	0	6
1	2	3	**Shots off target**	6	3	3
0	0	0	**Hit woodwork**	0	0	0
48	60	54%	**Possession**	46%	40	52

"I feel we can be in the same position as Torquay find themselves next season with the addition of two or three more players."

Steve Tilson

"This has got to be the best day of my life in football. We showed that we can battle as well as play good football."

Craig Taylor

Other Div 3 Results

Bury 2 Macclesfield 0, Cheltenham 1 Huddersfield 1, Doncaster 1 Carlisle 0, Hull 3 Bristol Rovers 0, Kidderminster 2 Boston Utd 0, Leyton Orient 0 Cambridge Utd 1, Mansfield 1 Northampton 2, Oxford Utd 2 Rochdale 0, Scunthorpe 0 Darlington 1, Swansea 0 York 0

8th May

Southend [1] 1 TORQUAY [2] 2

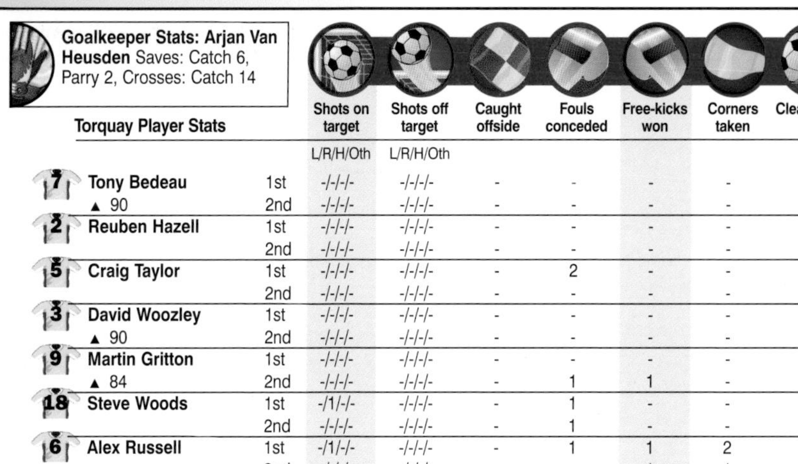

Goalkeeper Stats: Arjan Van Heusden Saves: Catch 6, Parry 2, Crosses: Catch 14

Torquay Player Stats		Shots on target	Shots off target	Caught offside	Fouls conceded	Free-kicks won	Corners taken	Clearances	Defensive blocks
		L/R/H/Oth	L/R/H/Oth						
7 Tony Bedeau	1st	-/-/-/-	-/-/-/-	-	-	-	-	-	-
▲ 90	2nd	-/-/-/-	-/-/-/-	-	-	-	-	-	-
2 Reuben Hazell	1st	-/-/-/-	-/-/-/-	-	-	-	-	2	-
	2nd	-/-/-/-	-/-/-/-	-	-	-	-	1	1
5 Craig Taylor	1st	-/-/-/-	-/-/-/-	-	2	-	-	1	-
	2nd	-/-/-/-	-/-/-/-	-	-	-	-	-	-
3 David Woozley	1st	-/-/-/-	-/-/-/-	-	-	-	-	-	-
▲ 90	2nd	-/-/-/-	-/-/-/-	-	-	-	-	-	-
9 Martin Gritton	1st	-/-/-/-	-/-/-/-	-	-	-	-	-	-
▲ 84	2nd	-/-/-/-	-/-/-/-	-	1	1	-	-	-
18 Steve Woods	1st	-/1/-/-	-/-/-/-	-	1	-	-	2	-
	2nd	-/-/-/-	-/-/-/-	-	1	-	-	1	-
6 Alex Russell	1st	-/1/-/-	-/-/-/-	-	1	1	2	-	2
	2nd	-/-/-/-	-/-/-/-	-	-	1	1	-	-
20 Liam Rosenior	1st	-/1/-/-	1/-/-/-	-	1	-	-	-	-
▼ 90	2nd	-/-/-/-	-/-/1/-	-	-	1	-	1	-
11 Kevin Hill	1st	-/-/-/-	-/-/-/-	-	-	2	-	-	-
	2nd	-/-/-/-	-/-/-/-	-	-	1	-	-	-
10 David Graham	1st	-/-/1/-	-/-/-/-	2	-	1	-	-	-
▼ 90	2nd	-/-/-/-	1/1/-/-	2	-	1	-	-	-
14 Matthew Hockley	1st	-/2/-/-	-/1/-/-	-	-	1	-	-	-
	2nd	-/-/-/-	-/-/-/-	-	-	-	-	1	-
12 Jo Kuffour	1st	-/-/-/-	-/1/-/-	1	-	-	-	-	-
▼ 84	2nd	-/-/-/-	-/-/-/-	-	-	1	-	-	-
17 Brian McGlinchey	1st	-/-/-/-	-/-/-/-	-	-	1	-	-	-
	2nd	-/-/-/-	-/-/-/-	-	-	-	-	-	1

Subs not used: Fowler, Canoville. - **Formation: 4-4-2**

Goalkeeper Stats: Darryl Flahavan Crosses: Catch 2

	Player Stats	Shots on target	Shots off target	Caught offside	Fouls conceded	Free-kicks won	Corners taken	Clearances	Defensive blocks
23	Lewis Hunt	-/-/-/-	-/-/-/-	-	1	-	-	-	2
11	Jim Corbett ▲ 36	1/-/-/-	-/-/-/-	-	-	-	-	-	-
24	Leon Constantine	1/2/-/-	-/-/-/-	-	-	3	-	-	1
27	Lawrie Dudfield	-/1/-/-	-/-/-/-	2	1	1	-	-	-
4	Leon Cort	-/-/-/-	-/-/-/-	-	-	-	-	4	1
9	Tesfaye Bramble	1/1/1/-	-/-/-/-	-	2	2	-	1	-
2	Duncan Jupp ▼ 75 ■ 66	-/-/-/-	-/-/-/-	-	3	-	-	1	-
17	Nicky Nicolau ▼ 80	-/-/-/-	-/-/-/-	1	-	1	-	-	-
8	Kevin Maher	-/-/-/-	-/3/-/-	-	1	-	5	-	-
19	Neil Jenkins ▲ 80	-/-/1/-	-/-/-/-	-	-	-	-	-	-
14	Che Wilson	-/-/-/-	-/-/-/-	-	1	-	-	2	1
26	Mark Bentley ▼ 36	-/-/-/-	-/-/-/-	-	3	-	-	-	-
10	Drewe Broughton ▲ 75	-/1/-/-	-/-/-/-	-	1	-	-	-	-

Subs not used: Stuart, Husbands. - **Formation: 4-4-2**

Torquay Played: 46 **Won** 23 **Drawn** 12 **Lost** 11 **For** 68 **Against** 44 **Pos** 3

...May Team Stats.....Team Stats......Team Stats......Team S

League table at the end of May

	HOME						AWAY						
	P	W	D	L	F	A	W	D	L	F	A	Pts	Df
Doncaster	46	17	4	2	47	13	10	7	6	32	24	92	42
Hull	46	16	4	3	50	21	9	9	5	32	23	88	38
Torquay	**46**	**15**	**6**	**2**	**44**	**18**	**8**	**6**	**9**	**24**	**26**	**81**	**24**
Huddersfield	46	16	4	3	42	18	7	8	8	26	34	81	16
Mansfield	46	13	5	5	44	25	9	4	10	32	37	75	14
Northampton	46	13	4	6	30	23	9	5	9	28	28	75	7
Lincoln City	46	9	11	3	36	23	10	6	7	32	24	74	21
Yeovil	46	14	3	6	40	19	9	2	12	30	38	74	13
Oxford Utd	46	14	8	1	34	13	4	9	10	21	31	71	11
Swansea	46	9	8	6	36	26	6	6	11	22	35	59	-3
Boston Utd	46	11	7	5	35	21	5	4	14	15	33	59	-4
Bury	46	10	7	6	29	26	5	4	14	25	38	56	-10
Cambridge U	46	6	7	10	26	32	8	7	8	29	35	56	-12
Cheltenham	46	11	4	8	37	38	3	10	10	20	33	56	-14
Bristol Rovers	46	9	7	7	29	26	5	6	12	21	35	55	-11
Kidderminster	46	9	5	9	28	29	5	8	10	17	30	55	-14
Southend	46	8	4	11	27	29	6	8	9	24	34	54	-12
Darlington	46	10	4	9	30	28	4	7	12	23	33	53	-8
Leyton Orient	46	8	9	6	28	27	5	5	13	20	38	53	-17
Macclesfield	46	8	9	6	28	25	5	4	14	26	44	52	-15
Rochdale	46	7	8	8	28	26	5	6	12	21	32	50	-9
Scunthorpe	46	7	10	6	36	27	4	6	13	33	45	49	-3
Carlisle	46	8	5	10	23	27	4	4	15	23	42	45	-23
York	46	7	6	10	22	29	3	8	12	13	37	44	-31

May matches table

	P	W	D	L	F	A	Pts
Hull	2	2	0	0	5	1	6
Northampton	2	2	0	0	5	3	6
Cambridge Utd	2	2	0	0	4	2	6
Kidderminster	2	1	1	0	3	1	4
Torquay	**2**	**1**	**1**	**0**	**3**	**2**	**4**
Swansea	2	1	1	0	2	1	4
Doncaster	2	1	1	0	1	0	4
Bury	2	1	0	1	4	3	3
Mansfield	2	1	0	1	4	3	3
Yeovil	2	1	0	1	4	4	3
Oxford Utd	2	1	0	1	3	2	3
Bristol Rovers	2	1	0	1	3	4	3
Darlington	2	1	0	1	2	2	3
Leyton Orient	2	1	0	1	2	2	3
Macclesfield	2	1	0	1	2	3	3
Cheltenham	2	0	2	0	2	2	2
Southend	2	0	1	1	2	3	1
Huddersfield	2	0	1	1	2	4	1
Carlisle	2	0	1	1	1	2	1
York	2	0	1	1	1	2	1
Rochdale	2	0	1	1	1	3	1
Boston Utd	2	0	1	1	0	2	1
Lincoln City	2	0	0	2	3	6	0
Scunthorpe	2	0	0	2	2	4	0

May team stats details

Club Name	Ply	Shots On	Shots Off	Corners	Hit W'work	Caught Offside	Offside Trap	Fouls	Yellow Cards	Red Cards	Pens Awarded	Pen Co
Boston Utd	2	5	6	18	0	9	6	29	4	0	- (-)	-
Bristol Rovers	2	14	9	13	0	13	4	34	3	0	- (-)	-
Bury	2	9	12	7	0	11	2	22	5	0	- (-)	-
Cambridge U	2	14	11	6	2	11	5	23	4	0	- (-)	1
Carlisle	2	13	8	4	0	7	5	25	4	0	- (-)	1
Cheltenham	2	13	17	11	0	4	6	23	1	1	- (-)	-
Darlington	2	6	7	14	0	5	1	17	1	0	- (-)	-
Doncaster	2	9	8	15	0	7	7	21	2	0	1 (-)	-
Huddersfield	2	11	15	9	0	4	5	22	2	0	- (-)	-
Hull	2	12	10	5	1	4	15	21	2	0	1 (1)	1
Kidderminster	2	11	12	12	1	4	7	25	5	0	- (-)	-
Leyton Orient	2	11	14	9	1	5	13	35	10	1	1 (-)	-
Lincoln City	2	11	5	9	0	2	12	24	6	0	- (-)	-
Macclesfield	2	17	11	15	1	5	8	19	4	1	- (-)	-
Mansfield	2	15	8	14	0	9	9	22	0	0	- (-)	-
Northampton	2	13	9	5	1	6	11	16	3	1	- (-)	-
Oxford Utd	2	6	11	9	0	5	9	25	0	0	- (-)	-
Rochdale	2	13	2	8	0	12	3	21	0	0	1 (-)	-
Scunthorpe	2	17	8	21	2	1	8	25	3	0	- (-)	-
Southend	2	13	7	13	0	3	11	27	2	0	- (-)	1
Swansea	2	11	12	8	1	4	3	27	3	0	- (-)	-
Torquay	**2**	**8**	**14**	**11**	**0**	**8**	**5**	**10**	**1**	**0**	**- (-)**	**-**
Yeovil	2	9	8	14	1	12	0	32	4	0	- (-)	-
York	2	7	5	7	0	8	4	31	1	0	- (-)	-

Monthly Match Details: Games 24 **Home Wins** 9 **Away Wins** 9 **Draws** 6

...May Player Stats..... Player Stats...... Player Stats......Pla

Monthly Top scorers

D Chillingworth (Cambridge Utd)	2
Paul Tait (Bristol Rovers)	2
David Graham (Torquay)	2
Junior Mendes (Mansfield)	1
Colin Larkin (Mansfield)	1
Kevin Nugent (Swansea)	1
Ian Ashbee (Hull)	1
Simon Yeo (Lincoln City)	1
Hugo Rodrigues (Yeovil)	1
John Cartledge (Bury)	1

Penalties scored

1 Stuart Green (Hull)

Assists

Chris Willmott (Northampton)	2
Gary Fletcher (Lincoln City)	2
Matthew Lockwood (Leyton O)	2
Pawel Abbott (Huddersfield)	2
Jefferson Louis (Oxford Utd)	1
Andy Preece (Carlisle)	1
Paul Tait (Bristol Rovers)	1

Quickest goals

2:43 mins - Steve Woods (Southend vs Torquay)

4:17 mins - Barry Conlon (Scunthorpe vs Darlington)

4:23 mins - Stuart Wise (York vs Leyton Orient)

6:31 mins - Paul Tait (Bristol Rovers vs Lincoln City)

7:43 mins - Luke Guttridge (Leyton Orient vs Cambridge Utd)

Top Keeper

	Mins	Gls
Boaz Myhill (Hull)	192	1
Neil Edwards (Rochdale)	97	1
Glenn Morris (Leyton O)	192	2
Michael Price (Darlington)	191	2
Paul Bastock (Boston Utd)	190	2
John Danby (Kidderminster)	95	1
Matthew Glennon (Carlisle)	190	2
A Van Heusden (Torquay)	190	2

Shots on target

Andy Booth (Huddersfield)	6
Steven MacLean (Scunthorpe)	5
Jonathan Parkin (Macclesfield)	5
Paul Tait (Bristol Rovers)	5
Ciaran Toner (Leyton Orient)	5
Rory Patterson (Rochdale)	5
Colin Larkin (Mansfield)	4
Marc Richards (Northampton)	4
Luke Guttridge (Cambridge Utd)	4
Paul Connor (Swansea)	4

Shots off target

David Graham (Torquay)	8
Matthew Tipton (Macclesfield)	6
Bradley Maylett (Swansea)	5
Simon Brown (Kidderminster)	5
D Chillingworth (Cambridge Utd)	5
Grant McCann (Cheltenham)	4
Jefferson Louis (Oxford Utd)	4
Pawel Abbott (Huddersfield)	4
Andrew Scott (Leyton Orient)	3
Tim Ryan (Doncaster)	3

Caught offside

David Graham (Torquay)	6
Paul Tait (Bristol Rovers)	5
Kevin Townson (Rochdale)	5
Lee McEvilly (Rochdale)	5
Lee Thorpe (Bristol Rovers)	5
Eric Sabin (Northampton)	4
Paul Connor (Swansea)	4
Shane Tudor (Cambridge Utd)	4
Liam George (York)	4

Free-kicks won

Darren Dunning (York)	8
David Graham (Torquay)	7
Andrew Scott (Leyton Orient)	7
Hugo Rodrigues (Yeovil)	7
Shane Tudor (Cambridge Utd)	7
Kevin Nugent (Swansea)	7
Graeme Jones (Boston Utd)	6
David Nugent (Bury)	6
Kevin Hill (Torquay)	6

Torquay v Southend

Fouls conceded

Brian Saah (Leyton Orient)	11
Damian Spencer (Cheltenham)	10
Graeme Jones (Boston Utd)	8
Darren Dunning (York)	7
Danny Williams (Bristol Rovers)	6
Kevin Nugent (Swansea)	6
Lee Thorpe (Bristol Rovers)	6
Gavin Williams (Yeovil)	6
Paul Ellender (Boston Utd)	6

Fouls without a card

Graeme Jones (Boston Utd)	8
Darren Dunning (York)	7
Danny Williams (Bristol Rovers)	6
Gavin Williams (Yeovil)	6
J Christiansen (Kidderminster)	6
Danny Allsopp (Hull)	6
Leon Britton (Swansea)	5
Leigh Wood (York)	5
Ben Futcher (Lincoln City)	5

Jo Kuffour takes on the Southend defense.
Southend v Torquay
HPL01587_TNA_012

Goal...goal...goal...Steve Woods is in mid air as he cleverly volleys home Torquay's opener.
Southend v Torquay
HPL01587_TNA_031

Leroy and Liam Rosenior celebrate promotion
Southend v Torquay
HPL01591_TNA_044

Fans shoe their support for United.
Southend v Torquay
HPL01591_TNA_020

Actual quote from Torquay playmaker Alex Russell: 'Don't do that, I don't want to get my photograph in the paper!'.
Southend v Torquay
HPL01591_TNA_023

Goal...goal...goal...David Graham stoops to head home Jo Kuffour's inch perfect pass.
Southend v Torquay
HPL01587_TNA_053

The Coca-Cola League One Fixture List 2004-2005

August		result
7 Bristol City	(A)	
10 Hull	(H)	
14 Sheff Wed	(H)	
21 Luton	(A)	
28 Walsall	(H)	
30 Milton Keynes Dons	(A)	
September		**result**
4 Stockport	(A)	
11 Brentford	(H)	
18 Hartlepool	(A)	
25 Tranmere	(H)	
October		**result**
2 Peterborough	(A)	
9 Huddersfield	(H)	
16 Doncaster	(A)	
19 Bournemouth	(H)	
23 Wrexham	(H)	
30 Swindon	(A)	
November		**result**
6 Oldham	(H)	
20 Port Vale	(A)	
27 Colchester	(H)	
December		**result**
7 Blackpool	(A)	
11 Barnsley	(H)	
18 Chesterfield	(A)	
26 Brentford	(A)	
28 Bradford	(H)	

January		result
1 Stockport	(H)	
3 Tranmere	(A)	
8 Huddersfield	(A)	
15 Hartlepool	(H)	
22 Bradford	(A)	
29 Peterborough	(H)	
February		**result**
5 Doncaster	(H)	
12 Wrexham	(A)	
19 Swindon	(H)	
22 Bournemouth	(A)	
26 Barnsley	(A)	
March		**result**
5 Chesterfield	(H)	
12 Hull	(A)	
19 Bristol City	(H)	
26 Sheff Wed	(A)	
28 Luton	(H)	
April		**result**
2 Walsall	(A)	
9 Milton Keynes Dons	(H)	
16 Port Vale	(H)	
23 Oldham	(A)	
30 Blackpool	(H)	
May		**result**
7 Colchester	(A)	
		EMBARGOED